DEBATING THE DONALD:

12 Primaries

and

Trump's Showdown with Hillary Clinton

Aaron Kall

Editor

Director of Debate

University of Michigan

<<<<<<<<<<<<<<<<<<<<<<<<<<<<O>>>>>>>>>>>>>>>>>>>>>>

SYNOPSIS

<<<<<<<<<<<<<<<<<<<<<<<<<<<<O>>>>>>>>>>>>>>>>>>>>>>

Republican presidential nominee Donald Trump entered the 2016 election race with no political or debate experience. He had extremely low expectations heading into his first primary debate hosted by Fox News in Cleveland, Ohio on August 6, 2015. Trump took advantage of this and easily won the first debate, which catapulted him to permanent frontrunner status and he never looked back. He participated in ten additional primary debates, while choosing to boycott the event in Des Moines, Iowa in January of 2016. Nearly 200 million viewers watched the GOP primary debates and Trump's reality television star background played a major role in this phenomenon. In "Debating The Donald", a dozen debate experts from around the United States analyze Trump's performances in the primary debates. They discuss what techniques were employed by the candidate to yield successful results. Finally, the authors predict how style and content from Trump's primary debates will influence his three general election showdowns with Hillary Clinton in the fall. The first Trump-Clinton debate at Hofstra University in New

York will have a Super Bowl-like atmosphere and will truly be must-see TV.

<<<<<<<<<<<<<<<<<<<<<<<<◇>>>>>>>>>>>>>>>>>>>>>

CONTRIBUTORS

<<<<<<<<<<<<<<<<<<<<<<<<◇>>>>>>>>>>>>>>>>>>>>>

Dr. Brett Bricker, Associate Director of and Specialist in the Department of Communication Studies at the University of Kansas

Dr. David Cram Helwich, Director of Debate and Senior Lecturer in Communication Studies at the University of Minnesota

Kurt Fifelski, MPA and Assistant Director of Debate at the University of Michigan and University of Michigan Debate Institute

Dr. Ryan Galloway, Assistant Professor of Communication Studies and Director of Debate at Samford University

Aaron Kall, Director of Debate at the University of Michigan and University of Michigan Debate Institute

Dr. Eric Morris, Associate Professor of Communication and Director of Forensics at Missouri State University

Dr. Will Mosley-Jensen, Director of Debate and Assistant Professor of Human Communication at Trinity University

Dr. Sarah Partlow-Lefevre, Professor of Communication and Rhetorical Studies and Director of Debate at Idaho

State University

Dr. Sarah Topp, Litigation Consultant at JurySync
and M.A. and Ph.D. in Communication Studies from the
University of Kansas

Dr. Ben Voth, Associate Professor of Corporate
Communications and Public Affairs and Director of Debate
at Southern Methodist University

Patrick Waldinger, Assistant Director of Debate and
Lecturer in the School of Communication at the University
of Miami

Dr. Kelly Young, Associate Professor of Communication
and the Director of Forensics at Wayne State University

AARON KALL, EDITOR

2015-2016 REPUBLICAN PRIMARY DEBATE SCHEDULE

CHAPTER ONE: Debate #1–Cleveland, Ohio, August 6, 2015

CHAPTER TWO: Debate #2–Simi Valley, California, September 16, 2015

CHAPTER THREE: Debate #3–Boulder, Colorado, October 28, 2015

CHAPTER FOUR: Debate #4–Milwaukee, Wisconsin, November 10, 2015

CHAPTER FIVE: Debate #5–Las Vegas, Nevada, December 15, 2015

CHAPTER SIX: Debate #6–North Charleston, South Carolina, January 14, 2016

CHAPTER SEVEN: Debate #7–Des Moines, Iowa, January 28, 2016

CHAPTER EIGHT: Debate #8–Manchester, New Hampshire, February 6, 2016

CHAPTER NINE: Debate #9–Greenville, South Carolina, February 13, 2016

CHAPTER TEN: Debate #10–Houston, Texas, February 25, 2016

CHAPTER ELEVEN: Debate #11–Detroit, Michigan, March 3, 2016

CHAPTER TWELVE: Debate #12–Miami, Florida, March 10, 2016

AARON KALL, EDITOR

<<<<<<<<<<<<<<<<<<<<<<<◇>>>>>>>>>>>>>>>>>>>>>>>
TABLE OF CONTENTS
<<<<<<<<<<<<<<<<<<<<<<<◇>>>>>>>>>>>>>>>>>>>>>>>

SYNOPSIS...**3**

CONTRIBUTORS..**5**

2015-2016 GOP PRIMARY DEBATE SCHEDULE......**7**

INTRODUCTION...**11**

CHAPTER ONE..**19**

CHAPTER TWO...**51**

CHAPTER THREE..**101**

CHAPTER FOUR..**123**

CHAPTER FIVE..**143**

CHAPTER SIX..**173**

CHAPTER SEVEN...**195**

CHAPTER EIGHT..**217**

CHAPTER NINE...**245**

CHAPTER TEN...**271**

CHAPTER ELEVEN...**289**

CHAPTER TWELVE...**317**

CONCLUSION 345

ACKNOWLEDGEMENTS 357

COPYRIGHT...359

CONTACT 361

PLEASE LEAVE A REVIEW 363

INTRODUCTION

<<<<<<<<<<<<<<<<<<<<<O>>>>>>>>>>>>>>>>>>>

Aaron Kall

<<<<<<<<<<<<<<<<<<<<<O>>>>>>>>>>>>>>>>>>>

On June 16, 2015 Donald Trump and his wife Melania rode down an escalator of the 68-story Trump Tower on Fifth Avenue in New York City to declare his candidacy for the Republican presidential nomination. Trump had teased about running for president on at least five previous occasions and as recently as 2011. The launching of his exploratory committee, delayed production of "The Apprentice," and hiring of staff in early voting states indicated a heightened level of seriousness this time. Trump was the twelfth candidate to enter the race and began the contest as a tremendous long shot. Among a crowded and distinguished field, he was polling in the low single digits nationally and there were initial legitimate concerns whether he would even qualify for the main debate stage in Cleveland. Although many media commentators said Trump's inaugural speech rambled on for nearly an hour, it was merely a preview of several themes that would become commonplace during his eleven primary debate performances. Trump mentioned making

America great again and spoke negatively about many immigrants that were coming to the United States from Mexico. Signature issues like Chinese currency manipulation and building a wall between Mexico and the U.S. border were discussed. Finally, Trump took a strong poke at frontrunner Jeb Bush, who had just announced his candidacy the previous day. It only took a few months for these major issues to make their way onto the political debate stage, which will never be the same after the 2016 Republican primary.

Seventeen Republicans would eventually declare their candidacies, which produced an extremely crowded field. This was the largest pool of candidates in the modern political era and first time since 1916 there were so many distinguished contenders. Numerous sitting Governors and Senators were part of the mix, intertwined with business executives and medical doctors. Since no debate stage would be able to accommodate seventeen candidates at one time, a separate main event and undercard would occur for the first time during this cycle. This produced an intense jockeying for top-tier status in the most reputable polls heading into the Cleveland debate. Only the top ten polling candidates would get the opportunity to separate themselves from the pack and, because of recent

Republican National Committee rule changes, there would be many fewer debates during the 2016 cycle.

After the fallout from the 2012 primary, the RNC determined that major changes were needed concerning the debate structure. The twenty odd debates from the previous cycle were referred to as ridiculous and a circus. They started in May of 2011, which was about eight months before votes would begin to be cast in Iowa. In January of 2012, two debates in New Hampshire were held less than twelve hours apart. A proliferation of debates was distracting from other essential campaign activities and the GOP autopsy report released in March of 2013 offered several proposals to reform the process, which would give Republicans a better chance to prevail in 2016. There was a consensus in having half as many this time and a fall start date. The RNC announced the formation of a standing committee that would select moderators and impose penalties on any candidates that didn't follow the new rules. Trump's campaign would have to successfully operate within these new parameters and spend the dog days of summer with Cleveland firmly on their radar.

In the slow summer months leading to the opening Cleveland debate, Trump was consuming all of the media spotlight and political oxygen. During late June his relationship with NBC Universal over the Miss USA and Miss Universe pageants was severed because of his disparaging language toward immigrants. Several celebrity chefs soon pulled out of high-profile ventures with Trump for similar reasons. In July he insulted war hero and Arizona Senator John McCain for getting captured during the Vietnam War. Later that month Trump called South Carolina Senator Lindsey Graham a lightweight and idiot before releasing his cell phone number to the public. If you operate under the assumption that all publicity is good publicity, Trump was having a politically successful summer. Most importantly, he was gradually improving his polling numbers, which was a prerequisite to shining in Cleveland. The campaign employed some additional creative tactics in the weeks leading up to the inaugural debate in order to manage expectations and best level the playing field for Trump.

At least half the battle to succeeding in a debate is the establishment of moderate or preferably low expectations. Nobody understands this better than Trump, who immediately hit the airwaves to hype up the political and debate experience of his opponents, while simultaneously highlighting his novel candidacy. During appearances on

Fox News and NBC he repeatedly pointed out that he had never debated and expressed some apprehension about the unique challenges the format presented. Not only was Trump a debate novice, his opponents were career politicians who had engaged in such events for decades, which would present a formidable challenge. As the frontrunner, he expected to take incoming fire from all sides during the first debate and equated the experience to being in a lion's den. Trump expected the debates to be civil affairs that focused on major policy issues. He pledged not to proactively attack any of his opponents on the stage, but reserved the right to counterpunch if necessary. Trump was fairly honest and transparent about his debate tactics and strategy. Most of Trump's opponents would get an up-close view of his pinpoint execution in due time.

Solid preparation is the cornerstone to any successful debate outcome, but there are various ways in which this can be accomplished. Trump has consistently engaged in relaxed and informal debate preparations with a small group of trusted advisors. He attended the Women's British Open at his Turnberry resort in Scotland the week before the Cleveland debate. This is not a decision most politicians would have similarly made while cramming for such an important engagement. Trump puts tremendous faith in his instincts and ability to read an audience. His debate preparation is consistent with his theme as a candidate and this has proven a recipe for success. Trump is the ultimate non-traditional candidate and his unorthodox debate preparations are perfectly consistent with this overall campaign philosophy.

Close to 4,500 people were in attendance for the Republican primary debate in Cleveland on August 6, 2015. Frontrunner Trump was at the center of the main stage, flanked by Governors Jeb Bush and Scott Walker. He was clearly the star of the show and 24 million viewers tuned-in to watch Trump debate and see what he would say and do next. With a simple raising of the hand, Trump refused to pledge his support to the ultimate Republican presidential nominee and immediately found himself on a political island. A heated exchange with Fox News moderator Megyn Kelly over disparaging remarks toward women and political correctness quickly followed. Trump commandeered the debate stage in Cleveland and never looked back. *Debating The Donald* critically analyzes all of Trump's primary debate performances, while previewing his trio of integral dates with Hillary Clinton. Trump's evolution as a candidate and debater has been a long and arduous process, but never lacked pizazz and excitement.

Look for this pattern to continue during the three fall debates with Clinton, which should be a battle royale for the ages.

CHAPTER ONE

<<<<<<<<<<<<<<<<<<<<<<<o>>>>>>>>>>>>>>>>>>>>>>

GOP Primary Debate #1
Cleveland, Ohio, August 6, 2015
Dr. David Cram Helwich

<<<<<<<<<<<<<<<<<<<<<<<o>>>>>>>>>>>>>>>>>>>>>>

High-profile events, such as televised debates, present candidates with both peril and opportunity—opportunity in the sense that candidates can raise their profile and reach out to potential supporters, and peril because of the looming threat of campaign-deflating missteps and lackluster performances. Although many campaign experts contend that election outcomes are driven strongly by underlying fundamentals, public debates still serve as rights-of-passage for presidential candidates in the United States, allowing the electorate to evaluate a potential president's performance and poise in a high-pressure environment. A campaign may not necessarily be won during a debate, but it certainly can be significantly damaged. One need only recall President Barack Obama's divergent performances in the 2012 presidential debates, where his poll numbers tanked after a very weak performance in the first debate in Denver, CO, and then rebounded after a much stronger showing in the second and third debates. Although Democratic nominee Hillary Clinton currently holds a significant lead over Republican nominee Donald Trump in both national and swing state opinion polls, Clinton's lead is not insurmountable, and Clinton will have to confront Trump's decidedly unorthodox debate style in a series of three presidential primary debates in the run-up to the November election. Trump has shown himself to be a surprisingly formidable debate opponent, drawing upon effective messaging strategies and his wealth of on-camera experience. Trump's performance in the slew of GOP primary debates shows a debater who is successful at controlling the tenor and content of the debate, who readily fends off challenging questions and personal attacks, and mobilizes potential supporters to his cause.

Successfully debating Donald Trump has proven to be difficult for candidates who follow the conventions of contemporary political debate, as shown by the GOP presidential primaries. In this chapter, I assess Trump's performance in the opening GOP presidential primary debate on August 6, 2015 in Cleveland, OH, broadcast on Fox News and moderated by Fox anchors Bret Baier, Megyn Kelly, and Chris Wallace. I both outline Trump's approach to responding to the seven questions directed toward him during the debate and discuss how these responses might implicate the upcoming presidential primary debates between Trump and Clinton. The Cleveland primary debate is significant because Trump's theatrics demonstrated that the candidate would refuse to follow the rules guiding a traditional campaign. He began the night declaring that he would not toe the line and support the GOP's eventual nominee, notably doing so in the very venue where he would accept the GOP's presidential nomination this past July. Just as Trump shaped both the style and content of the August 2015 debate, he subsequently dominated coverage of the entire nomination process.

Debate Format and Context

Even a seasoned campaign debater would be justified in feeling intimidated by the structural difficulties presented by the opening debate. At the time of the contest, there were 17 declared GOP candidates, far too many to include in a single two-hour debate. Fox News chose to use a polling average to split the candidates into two pools, with the ten highest-polling candidates invited to participate in the prime-time event, and the other seven candidates offered spots in a separate debate immediately preceding the main contest. Campaigns both decried the pool split upon Fox's announcement of their strategy, and worked diligently to position themselves to receive a coveted invitation to the main stage and avoid being relegated to the earlier, so-called "kiddie table" timeslot. As the aggregate poll leader, Trump was invited to the opening debate, along with Jeb Bush, Ben Carson, Chris Christie, Ted Cruz, Mike Huckabee, John Kasich, Rand Paul, Marco Rubio, and Scott Walker.

The stage in Cleveland was crowded, presenting strategic difficulties for the candidates and moderators. The candidates needed to balance their need to maximize their visibility against the risk of presenting themselves as a target for attacks from the other debaters. Limiting the field to ten debaters still stretched a two-hour debate format, presenting the three moderators with the challenge of balancing the desire to cover a wide array of issues with the need to allow each of the ten candidates to share their views. The moderators chose to open and close the contest with a general query affording each candidate an opportunity to respond, and to then focus the rest of their time on issue-specific questions that were directed at only a select number of candidates. Candidates were granted one minute to answer each question, with the possibility of 30-second follow-up responses from both the original candidate and the other debaters at the discretion of the moderators. Although the design seemed intended to afford relatively equal mic time to each candidate, Trump spoke for over 11 minutes, nearly two and a half minutes more than his opponent with the second greatest amount of speaking time (Bush), and nearly twice as much as any other candidate ("Republican Debate," 2015). Trump's advantage in speaking time reflected both the larger number of questions he received than many other candidates and Trump's tendency to provide answers considerably longer than the mandated, and only lightly enforced, 60-second time limit. Trump's performance was watched by over 24 million viewers, the most-watched primary debate ever, and nearly 6 times as many viewers as saw the first GOP primary debate in 2012. Many analysts posited after the debate that Trump's high name recognition, coupled with his well-earned reputation as a potential wild card, drove up the ratings for the debate (Stelter, 2015).

The criteria for "winning" a political debate vary considerably from the rules and norms of competitive academic debate contests. Although many observers and analysts often focus on a candidate's ability to "land punches on" and "score points against" their political opponents, such a narrow view ignores critical potential functions and potentialities of a successful debate performance for the candidate. For example, many low-interest and low-information potential voters are often less interested in the substance of a candidate's answers to particular questions than in whether a candidate appears to be "presidential" in their bearing. Candidates may decide to focus on projecting confidence and working to command the stage. Other audience members may not be interested in the minutiae of policy details when selecting a candidate, and instead focus on whether a candidate aligns with that person's values. A candidate's performance in a debate is also often judged by both voters and professional commentators against a set of expectations about a candidate's competency and debate skill. Indeed, it has now become something of a contest between candidates to lower audience and media expectations before each debate. A relatively recent example of this phenomenon are the contests between George W. Bush and Al Gore during the 2000 presidential race, where Gore easily prevailed in each debate "on points" as determined by debate and policy experts, but Bush was judged to have won at least two of the three debates by the audience. Bush's performances both far exceeded pre-debate expectations and demonstrated an ability to connect with voters. During the opening GOP primary debate, Trump may well have committed a number of "political faux pas" in vocalizing a number of highly controversial positions during the two-hour contest, but he also dictated the tone of the debate, seemingly foiled pointed questions from the moderators and a few attacks from the other candidates, and solidified his frontrunner status by dominating the media's subsequent coverage of the debate, one that *Politico* described in a headline the next day as "The Trump Show" (Cheney, 2015). From the perspective of "any press is good press," Trump won the Cleveland primary debate going away. However, we should review the political context within which the debate occurred.

Going into the debate, Trump likely expected considerable attention, including challenges to his announced policy stances and prior statements, from both the moderators and the other candidates. Trump entered the contest topping the polls in a crowded field, drawing support from roughly one-fourth of likely GOP voters. Most polls put Jeb Bush, former Florida Governor in second place, trailing Trump by ten or so points, with Governor Scott Walker of Wisconsin sitting in third (Dutton, De Pinto, Salvanto, & Backus, 2015). At the time of the first debate, most pundits and political professionals did not take Trump's candidacy seriously despite his early lead, with many prognosticators arguing that his "entertainer" style and propensity for generating controversy would eventually torpedo his campaign (Schlesinger, 2015). The conventional wisdom at this point was seemingly validated by a number of highly controversial comments offered by Trump during the early stages of the process. First, Trump launched his candidacy with a number of inflammatory remarks on undocumented immigration during his June 16, 2015 announcement speech, stating that "The U.S. has become a dumping ground for everyone else's problems" and claiming that "When Mexico sends its people, they are not sending their best," noting further that many Mexican immigrants are "bringing drugs," "bringing crime," and are "rapists" ("Donald Trump," 2015, npg). The resulting furor and Trump's defense of these comments led Univision, the broadcaster of Trump's Miss USA pageant, to sever all ties with Trump on June 25, 2015 ("Univision Ends," 2015). Trump then doubled-down on his anti-undocumented immigration stance during his first major campaign rally on July 11, 2015 in Phoenix, AZ, where Trump stated that although he "respected" Mexico, whose leadership he described as "too smart for our leaders," he accused them of "taking our jobs ... taking our manufacturing ... taking our money ... taking our everything, and they're killing us at the border" ("Trump Taking," 2015, npg). Trump also advanced a now stock campaign pledge to build a wall along the U.S.-Mexico border. Then, on July 18, Trump escalated an ongoing feud with 2008 GOP standard-bearer Senator John McCain, maintaining that the senator was only "a war hero because he was captured," noting that he "like[s] people that weren't captured" ("Presidential Candidate," 2015, npg).

Question One: Party Loyalty

One critical task faced by Trump during the first debate was persuading the Republican primary electorate that he shared the values and policy objectives of the Republican Party. Moderator Bret Baier's first question both challenged Trump's conservative bona fides and provided him with an opportunity to pledge his support for the party, asking for a show of hands among the participants on whether anyone was "unwilling tonight to pledge your support to the eventual nominee of the Republican Party..." ("Transcript," 2015, npg). Trump was the only one of the ten candidates to raise his hand, to a chorus of boos from the audience. When asked by Baier to clarify his stance, and challenged by the fact that an independent Trump run would "almost certainly hand the race over to Democrats", Trump claimed that he could not make that pledge because he had to "respect … the person that wins …," arguing that he wanted to "win as the Republican" and, strangely, pledging to not run as an independent "If I'm the nominee …." The answer is significant because it signaled to both Trump's opponents for the GOP presidential nomination, and the party leadership, that he remained willing to pursue his ambitions outside the party apparatus with an independent run, a gambit unacceptable to the GOP because it would almost certainly lock in a Democratic victory in November 2016. Trump later described this situation as giving him "leverage" over the GOP establishment.

The audience's response to both Baier's question and Trump's response included a loud mix of cheers and boos, something of a departure from most presidential debates, which see relatively restrained audiences, often at the direction of the moderators. The audience reaction set the tone for the rest of the debate, which featured a number of positive and negative audience reactions to moderator questions and candidate responses, particularly those questions about, or addressed to, Trump. These audience responses both reflected the sometimes raucous nature of many of Trump's public events prior to this opening debate, and presaged a much more significant role for audience-directed appeals and vocal participation in later primary debates and on the campaign trail. The path to the notorious "hand size," "Lyin' Ted" and "Little Marco" exchanges the March 3, 2016 GOP debate held in Detroit, MI apparently had its beginning on this night in Cleveland ("Republican Candidates," 2016). We can expect a similarly elevated level of audience participation in this fall's debates.

Trump's approach answering this question illustrates how he defines himself as a political outsider. His refusal to pledge support to the GOP's nominee is part of Trump's strategy of rallying potential voters who find themselves deeply alienated from the current political process. Trump frequently attacks both the political establishment, which he labels as "corrupt" and unable "to get things done," and the news media, which he often accuses of treating him and his campaign "unfairly." Trump's public statements during the early stages of the general campaign demonstrate that he will likely attempt to brand Clinton as an ineffective, "corrupt" politician during this fall's debates while projecting his own candidacy as an opportunity to reset a dysfunctional Washington by introducing alleged private sector-linked values like decisiveness and effective bargaining. Clinton will face the test of clearly and persuasively explaining to an electorate increasingly disenchanted with government why they should entrust the responsibility for reforming the Washington establishment to a prominent member of that establishment.

Question Two: 'War On Women'

The strongest challenge that Trump faced on the night, and one that dominated post-debate coverage, occurred during his second question. Kelly asked Trump whether Democratic candidate Hillary Clinton was correct in describing Trump as "part of the war on women...," with Kelly noting that Trump had "called women you don't like 'fat pigs, dogs, slobs, and disgusting animals.'" Kelly also asked Trump to justify statements on his Twitter account, which had "several disparaging comments about women's looks. You once told a contestant on Celebrity Apprentice it would be a pretty picture to see her on her knees. Does that sound to you like the temperament of a man we should elect as President?"

Trump's body language signaled that he found Kelly's question off-putting, and he eventually offered three responses. First, in an attempt to minimize the impact of Kelly's argument, Trump claimed that the arguably most offensive comments were only directed at TV talk show host and actress Rosie O'Donnell, with whom Trump has feuded publicly for years. Kelly subsequently contested this argument in a back-and-forth that followed. Second, Trump disparaged concerns about his descriptions of women as part of the country's "big problem" with political correctness, noting, "I don't frankly have time for total political correctness." He pivoted to a favored messaging theme, noting that "We don't win anymore..." and "We lose to everybody... ," implying that focusing on the language used by politicians weakened the country and distracted the nation's leadership from addressing real problems. Instead, Trump argued, "we need strength, we need energy, we need quickness and we need [a] brain in this country to turn it around." Third, Trump claimed that his statements were "kidding," and that "We have a good time. What I say is what I say." This part of his answer also included a statement that sparked a headline-grabbing post-debate controversy, with Trump stating: "And honestly Megyn, if you don't like it, I'm sorry. I've been very nice to you, although I could probably maybe not be, based on the way you have treated me. But I wouldn't do that."

In the post-debate spin-room, Trump told a group of reporters that the "questions to me where much tougher than to other people," singling out Kelly for particular criticism, stating, "the questions to me were not nice. I didn't think they were appropriate. And I thought Megyn behaved very badly, personally" (as cited in Weigel, 2015, npg). Later that night, Trump expressed similar sentiment in a number of tweets in the wee hours of August 7, 2015, including:

- "@RubenMMoreno: @realDonaldTrump The biggest loser in the debate was @megynkelly. You can't out trump Donald Trump. You will lose!

- "@timjcam: @megynkelly @FrankLuntz @realDonaldTrump Fox viewers give low marks to bimbo @MegynKelly will consider other programs!"

- Wow, @megynkelly really bombed tonight. People are going wild on twitter! Funny to watch.

- I really enjoyed the debate tonight even though the @FoxNews trio, especially @megynkelly, was not very good or professional!

- "@Reid2962: @realDonaldTrump @FoxNews I expected better from @megynkelly, wondering what is her hidden agenda (Trump, 2015, npg)

Trump escalated his attacks on Kelly in an interview on CNN Tonight on August 7, where he said "she starts asking me all sorts of ridiculous questions and you know, you can see there was blood coming out of her eyes, blood coming out of her wherever..." (Trump, 2015, npg). Trump's statement drew significant criticism from many quarters, including media commentators, Republicans, and Democrats, many of whom described the statement as validating the necessity of Kelly's original question (Yan, 2015).

Although Trump later made a conciliatory gesture by granting Kelly an exclusive, broad-ranging interview ("Megyn Kelly Special," 2016, npg), this question and the ensuing controversy demonstrate that there is a potential opening for Clinton to both discombobulate Trump during their debates and to consolidate the significant gender gap reflected in current polls (Monmouth University, 2016, npg). Notably, Trump interrupted Kelly while she was asking the initial question, and there is a distinct possibility that Trump will show similar verbal aggression towards Clinton. Clinton thus may have ample opportunity to validate her campaign's contention that Trump's "tone" is too often inappropriate and that Trump tends to act as a "bully," rendering him unfit to occupy a position of moral leadership, like the presidency.

Question Three: Politically Incorrect Provocateur (Immigration)

Trump's third question, posed by Chris Wallace and addressing Trump's highly controversial position on undocumented immigration, contested whether Trump's stances were truthful and realistic enough to shape federal policy. Wallace asked:

> "You say that the Mexican government is sending criminals—rapists, drug dealers, across the border... and you have repeatedly said you have evidence that the Mexican government is doing that, but you have evidence you have refused or declined to share. Why not use this first Republican presidential debate to share your proof with the American people?"

Although Trump's answer was a bit convoluted, he advanced three responses. First, he took credit for elevating the status of immigration policy in the campaign, claiming "If it weren't for me, you wouldn't even be talking about illegal immigration." Second, Trump again engaged in his favored strategy of attacking the media, arguing that his statements on the issue had been misreported, and describing journalists as "a very dishonest lot... in the world of politics..." Third, Trump maintained that events subsequent to his statement had validated his claims, noting that "since then, many killings, murders, crime, drugs pouring across the border, are money going out and the drugs coming in," then pivoting to a go-to applause line about the need to "build a wall" along the U.S. Mexico border. Wallace then pressed Trump for "specific evidence that the Mexican government is sending criminals across the border..." Trump claimed that officials in the Border Patrol that he had spoken with at the border supported his claims. Trump then voiced another applause line, noting that "our leaders are stupid...," contrasting them with those of Mexico, who are "much smarter, much sharper, much more cunning."

This exchange illustrates several important elements of Trump's overall strategy. He frames his campaign as the only one willing to speak uncomfortable truths about difficult political issues, and often asserts that he says what other people are thinking, but are afraid to say in public. Trump also frequently attacks the mainstream media as elitist and dishonest, which both potentially inoculates himself from media criticism and burnishes his anti-establishment credentials. Further, when challenged on the factual basis of a statement, Trump often cites unnamed sources as supporting his position, making it difficult to concretely invalidate any particular statement. Trump is also careful to blame the purported incompetence of our government officials for the problem of undocumented immigration, both potentially deflecting charges of racial animus and supporting his broader campaign theme of the need to bring private sector executive experience to the White House.

A candidate preparing to debate Trump should be prepared for a similar strategy in addressing controversial statements. Although Trump's post-convention decline in national polls may indicate that he is not entirely insulated from the furor generated by many of his public comments, the past year demonstrates how Trump seems to defy a conventional understanding of national campaign rhetoric. Not only is it difficult to make ostensibly damaging statements "stick" to Trump, but many of his supporters are energized by Trump's demonstrated disdain for "political correctness." When Clinton takes on Trump starting in September, she is unlikely to make much headway in reaching out to the segments of the electorate who agree with Trump, nor is it necessarily productive for Clinton to invest much debate time in a point-by-point refutation of

Trump's more controversial assertions. Instead, a potentially fruitful strategy is to approach responding to inflammatory Trump statements as an opportunity to identify with the members of her prospective electoral coalition who find such statements to be harmful, and potentially as evidence of an underlying animus.

Questions Four & Six: Conservative Credentials (Health Care, Abortion)

Perhaps the strongest test of Trump's credentials as a "real" conservative came during the debate's third theme question, when moderator Baier probed Trump on why he now labels Obamacare "a disaster," when "15 years ago, you called yourself a liberal on health care. You were for a single payer system, a Canadian-style system." Baier challenged Trump, asking "Why were you for that then and why aren't you for it now?"

The opening to Trump's answer had nothing to do with health care policy, pivoting back to the immediately preceding exchange among several of the other candidates about the threat posed by the Islamic State and various criticisms of the Obama administration's foreign policy, noting his strong, early opposition to the war in Iraq, claiming that he was vindicated in arguing in July of 2004 that "it was going to destabilize the Middle East." This strategy of using time allocated for answering one question to interject an argument about a previously-discussed issue appears frequently in political debates. This type of response can aid a candidate in at least two ways, since it regularly results in additional speaking time as the candidate's inevitably truncated response to the initial query spurs the moderator to ask a related follow-up, and it also capitalizes on the debate's response rules to make it difficult for an opponent to immediately respond to a new attack.

Trump then responded to Baier's question, observing that a single payer system has its merits, working in both Canada and Scotland, and in America "could have worked in a different age, which is the age you are talking about here." Trump clearly was attempting to distance himself from a policy position that has become anathema to Republican voters. Trump then touted his only to-date health care proposal, noting that "What I'd like to see is a private system without artificial lines around every state," claiming that a lack of competition, which he has seen in his own business, is the root of the problem. Trump turned to a core campaign theme, namely the corruption and incompetence of politicians, explaining, "You know why?

Because the insurance companies are making a fortune because they have control of the politicians, of course, with the exception of the politicians on this stage. But they have total control of the politicians. They're making a fortune."

The question also subsequently afforded Trump an opening to humble an opponent and highlight his argument that money is corrupting the American political system. Rand Paul objected to Trump's effort to divorce himself from his prior support of a single-payer system, observing that "News flash, the Republican Party's been fighting against a single-payer system... for a decade. So I think you're on the wrong side of this if you're still arguing for a single-payer system." Trump used this as an opportunity to interject an assessment of Paul's debate performance, claiming that Paul misheard Trump, and noting that "You're having a hard time tonight." Baier then asked a more pointed follow-up, noting that Trump had "also supported a host of other liberal policies" and "donated to several Democratic candidates, Hillary Clinton included, Nancy Pelosi." Baier invited Trump to explain a recent statement by the candidate justifying those donations, "When you give, they do whatever the hell you want them to do." After some joking cross-talk between Trump and several other candidates, Trump launched into a now-familiar indictment of the political process, stating that "our system is broken" and nothing that as "a businessman, I give to everybody. When they call, I give." Trump claimed that these donations gave him influence and access, noting that "When I need something from them two years later, three years later, I call them, they are there for me."

Trump's sixth question also questioned his commitment to core Republican principles. Again facing Kelly, citing critics who "say you often sound more like a Democrat than a Republican," Trump was asked to explain previous statements about being "very pro-choice" and describing other GOP candidates as "clowns and puppets." Trump immediately pivoted to the great conservative icon, Ronald Reagan, whom Trump claimed had, like himself, "evolved on many issues." Trump described himself as "pro-life," and as always having "hate[d] the concept of abortion." Trump also related an anecdote of friends who decided to forego an abortion, having a child that "today is a total superstar...." Trump also justified his criticism of some Republican policies, claiming that his experiences living in New York City, which he described as "almost exclusively Democrat" had permitted him to "see some of the negatives" of George W. Bush's administration, which he blamed for Obama's victory in 2008.

A future Trump opponent can learn a great deal from Trump's responses to these questions. First, Trump is practiced at dissociating himself from previous positions and public statements, with the candidate often either insisting that he was being misquoted, or that some intervening event had compelled him to change his perspective. Second, Trump will seize the opportunity to demonstrate his own strength by portraying an opponent as weak. Not only does Trump frequently refer to his poll numbers when he is on the debate stage (at least when he is ahead), but he often attaches demeaning labels to his opponents. Finally, Trump seemingly enjoys attacking his opponents for being beholden to a "crooked" political system, contrasting the dependence of traditional politicians on the donor class with his own financial muscle, which Trump claims makes him immune to donor demands. Trump's ability to direct his answers and public statements towards the outsized role of money in campaigns and the lawmaking process both plays on the public's fear that their interests are not reflected in government policy and to highlight his independence and wealth, a major campaign theme.

Questions Five & Seven: Trump's Competence (Economy, Foreign Policy)

Wallace chose to take on Trump's ability to improve the nation's economy, asking "why should we trust you to run the nation's business?" Wallace framed the question around a challenge to Trump's business record, noting that "Trump corporations, casinos, and hotels, have declared bankruptcy four times over the last quarter-century…" and citing "financial experts involved in those bankruptcies" who claimed that "lenders to your companies lost billions of dollars…" challenging Trump's strongest argument to leadership competence, namely his purported success in the business world.

Trump began his response with a campaign trail-tested argument defending his utilization of bankruptcy laws, claiming that he "used the laws of this country just like the greatest people you read about every day in business have used the laws of this country, the chapter laws, to do a great job for my company, for myself, for my employees, for my family, et cetera." He also denied that he had ever personally gone bankrupt, noting that "Out of the hundreds of deals that [he'd] done… on four occasions, [he'd] taken advantage of the laws of this country…" much like "virtually every person that you read about on the front of the business sections..." whose bankruptcies, unlike Trump's are ignored by the press. Trump also defended his business record, claiming that he had "built a network of more than $10 billion..." that "employ[s] thousands of people...."

When pushed by Wallace about the 2009 failure of Trump entertainment resorts, where Wallace claimed that "lenders to your company lost over $1 billion and more than 1,100 people were laid off..." Trump minimized the alleged harm, nothing that "these lenders aren't babies. These are total killers. These are not the nice, sweet little people that you think, OK?" Trump also claimed that his business problems were endemic to the climate of Atlantic City, where "every company virtually in Atlantic City went bankrupt." Trump even credited himself for having the foresight to leave Atlantic City "before it totally cratered..." concluding that he "made a lot of money in Atlantic City, and I'm very proud of it. I want to tell you that. Very, very proud of it." He also said the country was in debt $19 trillion, implying that his bankruptcy experience would help him "straighten out that mess."

Baier later tested Trump's credentials on foreign policy. Baier asked Trump how he would respond to the news that General Qassem Soleimani, "blamed for hundreds of U.S. troops death in Iraq, and Afghanistan" was visiting Iran, with such a visit defying "U.N. Security Council Resolutions to confine him to Iran." Trump did not answer the question directly, but instead took the opportunity to attack the Obama administration's Iran policy. Trump said that "[w]e have a president who doesn't have a clue. I would say he's incompetent, but I don't want to do that because that's not nice..." and instead said a Trump policy would be "the polar opposite...." Trump maintained that the administration was responsible for giving the Iranian government "$150 billion dollars plus," comparing Iran to a stock that "you folks should go out and buy it right now because you'll quadruple...." Trump closed to applause by describing Obama's policy as a "disgrace" that is "going to lead to destruction in large parts of the world."

Both of these questions reveal potential weaknesses that Clinton could exploit in future debates. Much of Trump's candidacy is built around a narrative of business acumen and significant personal wealth. Trump claims to have a net worth of over $10 billion, and commonly argues that his sharp deal-making capabilities provide him with the unique capacity to broker the bargains needed to solve the nation's problems. However, many elements of Trump's business dealings, including the aforementioned bankruptcies, could be leveraged to undermine Trump's narrative. Obama successfully turned Mitt Romney's business success against him during the 2012 campaign, fusing claims about job losses related to many Romney-led corporate takeovers with anecdotes from Romney's personal life (car elevator, dog riding on the station wagon roof) to demonstrate that Romney was out of touch with the needs of ordinary voters. Similarly Clinton could use the debates to solidify a counter-narrative that portrays Trump as a shady businessman and self-promoter whose professional accomplishments are both exaggerated and built upon unethical business practices. Trump's defense of his corporate bankruptcies depend on a distinction between personal and corporate finances that many potential voters may find difficult to follow. Clinton also has an opportunity to showcase her foreign policy experience. Trump's responses to foreign policy questions, including Baier's, can often fairly be described as awkward and short on detail, likely reflecting his relative lack of professional expertise with foreign policy matters. Clinton's ability to discuss such matters in both detail and at length may serve her well during the debates, not necessarily because she can persuade the audience that she is right on any particular issue, but because she can bolster the perception among some parts of the electorate that she is more competent to address critical national security issues.

Trump's approach to campaign debates defies convention. However, despite "breaking" most of the rules of presidential debating and campaigning, he emerged victorious from a crowded Republican field. Trump's performances during the primary debates exceeded the expectations of both mainstream pundits and professional political operatives alike, and his sometimes heretical methods confounded many of Trump's opponents. The Cleveland primary debate shows that debating Trump successfully will require Clinton to be prepared to fend off belittling monikers, attacks against the ineffectiveness and corruption of the governing elite, and accusations of embracing "political correctness" over decisive action. Trump has also displayed a sometimes overly-aggressive debating style and lower comfort level in discussing both foreign policy details and some of his past political positions and business dealings. If Clinton can exploit these weaknesses while deflecting Trump's likely criticisms, we may witness some truly memorable debates this fall.

References

Cheney, K. (2015, August 6). Yes, It's the Trump Show. *Politico*. Retrieved from http://www.politico.com/story/2015/08/republican-debate-donald-trump-121114

Donald Trump Live on 'CNN Tonight' (2015, August 7). *CNN Tonight*. Retrieved from http://transcripts.cnn.com/TRANSCRIPTS/1508/07/cnnt.01.html

Donald Trump Transcript: 'Our Country Needs a Truly Great Leader' (2015, June 16). *Wall Street Journal*. Retrieved from http://blogs.wsj.com/washwire/2015/06/16/donald-trump-transcript-our-country-needs-a-truly-great-leader

Dutton, S., De Pinto, J., Salvanto, A., & Backus, F. (2015, August 4). CBS News Poll: Donald Trump Leads GOP Field in 2016 Presidential Race. *CBS News*. Retrieved from http://www.cbsnews.com/news/cbs-news-poll-donald-trump-leads-gop-field-in-2016-presidential-race

Megyn Kelly Special: Trump Defends Tone, Says Bid Will Be 'Complete Waste' if He Doesn't Win (2016, May 18). *Fox News*. Retrieved from http://www.foxnews.com/politics/2016/05/18/megyn-kelly-special-trump-defends-tone-says-bid-will-be-complete-waste-if-doesn-t-win.html

Monmouth University Polling Institute. (2016, August 8). Clinton Opens Post-Convention Lead. Retrieved from http://www.monmouth.edu/polling-institute/reports/MonmouthPoll_US_080816

Presidential Candidate Donald Trump at the Family Leadership Summit [Video File] (2015, July 18). *C-SPAN*. Retrieved from https://www.c-span.org/video/?327045-5/presidential-candidate-donald-trump-family-leadership-summit

Republican Candidates Debate in Detroit, Michigan. (2016, March 3). *American Presidency Project*. Retrieved from http://www.presidency.ucsb.edu/ws/index.php?pid=111711

Republican Debate: Analysis and Highlights. (2015, August 6). *New York Times*. Retrieved from http://www.nytimes.com/live/republican-debate-election-2016-cleveland/a-final-count-of-candidate-speaking-time/

Schlesinger, R. (2015, August 3). A Passing Fancy for the GOP. *U.S. News & World Report*. Retrieved from http://www.usnews.com/opinion/blogs/robert-schlesinger/2015/08/03/the-gop-doesnt-take-donald-trump-seriously-as-candidate-for-president

Stelter, B. (2015, August 7). Fox's GOP Debate Has Record 24 Million Viewers. *CNN Money*. Retrieved from http://money.cnn.com/2015/08/07/media/gop-debate-fox-news-ratings

Transcript: Read the Full Text of the Primetime Republican Debate (2015, August 6). *Time*. Retrieved from http://time.com/3988276/republican-debate-primetime-transcript-full-text/

Trump, D. (2015, August 7). Twitter. Retrieved from https://twitter.com/realDonaldTrump/status/629553442944602112; https://twitter.com/realDonaldTrump/status/629553612839124992;

https://twitter.com/realDonaldTrump/status/629553612
839124992;
https://twitter.com/realDonaldTrump/status/629561051
982495744;
https://twitter.com/realDonaldTrump/status/629562617
548378112

Trump Taking His Message To Phoenix (2015, July 11).
    CNN Newsroom. Retrieved from
    http://www.cnn.com/TRANSCRIPTS/1507/11/cnr.08.
    html

Univision Ends Miss Universe Business Deal Over Trump
    Mexico Comments (2015, June 25). *NBC News*.
    Retrieved from:
    http://www.nbcnews.com/news/latino/univision-no-
    miss-universe-due-trump-mexico-comments-n381696

Weigel, D. (2015, August 7). Donald Trump: Fox Anchor
    'Megyn [Kelly] Behaved Very Badly'. *Washington
    Post*. Retrieved from
    https://www.washingtonpost.com/news/post-
    politics/wp/2015/08/07/donald-trump-fox-anchor-
    megyn-kelly-behaved-very-badly

Yan, H. (2015, August 8). Donald Trump's 'Blood'
    Comment about Megyn Kelly Draws Outrage. *CNN
    Politics*. Retrieved from
    http://www.cnn.com/2015/08/08/politics/donald-
    trump-cnn-megyn-kelly-comment

CHAPTER TWO

<<<<<<<<<<<<<<<<<<<<O>>>>>>>>>>>>>>>>>>

GOP Primary Debate #2
Simi Valley, California, September 16, 2015
Sarah Partlow-Lefevre

<<<<<<<<<<<<<<<<<<<<O>>>>>>>>>>>>>>>>>>

Donald Trump led the pack of Republican candidates racing to the second GOP primary debate in Simi Valley, California. The day before the debate (September 15), his poll numbers were at 30.2% (Wall Street Journal, 2016). On September 16, 2015, the debate among the eleven leading Republicans lasted more than three hours, and Trump's performance did not impress most debate analysts. Indeed, Trump lost ground in the polls, but managed to maintain his lead. CNBC's average poll number of 25.22% allowed Trump to qualify for the third debate as the frontrunner with Ben Carson in second place at 19.78% (Thompson & Yeip, 2015). While Trump's performance in the debate was lackluster, structural, content, and strategic approaches allowed him to stay in the race. In this essay, I examine his debate performance to understand the reasons that Simi Valley wasn't fatal to his campaign. First, structural and procedural components such as candidate positioning, the right to reply, and questions addressed to

Trump allowed him to speak more than other candidates and aided his performance. Second, he conveyed two core themes: that he is a celebrated businessman who knows how to manage and make decisions; and, that he can make America great again. While Trump was persistently vague on policy, he constructed himself as an agenda-setter on the immigration debate and successfully tapped into public disaffection with the political status quo. Finally, other tactics aided in his performance and supported his continued popularity including; strategic nonparticipation, intentional ambiguity, placation, refusing to apologize, addressing other candidates by their first names, and interruption of other candidates. In this essay I first outline Trump's key exchanges of the debate and explore how Trump's nontraditional debate style might appeal to disaffected voters. On structural, thematic, and tactical levels, Trump's performance allowed him to maintain his lead and effectively continue his campaign.

Trump's Role in the Debate

The second Republican primary debate featured 11 candidates standing in a slight arc in front of Ronald Reagan's Air Force One in his Presidential Library. Moderators were Jake Tapper (CNN), Dana Bash (CNN), and Hugh Hewitt (Salem Radio Network). Debate rules required one-minute answers, 30-second follow-ups, and the right to respond to criticism. Candidates introduced themselves and responded to questions raising issues from social security to foreign policy.

Despite Trump speaking far more than others, many analysts declared Fiorina the winner (Hohmann & Viebeck, 2015; Lapinski & Kopicki, 2015; Perticone, 2015; Silver, 2015b; Walsh, 2015). After the debate, Trump stated, "All of the polls seem to say I did very well. . . . The Drudge Report right now has me at 64%. . . . Every poll right now has me winning it" (Trump assesses second GOP debate performance, 2015). Trump declared himself the winner and some informal online polls agreed: A Drudge Report poll gave Trump 53.35% (as cited in Headlines and Global News, 2015); A Slate reader's poll put Trump at 44% (Kirk, 2015); and, a Time reader's poll logged almost 139 thousand votes and placed Trump at 55% (Lacey, 2015). These results foreshadowed a continuing disconnect between the media, debate analysts, and GOP voters.

Trump's Introduction

In his introduction, Trump represented the core themes of his strength as a leader and businessman, the promise of a return to a better past, a renewal of American wealth,

elimination of Obamacare and support for the military.
Trump introduced himself,

> "I'm Donald Trump. I wrote *'The Art of the
> Deal* . . . I've made billions and billions of
> dollars dealing with people all over the
> world, and I want to put whatever that talent
> is to work for this country so we have great
> trade deals, we make our country rich again,
> we make it great again. We build our
> military, we take care of our vets, we get rid
> of Obamacare, and we have a great life
> altogether" (Peters & Woolley, 2015).

Thus, Trump introduced himself as a wildly successful
businessman who could craft deals in any context, make
America wealthy, and restore American greatness.
Repeated use of "we" invited supporters to assume they
would reap the benefits of "a great life altogether."

Character & Nuclear Access

The next significant exchange involving Trump was in
response to the question of whether Fiorina would "feel
comfortable with Donald Trump's finger on the nuclear
codes?" (Peters & Woolley, 2015). In response, Fiorina
called Trump, "a wonderful entertainer" and suggested
each candidate's "character and capability" would be

"revealed over time and under pressure" (Peters & Woolley, 2015). He responded directly, affirming his monetary success and shifting the topic to his business acumen. He stated, "What I am far and away greater than an entertainer is a businessman, and that's the kind of mindset this country needs to bring it back, because we owe $19 trillion right now" (Peters & Woolley, 2015). Trump claimed also be strong on the international stage. He stated. "Believe me, my temperament is very good, very calm. But we will be respected outside of this country. We are not respected now" (Peters & Woolley, 2015).

In his answer, he also criticized Rand Paul's participation in the debate because of low poll numbers. Paul criticized Trump for using a "non-sequitur" and suggested that Trump had a "sophomoric quality" (Peters & Woolley, 2015). Paul stated, Trump's "visceral response to attack people on their appearance — short, tall, fat, ugly — my goodness, that happened in junior high . . . Would we not all be worried to have someone like that in charge of the nuclear arsenal?" (Peters & Woolley, 2015). In response, Trump joked, "I never attacked him on his look, and believe me, there's plenty of subject matter right there" (Peters & Woolley, 2015). While Rand Paul seemed to speak only to educated voters through the use of words such as non- sequitur and sophomoric, Trump incorporated humor at Paul's expense.

Trump Versus Insider Politicians

Tapper asked Trump to, "Tell Governor Bush why you are a serious candidate and what your qualifications are to be commander-in-chief?" (Peters & Woolley, 2015). Trump suggested, "I've actually been in politics all my life ... on that side as opposed to this side. I'm now a politician ... Obviously, I'm doing pretty well. I'm number one in every poll by a lot" (Peters & Woolley, 2015). He again turned the discussion to his success. He said,

> "I've ... been successful all over the world. Everything I've done virtually has been a tremendous success ... I've made a tremendous amount of money in Atlantic City. I left seven years ago, I've gotten great credit for my timing, and that's what I'm all about" (Peters & Woolley, 2015).

Trump distinguished himself from the other candidates, suggesting that only a businessman can restore wealth to America. He said,

> "I'm a businessman, did really well ... I want to ... put that ability into this country to make our country rich again. And I can do

that, and I'm not sure that anybody else in the group will be able to do that" (Peters & Woolley, 2015).

Bush responded attacking Obama rather than directly addressing Trump's qualifications. He said,

"This administration, with President Obama and Hillary Clinton, has created insecurity the likes of which we never would've imagined. There's not a place in the world where we're better off today than six and a half years ago" (Peters & Woolley, 2015).

Bush obliquely attacked Trump without directly addressing Trump's qualities. He opted to stress his own qualifications. He continued, "That requires an understanding and appreciation of American leadership in the world. You can't just ... insult leaders around the world and expect a good result. You have to do this with a steady hand ... I have those skills" (Peters & Woolley, 2015). At this point, Walker suggested it wasn't a real debate. He said, "We're not talking about real issues. And Mr. Trump, we don't need an apprentice in the White House [applause]" (Peters & Woolley, 2015).

An unmoderated exchange between Walker and Trump followed. Trump accused Walker of losing "2.2 billion" in Wisconsin "right now" while Walker suggested that Trump could never balance a budget because Trump "took four major projects to bankruptcy over and over and over again" (Peters & Woolley, 2015). Trump defended his actions and continued to attack Walker. Trump stated, "I never went bank bankrupt … I used the law four times … I did a very good job … people are very, very impressed with what I've done, the business people" (Peters & Woolley, 2015). Trump attacked Walker for losing 2.2 billion in Wisconsin. Trump said, "You were supposed to make a billion … You lost 2.2 … That's a fact. And when the people of Iowa found that out, I went to No. 1 and you went down the tubes" (Peters & Woolley, 2015).

Trump's next significant interaction pitted Trump as businessman against Bush and politicians. Tapper asked Bush about perceptions that he was a "puppet for … donors" as opposed to Trump who was not "bought and paid for by wealthy donors" (Peters & Woolley, 2015). In response, Bush shifted Trump into the position of a wealthy donor whose influence he had resisted by denying legalized casino gambling in Florida. Trump rejected Bush's version of events suggesting he would have gotten it if he'd wanted it. Trump and Bush spoke over each other. Finally, Trump said, "the donors, the special interests, the lobbyists have very strong power over these people" (Peters & Woolley, 2015). In contrast, Trump said his wealth exempted him from obligations to donors. He stated,

> "I'm spending all of my money ... I turn down so much ... I could have double and triple what he's got ... I understand the game ... And they have a lot of control over our politicians ... I am not accepting any money from anybody. Nobody has control of me other than the people of this country. I'm going to do the right thing" (Peters & Woolley, 2015).

Trump built his character as uniquely honest and willing to do the right thing because he was not a politician. Then Bush criticized Trump for supporting Clinton previously. To this, Trump replied, "I was a businessman, I got along with Clinton, I got along with everybody. That was my job" (Peters & Woolley, 2015). When Bush pushed the attack, Trump joked, "OK, more energy tonight. I like that" (Peters & Woolley, 2015). Trump extended his argument, "It was my obligation as a businessman to my family, to my company, to my employees, to get along with all politicians … I did a damn good job in doing it" (Peters & Woolley, 2015). Trump argued that his proper role as a businessman was to get along with everyone. Again, Bush attempted to reorient the conversation to Trump's pursuit of gambling. Trump repeated, "Don't make things up" (Peters & Woolley, 2015). Ben Carson ended the exchange, suggesting that he was able to raise money without getting "in bed with special interest groups" or licking "the boots of billionaires" (Peters & Woolley, 2015). Carson ended the exchange. He said, "The pundits forgot about … the people. And they are really in charge" (Peters & Woolley, 2015). Bush lost the exchange. He did not defend politicians as a class or his dealings with lobbyists. Trump, on the other hand, portrayed himself as unbiased and an independent thinker who could fill roles as appropriate.

Foreign Policy

Trump also spoke about foreign policy, including relations with Putin and Russian involvement in Syria. Trump stated that he would not only get along with Putin, but that he would demand respect. He said, Putin "has absolutely no respect for President Obama. Zero" (Peters & Woolley, 2015). He suggested that the United States shouldn't be fighting ISIS in Syria. Instead, we should "let them fight each other and pick up the remnants" (Peters &

Woolley, 2015). He claimed he would get along with Putin broadening the claim to all world leaders (Peters & Woolley, 2015). Trump said he would demand respect and promote global stability. He stated,

> "I would get along with him … I would get along with a lot of the world leaders that this country is not getting along with … China … the heads of Mexico. We don't get along with anybody, and … they rip us left and right. They take advantage of us economically and every other way … I will get along … and we will have a much more stable … world" (Peters & Woolley, 2015).

When asked about specific actions in regard to Putin, Trump generalized, "I will get along … we won't have the kind of problems that our country has right now with Russia and many other nations" (Peters & Woolley, 2015). Tapper asked Trump to compare his response to Obama's response to Assad in Syria. Tapper said, "We now have 4 million refugees, Syria is a living hell … what would you have done when Bashar Assad crossed the line?" (Peters & Woolley, 2015). Trump responded, "I wouldn't have drawn the line" and indicated that there was an obligation to act once the line was drawn (Peters & Woolley, 2015). Trump said, Obama "just doesn't have courage … Had he … really gone in … with tremendous force, you wouldn't have millions of people displaced all over the world" (Peters & Woolley, 2015). Trump constructed himself as a leader who would demand respect from the world and follow through on his word without proposing a single policy action.

Women's Health & Carly Fiorina's Looks

In this segment, Tapper asked Bush about Trump's claim that Bush's comment that he was "not sure we need a half billion for women's health issues" would "haunt" him (Peters & Woolley, 2015). Bush responded by restating his support for defunding Planned Parenthood and opposing abortion (Peters & Woolley, 2015). Tapper redirected the question to Trump who contrasted Bush's lack of care for women with his assertion he would "take care of women" and "respect" women (Peters & Woolley, 2015). Then, Trump began to discuss Iran and North Korea and the dangerous world. He said,

> "I would like to get back to the Iran situation … The agreement was terrible … One of the worst contracts of any kind. … And … North Korea where you have this maniac sitting there and he actually has nuclear

weapons and somebody better start thinking about North Korea" (Peters & Woolley, 2015).

Trump spent 71 words generically decrying Bush's position on women's health, he advanced no policy and used the remaining 145 words of his answer to appeal to fear by discussing threats posed by Iran and North Korea. Tapper turned to Bush. Bush's rejoinder was then interrupted continuously by Trump repeatedly demanding that Bush "said it" (Peters & Woolley, 2015). During the eighty-word exchange, Trump used the variations words "say it" or "said it" seven times. Bush and Trump spoke over one another and Trump interrupted Bush multiple times.

Tapper then asked Fiorina about a comment Trump made about her face. Tapper quoted Trump saying, "Look at that face. Would anyone vote for that? Can you imagine that, the face of our next president?" and Trump's later correction that he was discussing Fiorina's "persona, not ... appearance" (Peters & Woolley, 2015). Fiorina looked directly at the camera and scored applause, saying, "Mr. Trump said that he heard Mr. Bush very clearly and what Mr. Bush said. I think women all over this country heard very clearly what Mr. Trump said (Peters & Woolley,

2015). The exchange ended with Trump's statement, "I think she's got a beautiful face, and I think she's a beautiful woman" before Tapper cut to a commercial break (Peters & Woolley, 2015).

Immigration

On immigration, Tapper asked Trump about his plan to "forcibly deport 11 to 12 million people" (Peters & Woolley, 2015). Trump supported his deportation plan, specifying the need to "build a wall that works" (Peters & Woolley, 2015). He claimed that he would deport "a lot of really bad dudes . . . from outside" (Peters & Woolley, 2015). He said. "If I get elected, first day they're gone. Gangs all over the place. Chicago, Baltimore . . ." (Peters & Woolley, 2015). He mentioned Katie who was shot, in San Francisco, by an illegal immigrant. Trump claimed he initiated the immigration debate,

> "I don't think you'd even be talking about illegal immigration if it weren't for me. So, we have a country of laws . . . If they've had a bad record, if they've been arrested, if they've been in jail, they're never coming back . . . Right now, we don't have a country, we don't have a border, and we're

going to do something about it" (Peters & Woolley, 2015).

Trump linked illegal immigration to American decline. His phrasing also positioned Trump as the one who would literally revive the United States by restoring geographic boundaries.

Jeb Bush's Wife

Dana Bash asked about Trump's suggestion that Bush's views on immigration were swayed by his wife. She said, "Did Mr. Trump go too far in invoking your wife?" (Peters & Woolley, 2015). Bush, took the opportunity to demand an apology. He said, "To subject my wife into the middle of a raucous political conversation was completely inappropriate, and I hope you apologize for that, Donald" (Peters & Woolley, 2015). Trump deflected the demand, calling Bush's wife a "lovely woman" (Peters & Woolley, 2015). Bush said, "She is absolutely the love of my life, and she's right here . . . why don't you apologize to her right now" (Peters & Woolley, 2015). To which Trump responded, "No, I won't do that, because I've said nothing wrong. . . . But I do hear she's a lovely woman" (Peters & Woolley, 2015). During this exchange, Bush and Trump interrupted each other several times. After Trump refused to apologize, Bush turned to the task of defending his wife. He said,

> "My wife is a Mexican-American. She's an American by choice. She loves this country . . . and she wants a secure border. But she wants to embrace the traditional American values . . . Are we going to take the Reagan approach, the hopeful optimistic approach . . . Or the Donald Trump approach? The approach that says that everything is bad, that everything is coming to an end" (Peters & Woolley, 2015).

Trump cut Bush off, "Jeb said . . . they come into our country as an act of love . . . this is not an act of love. He's weak on immigration . . . He doesn't get my vote" (Peters & Woolley, 2015).

Birthright Citizenship

Part of the immigration debate, birthright citizenship was the next topic on which Trump focused. Tapper asked about Trump's suggestion that birthright citizenship should be eliminated. Trump attacked the 14th Amendment stating, "it is wrong" according to "great legal scholars" (Peters & Woolley, 2015). Trump argued against granting birthright citizenship and suggested it could probably be changed without Congressional action. He said, "A woman gets pregnant. She's nine months, she walks across the border, she has the baby in the United States, and we take care of the baby for 85 years. I don't think so" (Peters & Woolley, 2015). He said most other countries don't have birthright citizenship, "Mexico and almost every other country anywhere in the world doesn't have that. We're the only ones dumb enough, stupid enough to have it" (Peters & Woolley, 2015). He said, "This is not just with respect to Mexico. They are coming from Asia to have babies here" (Peters & Woolley, 2015). He repeated his claim that it strained Americans, "All of a sudden, we have to take care of the babies for the life of the baby . . . We're going to take care of those babies for 70, 75, 80, 90 years? I don't think so" (Peters & Woolley, 2015). Fiorina responded that changing the Constitution is difficult, "You can't just wave your hands and say 'the 14th Amendment is gonna go away.' It will take an extremely arduous vote in Congress, followed by two-thirds of the states" (Peters & Woolley, 2015). To this, Trump reasserted that the 14th Amendment could be interpreted to disallow birthright citizenship. He said, "A reading of the 14th Amendment allows you to have an interpretation where this is not legal and where it can't be done . . . some of the greatest scholars agree with me" (Peters & Woolley, 2015).

Trump vs. Fiorina on Business Credentials

Trump's next significant interaction revolved around comparing his business credentials with Fiorina's. Tapper cited Trump's statement that Fiorina "ran HP into the ground" and asked why she was a better executive than Trump (Peters & Woolley, 2015). Fiorina said, she "led Hewlett Packard through . . . the worst technology recession in 25 years" (Peters & Woolley, 2015). Yet, she made "tough choices," preserved "80,000 jobs," and grew "160,000 jobs" (Peters & Woolley, 2015). She claimed that her former detractor, Tom Perkins, believed that she would be "a magnificent president of the United States" (Peters & Woolley, 2015). Tapper then asked Trump about his job creation potential. Trump claimed that Fiorina failed as CEO at HP and at Lucent. He said, "The company [HP] is a disaster and continues to be a disaster . . . Today, on the front page of the Wall Street Journal, they fired another 25 or 30,000 people . . . revenues went up . . . because she bought Compaq, it was a terrible deal, and it really led to the destruction of the company . . . Lucent turned out to be a catastrophe also . . . She can't run any of my companies" (Peters & Woolley, 2015).

Fiorina called Sonnenfeld "a well-known Clintonite" who "had it out for me from the moment I arrived at Hewlett Packard" and turned to Trump's corporate bankruptcies (Peters & Woolley, 2015). She said,

> "You ran up mountains of debt, as well as losses, using other people's money, and you were forced to file for bankruptcy not once . . . a record four times. Why should we trust you to manage the finances . . . of this nation any differently than you managed the finances . . . of your casinos?" (Peters & Woolley, 2015).

Throughout this attack, Trump interrupted. Stating that "Atlantic City is a disaster" and "almost everybody is in trouble" (Peters & Woolley, 2015). He argued that he made "over $10 billion" and that he "did great in Atlantic City" because he "knew when to get out" (Peters & Woolley, 2015). He suggested he would make "great deals for this country" (Peters & Woolley, 2015).

Lack of Extensive Foreign Policy Knowledge

Trump's next exchange involved Rubio's concern about Trump's foreign policy credentials. Tapper asked, how Trump could be commander-in-chief if he "didn't seem to know the details about some of the enemies the U.S. faces" (Peters & Woolley, 2015). Trump responded,

> "Hugh was giving me name after name, Arab name, Arab name, and there are few people anywhere, anywhere that would have known those names. I think he was reading them off a sheet . . . I will have the finest team that anybody has put together and we will solve a lot of problems" (Peters & Woolley, 2015).

Trump said that as a business man he was "not sitting in the United States Senate" but that he would "know more about the problems of this world by the time I sit" (Peters & Woolley, 2015). Trump's argument required him to learn rather than rely on previous knowledge. He didn't claim expertise. Rather, he claimed to be an expert at harnessing and channeling other people's expertise.

Opposition to the Iraq War

Hewitt followed up on Trump's claim to managing experts, asking,

> "You promised us great leaders . . . Bush has laid out 20 different people that have experience around the world . . . When are we going to get some names on your

military and your foreign policy advisers?"
(Peters & Woolley, 2015).

Trump said he was "meeting with terrific people" and that "it's about judgment" (Peters & Woolley, 2015). He argued that he proved his judgment by opposing the second Iraq invasion. He said, "You have to know when to use the military. I'm the only person up here that fought against going into Iraq" (Peters & Woolley, 2015). Trump cut off Paul's attempt to respond claiming Paul had little popular support. Bush questioned Trump's judgment, arguing that Trump believed that Clinton was the "best negotiator" for the Iran deal which was "really dangerous" (Peters & Woolley, 2015). Trump attacked Bush's brother, former President George W. Bush, stating, "Your brother's administration gave us Barack Obama, because it was such a disaster . . . that Abraham Lincoln couldn't have been elected" (Peters & Woolley, 2015). In response, Bush invoked the image of a firefighter in the ruins of the World Trade Center and said, "There's one thing I know for sure. He kept us safe. . . . He sent a clear signal that the United States would be strong and fight Islamic terrorism" (Peters & Woolley, 2015). Trump denied Bush's claim, "You feel safe right now? I don't feel so safe" (Peters & Woolley, 2015). When Paul interjected that Obama was to blame,

Trump referenced "the collapse of the economy" (Peters & Woolley, 2015).

Social Security

Dana Bash prefaced her social security question by quoting Trump's claims that he's "by far the richest person on this stage" (Peters & Woolley, 2015). She asked whether Trump agreed with Christie's assertion that "billionaires like you . . . should no longer get Social Security, or at least there should be limits based on . . . their income" (Peters & Woolley, 2015). Trump personalized his response, saying that he would be willing to "check it off, and say I will not get Social Security" (Peters & Woolley, 2015). When asked to articulate a policy, Trump asserted his policy would be popular. He said.

> "As a policy, I would almost leave it up to the people. Don't forget they pay in . . . There are people that truly don't need it, and there are many people that do need it very, very badly. And I would be willing to write mine off 100 percent, Dana" (Peters & Woolley, 2015).

Vaccines & Autism

Tapper introduced the vaccine debate, highlighting the "backlash against vaccines that was blamed for a measles outbreak here in California" (Peters & Woolley, 2015). Tapper asked Dr. Carson if Trump should stop connecting "childhood vaccines to autism, which, as you know, the medical community adamantly disputes" (Peters & Woolley, 2015). Carson said, "numerous studies . . . have not demonstrated that there is any correlation between vaccines and autism" and that "vaccines are very important" (Peters & Woolley, 2015). He noted that some vaccines were less important and "there should be some discretion in those cases" (Peters & Woolley, 2015). Of Trump, Carson said, "I think he's an intelligent man and will make the correct decision after getting the real facts" (Peters & Woolley, 2015). Trump reaffirmed his belief that vaccines cause autism, arguing vaccines should be spread out with smaller doses. He said, "It looks just like it's meant for a horse, not for a child." He used a single example to claim a link to autism. He said, "Just the other day, two years old . . . a beautiful child went to have the vaccine, and came back, and a week later got a tremendous fever, got very, very sick, now is autistic" (Peters & Woolley, 2015). Trump concluded that administering vaccines "in little sections" would "see a big impact on autism" (Peters & Woolley, 2015). Carson denied the link between vaccines citing "extremely well-documented proof" and affirmed Trump's position supporting a reduction in "the number and proximity" of doses (Peters & Woolley, 2015). By agreeing with Trump's prescription, Carson enhanced Trump's credibility while denying links between vaccines and autism.

Who Won the Debate?

Pundits quickly began declaring Fiorina the winner (Enten, 2015). After the debate, FiveThirtyEight asked twelve staff members to grade each candidate. "Everyone gave Fiorina and A-. A or A+" (Silver, 2015). In contrast, the FiveThirtyEight staff gave Donald Trump an average C+ with a high B+ and a low of D (Silver, 2015a). Approximately a week later, Enten analyzed eight national polls (IPSOS, Morning Consult, Zogby, Survey Monkey, CNN, FOX, Bloomberg, and Quinnipiac) and argued that they supported Fiorina's victory. Post-debate, Fiorina's average support increased by +5.2 (2015). Enten found, "A solid plurality of Republicans who watched the debate declared Fiorina the debate's winner (Trump came in a distant second)" (2015). Trump's post-debate numbers decreased by -3.1 on average (CNN found -8 while FOX found -1). Enten explained, "Even though a number of Republicans thought he won the debate, a larger percentage of Republicans said he did the worst job in it" (Enten, 2015).

Despite pundits and polls, Trump declared victory. Trump repeatedly stated that he was "very happy" about the debate and said "all of the polls seem to say I'm doing well" (Trump assesses second GOP debate performance, 2015). When asked about Fiorina's applause line, he said, "I think I got some of the biggest applause tonight" (Trump assesses second GOP debate performance, 2015). He stated, "Every poll right now has me winning it" (Trump assesses second GOP debate performance, 2015). Some online polls did declare Trump the winner including the Drudge Report (53.35%) (as cited in Headlines and Global News, 2015), Slate's reader's poll (44%) (Kirk, 2015), and Time (55%) (Lacey, 2015). Differences in the numbers hinted at a divide between debate analysts and those who found Trump persuasive. Trump credited his lack of political correctness with garnering the people's support. "I think one of the reasons I'm leading in every poll is because I'm not so politically correct. People get it."(Trump assesses second GOP debate performance, 2015). Whether Trump won or lost the debate, one thing is clear. He participated in the third debate as the leading Republican candidate for president.

Structural and Procedural Aspects of the Debate

Structural and procedural components including candidate positioning, the right to reply, and direct questions aided Trump's performance. Trump's position at center stage ensured plenty of camera time and made Trump visually dominant, implying his position as leader (for more about how visual argumentation functions see Birdsell & Groarke, 2007; Finnegan, 2001; Smith, 2007). Candidate positioning suggested, but did not explicitly state, that Trump was the candidate to beat. Tapper clarified, "These 11 Republicans are positioned on the stage based on their ranking in recent national polls" (Peters & Woolley, 2015). Trump's placement featured him prominently in photographic and video representations. The first video frames of the debate pictured all of the candidates. The camera then focused on the three front-runners and progressively showed candidates in rough order of their position in the polls.

Rules ensuring a right to reply and question distribution also advantaged Trump. Tapper explained,

"I will ask follow-up questions, I will attempt to guide the discussion. Candidates, I will try to make sure each of you gets your fair share of questions. You'll have one minute to answer and 30 seconds for follow-ups and rebuttals. I'll give you time to respond if you've been singled out for criticism" (Peters & Woolley, 2015).

Thirty-second introductions began with Paul and questioning proceeded from there. Trump spoke much more than any other candidate, topping out at 18:47 while Walker spoke for a mere 8:29 (Sprunt & Mutnick, 2015). Bush clocked in at 15:48, Fiorina at 13:30, Carson at 12:56, and Christie at 12:36, rounding out the top five candidates (Sprunt & Mutnick, 2015). Equal speaking time should have hovered around twelve minutes for each candidate (Byler, 2015). Trump, however, spoke for 6:38 more than average (Byler, 2015). The moderators' questions gave Trump an advantage because they asked Trump 13 direct questions, four more than Bush and ten more than Huckabee (Libresco, 2015b). The right to reply gave Trump more opportunities to speak because his status as front runner made other candidates more likely to criticize him, opening speaking opportunities for Trump (Byler,

2015). Trump had the right to reply nine times while Bush had it 10 times (Libresco, 2015b). All other candidates accessed the right to reply an average of 2.2 times during the debate (Libresco, 2015b). In fact, neither Kasich nor Huckabee used it at all (Libresco, 2015b). Additionally, the number of times moderators and other candidates addressed Trump gave the sense that he was a legitimate candidate. Trump was addressed 22 times – all other candidates were addressed an average of 8.7 times (Libresco, 2015b). Only Bush came close to Trump as he was addressed 19 times (Libresco, 2015b). Additionally, Trump was named and criticized far more than any other candidate. Second only to 29 negative mentions of Obama, Trump was named in a negative context 21 times (Koeze, 2015). Kasich and Huckabee were not attacked by name (Koeze, 2015). Negative attacks can also serve as an indication that the candidate is leading. Thus, structural and procedural elements such as visual representation, moderators' questions, and the right to reply advantaged Trump. Indeed, visual representations of Trump were more prominent and he spoke far more than any other candidate.

Minor Tactics

Several minor tactics may have helped to keep Trump on top in the GOP primary race. These included: strategic non-participation, intentional ambiguity, placation and refusal to apologize, addressing other candidates by their first names or not at all, and interrupting other candidates.

First, for a long period of time during the second half of the debate, Trump did not speak. During these questions, he didn't have to take a position or demonstrate knowledge on subjects such as global warming and Supreme Court nominations. He was still able to speak substantially more than anyone else in the debate. Trump forwarded ambiguous policy prescriptions. He made promises to manage well, to get the best team, and to restore America. But, he provided no concrete plans for action. He promised a future tax plan while rejecting proposals for a flat tax. He said, "I'll be putting in the plan in about two weeks . . . people are going to like it" (Peters & Woolley, 2015). Similarly, on social security, he promised to forgo his social security but provided no policy recommendations. In a traditional debate, such lack of specifics can be a detriment. But, Trump evidenced his ability to get things done with his wealth and prosperity. As long as Trump won the argument that he was a successful businessman, voters could believe that he could transfer his success to the United States without needing to evaluate policy prescriptions in advance.

The third minor tactic Trump used to reaffirm his personal appeal was placation and refusal to apologize. He was confronted twice during the debate with comments he had made that insulted Carly Fiorina and Jeb Bush's wife. In both exchanges, he used a compliment to placate the wronged party and denied or refused to acknowledge the original slight. First, Tapper referred to a comment Trump had made about Fiorina's face. Fiorina looked directly at the camera and said, "You know, it's interesting to me, Mr. Trump said that he heard Mr. Bush very clearly . . . I think women all over this country heard very clearly what Mr. Trump said" (Peters & Woolley, 2015). Trump did not address the original comment, which, he had previously clarified as referring to her persona. Instead he said, "I think she's got a beautiful face, and I think she's a beautiful woman" and the debate went to a commercial break (Peters & Woolley, 2015). In a similar exchange, Bush demanded an apology from Trump for saying "If my wife were from Mexico, I think I would have a soft spot for people from Mexico" (Peters & Woolley, 2015). When asked to apologize, Trump replied with a compliment and didn't negate his original statement. He said, "I hear phenomenal things. I hear your wife is a lovely woman . . . " (Peters & Woolley, 2015). When Bush pressed for an apology,

Trump replied, "No, I won't do that, because I've said nothing wrong . . . But I do hear she's a lovely woman" (Peters & Woolley, 2015). In each case, he used a compliment to mitigate the impact of his prior statements while refusing to apologize. These exchanges have gendered undertones and serve as power plays. Trump's assumption that complimenting a woman's appearance would smooth over a situation indicates that he sees appearance as a woman's most valuable asset. His response strategy also augmented Trump's personal power and tracked with Trump's post-debate claims that his supporters liked him because of his refusal to be politically correct.

Another minor, but potentially effective tactic was Trump's choice to not refer to other candidates or to refer to them by their first names. He referred to Ben Carson as Ben. He addressed Carly Fiorina as Carly six times. He referred to Rand Paul by his full name once and called him Rand twice (Peters & Woolley, 2015). Finally, he called Jeb Bush Jeb eight times in the debate. While some other candidates called him Donald, he was most often referred to as Donald Trump or Mr. Trump throughout the debate.

Finally, Trump interrupted other candidates. In particular, one interaction with Bush illustrates his fight for verbal dominance and the last word. In whether or not

Trump wanted to legalize casino gambling in Florida, Bush said, "One guy . . . that tried to get me to change my views on something — that was generous and gave me money — was Donald Trump. He wanted casino gambling in Florida" (Peters & Woolley, 2015). Trump immediately replied, "I didn't" and Bush said, "Yes you did" (Peters & Woolley, 2015). Trump said, "Totally false . . . I would have gotten it" (Peters & Woolley, 2015). The exchange continued with both denying the claims of the other and interrupting each other. When Trump argued that he couldn't be bought since his campaign was self-funded, Bush attempted to link him to Clinton and Pelosi. The extended back and forth ended with Trump repeatedly interrupting Bush to tell him not to "make things up" (Peters & Woolley, 2015). Trump's interruptions conveyed the message that he was in charge and would always have the last word.

While minor tactics did not win the debate, they might have conveyed a sense of Trump as a man and a leader who would, in his supporters' views, not be beholden to political correctness. Indeed, strategic non-participation, intentional ambiguity, placation and refusal to apologize, addressing other candidates by their first names or not at all, and interrupting other candidates all served to enhance Trump's core theme of Trump himself as a product. Trump wasn't selling specific plans or even a particular political ideology. Instead, he was selling himself in the second GOP primary debate. He was selling himself as a success, as a leader, and as businessman who could control any conversation.

Core Themes

From a traditional debate perspective, Trump lacked logical argumentation. For example: he professed a long disproven link between vaccines and autism; and, others attacked his lack of foreign policy knowledge and impractical nature of his immigration policy. Analysts of debate as argument would agree that the content of Trump's speech lacked argumentative substance. However, trained argumentation critics weren't judging these debates. To understand why some found his arguments persuasive, it is important to interrogate the themes he conveyed and to examine why such themes might have resonated. Trump conveyed two major themes: 1. Trump portrayed himself as a fantastic businessman, as a manager who can learn, set the agenda, and make decisions in any context; 2. He argued that he would make America great again.

From the beginning, Trump offered little in the way of concrete facts, focusing instead on his prowess as a businessman. He introduced himself as the author of *The Art of the Deal,* a successful businessman, who had "made billions and billions of dollars with people all over the world," who would use "that talent to work for this country" (Peters & Woolley, 2015). He repeatedly relied on his business acumen and decision-making ability throughout the debate. When Fiorina tried to discount his qualifications by calling him an entertainer and businessman, he argued that business experience was a unique qualification. He said, "What I am far and away greater than an entertainer is a businessman, and that's the kind of mindset this country needs to bring it back" (Peters & Woolley, 2015). Trump repeated his core message throughout. The words business or businessman were used 29 times including 16 times by Trump (Peters & Woolley, 2015). To justify his qualifications as a potential commander-in-chief, Trump repeated themes of business and success. He said, "I've dealt with people all over the world, been successful all over the world. Everything I've done virtually has been a tremendous success" (Peters & Woolley, 2015). He suggested his business skills would translate directly to successful policymaking and produce wealth, "I'm a businessman . . . I want to . . . put that ability into this country to make our country rich again" (Peters & Woolley, 2015).

Later in the debate, Trump was attacked for his use of corporate bankruptcy laws. He both denied going bankrupt and suggested it was part of business acumen to use the bankruptcy law. He said, "I'm in business, I did a very good job" (Peters & Woolley, 2015). Trump turned arguments against him into assets by reframing them in business terms and implying that he could bring business experience to the project of governing the United States.

In business, Trump suggested it was imperative to have good relationships with a variety of people. He turned accusations of past affiliation with Hillary Clinton into an asset. While he did not explicitly state it, the ability to get along with political foes might also imply the ability to create bipartisan ties. He said, "I was a businessman, I got along with Clinton. I got along with everybody. That was my job, to get along with people . . . and I did a damn good job doing it" (Peters & Woolley, 2015). In foreign policy contexts, Trump sold his business expertise. He said, "I will get along . . . with Putin, and I will get along with others, and we will have a much more stable-stable world" (Peters & Woolley, 2015). Trump repeated the phrase "get along" thirteen times, suggesting he would also get along with China, Mexico, and many other nations.

Trump also used his status as a businessman to justify his lack of specific knowledge about foreign policy issues and suggested that he would get the best advisors and learn what he needed to know. His argument stressed the idea that judgment was more important than knowledge. He said, "I will have the finest team anybody has put together and we will solve a lot of problems. . . . We will have great teams and great people"(Peters & Woolley, 2015). When Rubio argued that he had knowledge that was needed the "first day in office," Trump replied, "I am not sitting in the United States Senate . . . I'm a businessman doing business transactions . . . I will know more about the problems of the world by the time I sit" (Peters & Woolley, 2015). He added, "Look at what's going in this world right now by people who supposedly know, this world is a mess" (Peters & Woolley, 2015). Trump highlighted his ability to learn and to transfer business skills to a political realm. He also indicted politicians and their foreign policy. This argument functioned on two levels. If it was true that the world was a mess, then either politicians didn't know what they were talking about or the value of knowledge was empirically denied because it had failed to produce good results. Trump used his qualifications as a businessman to answer arguments to construct himself as an outsider who had better judgment than politicians and could create prosperity for all Americans.

Coupled with this approach, Trump's second core theme was his pledge to make American great again. In his opening statement, he said he would like to use his business acumen "so we have great trade deals, we make our country rich again, we make it great again . . . and we have a great life all together" (Peters & Woolley, 2015). He argued that his business skills could "make our country rich again" and softened his deportation stance by saying, "the great ones will come back" implying that illegal immigrants who would help the country to excel might be allowed to return. He stressed the return to greatness in his closing statement. He said, "If I become president, we will do something really special. We will make this country greater than ever before. We'll have more jobs. We'll have more of everything" (Peters & Woolley, 2015). He swore not to forget his promises and to improve the United States' status in the world. He said, "If I'm president, many of the things that we discussed tonight will not be forgotten. We'll find solutions" (Peters & Woolley, 2015). In this way he promised to solve problems without the burden of proof. Normally, a debater would be asked to forward a plan of action and some proof that a plan would be effective.

Trump avoided this requirement altogether by focusing on visions of the "great." He crowned this utopian vision with thoughts of world harmony and respect. He said, "And the world will respect us. They will respect us like never before. And it will be actually a friendlier world" (Peters & Woolley, 2015).

The idea that Trump could make others respect us and restore a vision of a great America may have appealed to disaffected voters who felt disrespected. A large segment of American voters were feeling dissatisfied with the political system or economically alienated. The Wall Street Journal reported that 44% of the electorate agreed with the statement, "I feel angry because our political system seems to only be working for the insiders with money and power . . . rather than it working to help everyday people get ahead" (Wall Street Journal, 2015). At the same time, 28% agreed with the statement, "I feel anxious and uncertain because the economy still feels rocky and unpredictable so I worry about paying my bills, day to day living costs, and whether I can count on my own situation being stable" (Wall Street Journal, 2015). Trump's core themes of managing via a business model and making America great again may have resonated with voters who were tired of politicians or who feared loss of economic prosperity.

Indeed, post-debate polls of likely GOP voters from September 21, 2015 suggested that Trump was trusted on economic issues (44%), immigration (47%), and foreign policy (22%) (Bradner, 2015). Despite no concrete policy prescriptions, Trump portrayed himself as a businessman would could make America great again through fiat and a utopian vision of economic growth, prosperity, and international amity and respect with Trump at the center sharing the realization of these goals with Americans.

Immigration and birth right citizenship were the only issues where Trump chose to suggest policies. He defended his plan to deport approximately eleven million illegal immigrants and supported changing the interpretation of the 14th amendment to disallow birthright citizenship. In the context of making American great, Trump needed someone to blame. His immigration statements created immigrant others who were criminals or desperate for their children to take advantage of Americans. These people, he said, would be subject to deportation. Skinner explained how such appeals to voters create a racialized other. He wrote,

> "No issue defines Trump's campaign more .
> . . He has been willing to use racially
> charged language in support of his positions.
> He also talks tough on trade and "law and

order," using polarizing language reminiscent of Patrick Buchanan or George Wallace" (Skinner, 2015).

While Cruz portrayed himself as "the son of an Irish-Italian mom and Cuban immigrant who fled oppression and came to America seeking freedom," and Bush defended American values as consistent with some level of immigration, Trump claimed he would restore America's status as a nation by ejecting illegal immigrants. He sought agenda-setting credit for talking about immigration, "I don't think you'd even be talking about illegal immigration if it weren't for me" (Peters & Woolley, 2015). He stressed the idea that illegal immigrants were, by definition, lawbreakers. He said, "We have a country based on laws. I will make sure that those laws are adhered to. These are illegal immigrants" (Peters & Woolley, 2015). Illegal immigrants were excluded from the "we" for whom Trump promised to make America great again. Specifically, he argued that the presence of illegal immigrants was a threat to the integrity of the United States and to individual safety. He said those that opposed his hard line on immigration "found out with the killing of Katie, from San Francisco, and so many other crimes, they found out that I was right" (Peters & Woolley, 2015). He also suggested that illegal immigrants had committed crimes that should make them ineligible to return. He said, "If they've had a bad record, if they've been arrested, if they've been in jail, they're never coming back" (Peters & Woolley, 2015). In fact, he argued that illegal immigration was responsible for the destruction of our country. He said, "We're going to have a country again. Right now, we don't have a country, we don't have a border, and we're going to do something about it" (Peters & Woolley, 2015). He continued, "the good ones will come back" through an "expedited" process, "legally" (Peters & Woolley, 2015). Trump suggested that assimilation through speaking English was an essential component of the American system. He said, "We have a country, where, to assimilate, you have to speak English . . . to have a country, we have to have assimilation . . . This is a country where we speak English, not Spanish" (Peters & Woolley, 2015). Trump also constructed birthright citizenship as a sign that American policy was "dumb" or "stupid" and was creating a drain on the American system. He said,

> "A woman gets pregnant. She's nine months,
> she walks across the border, she has the
> baby in the United States, and we take care
> of the baby for 85 years . . . we're going to
> take care of those babies for 70, 75, 80, 90

years? I don't think so" (Peters & Woolley, 2015).

His argument ignored the ways that citizens contribute to the economy. Instead he constructed babies born to Mexican or Asian parents in the United States as a perpetual drain on the system. Trump gave disaffected voters someone to blame—either illegal immigrants, who he labeled as criminals, or babies born to illegal parents who, according to Trump, were straining American resources. The implication was that once those immigrants were gone, there would be more resources for law abiding, legal Americans. Functionally, ridding the country of the threat posed by illegal immigrants would be a key step to realizing Trump's vision of economic prosperity for Americans.

Trump's promises to make America great again may have been early signs of his appeal to working-class white voters who felt abandoned by economic and social change. Cox explained, "It's a visceral feeling of being left behind . . . Economically they are being left behind, but culturally, too . . ." (as quoted in Brownstein, 2016). Trump's reference to an earlier nostalgic time that can only exist for white working class voters remedies their "pervasive sense of loss among many of his supporters—the belief that the changes molding modern America have marginalized them economically, demographically, and culturally" and promises a return to "a hazy earlier time when American life worked better for the overwhelmingly white, heavily blue-collar coalition" (Brownstein, 2016). These arguments and later statements have cemented Trump as the candidate who appeals to "voters most anxious about demographic change" (Brownstein, 2016). Others have argued that Trump is popular among white men because they "believe they're slowly losing their . . . grip on societal power" (Cesca, 2016). Recent studies suggest that while Trump voters aren't poor as a group, "they are living in places that lack economic opportunity for the next generation (Ehrenfreund & Guo, 2016). Indeed, "both economic and racial anxieties are driving supporters to Trump" (Ehrenfreund & Clement, 2016). Rothwell, found "clear evidence that those who view Trump favorably are disproportionately living in racially and culturally isolated zip codes and commuting zones" and therefore lack exposure to immigrant populations (Rothwell, 2016).

Trump's promises to share his success with his supporters were buoyed by his construction of racialized others who could be blamed for their unhappiness. Trump provided a utopian vision of a wealthy future that voters could literally see in every golden building affixed with Trump's name while providing scapegoats. Mass deportation was the only specific mechanism Trump identified on the path to making America great again. In a traditional debate framework, Trump's performance lacked the substance and specificity necessary to prove his candidacy. But, his supporters did not agree. Thus, despite losing some ground after the second debate, Trump remained the frontrunner leading up to the third GOP primary debate.

Understanding Trump's performance in the GOP primary debates may provide some insight into his plans for the general election. Trump has recently been saying that he will seek changes in the general election debates. Whether, the Commission on Presidential Debates complies, remains to be seen. However, Schroeder argued,

> "Trump got away with making demands during the primaries because the cable news networks that sponsored the debates needed his participation to boost ratings. General election match-ups do not include commercials, and haven't since their inception in 1960. The ratings for presidential debates, huge as they are,

cannot be monetized. Debates are pure civic virtue—that's one of their attractions" (Schroeder, 2016).

Regardless of whether Trump successfully demands changes in format, general election debates have a strong influence on who wins the election. May argued,

> "Since 1960, when John F. Kennedy and Richard Nixon first met in Chicago, no other single moment has been more important in affecting the outcome of our elections . . . television's laser-like eye reveals the candidates' fitness for the presidency—their knowledge of domestic and foreign policy, their ability to answer reporters' probing questions, their coolness under fire, the image they project—all tell voters which person should occupy the Oval Office" (May, 2016).

Familiarity with Trump's argumentative strategy and tactics may help voters to more accurately assess his qualifications to be the President. His ability to capitalize on procedural advantages, his attention to minor tactics and his core themes that lack specifics are reasons voters continued to support him in the Republican primary. Trump's strategies must be effectively addressed in the general election if Hillary Clinton hopes to prove she is the best woman for the job.

References

Birdsell, D. S., & Groarke, L. (2007). Outlines of a theory of visual argument. *Argumentation and Advocacy*, 43 (3-4), 103.

Bradner, E. (2015, September 21). Carly Fiorina rockets to No. 2 behind Donald Trump. *CNN*. Retrieved from http://www.cnn.com/2015/09/20/politics/carly-fiorina-donald-trump-republican-2016-poll/index.html

Brownstein, R. (2016, June 2). Trump's Rhetoric of White Nostalgia. *The Atlantic*. Retrieved from http://www.theatlantic.com/politics/archive/2016/06/tr umps-rhetoric-of-white-nostalgia/485192

Byler, D. (2015, September 17). Trump Got Double Walker's Speaking Time. *RealClearPolitics*. Retrieved from http://www.realclearpolitics.com/articles/2015/09/17/tr ump_got_double_walkers_speaking_time__128116.ht ml

CNN. (2015). *CNN Republican Presidential Debate 2016 Simi Valley California (September 16, 2015) [Main Debate]*. Retrieved from https://www.youtube.com/watch?v=Mdm6zEup7Vg

Ehrenfreund, M., & Guo, J. (2016, August 12). A massive new study debunks a widespread theory for Donald Trump's success. *Washington Post*. Retrieved from https://www.washingtonpost.com/news/wonk/wp/2016

/08/12/a-massive-new-study-debunks-a-widespread-theory-for-donald-trumps-success

Enten, H. (2015, September 24). Was The Second Debate The Beginning Of The End For Donald Trump? *FiveThirtyEight*. Retrieved from http://fivethirtyeight.com/datalab/was-the-second-republican-debate-the-beginning-of-the-end-for-donald-trump

Finnegan, C. A. (2001). The Naturalistic Enthymeme and Visual Argument: Photographic Representation in the "Skull Controversy." *Argumentation and Advocacy*, 37 (Winter), 133–149.

Headlines and Global News. (2015, September 17). Donald Trump Wins Second Republican Debate. Retrieved from http://www.hngn.com/articles/130789/20150917/donald-trump-wins-second-republican-debate-landslide-according-numerous-polls.htm

Hohmann, J., & Viebeck, E. (2015, September 17). The Daily 202: Fiorina big winner in Reagan debate, pundits across the spectrum agree. *Washington Post*. Retrieved from https://www.washingtonpost.com/news/powerpost/wp/2015/09/17/the-daily-202-fiorina-big-winner-in-reagan-debate-pundits-across-the-spectrum-agree

Kirk, C. (2015, September 16). Who Won the GOP Debate? *Slate*. Retrieved from http://www.slate.com/articles/news_and_politics/politics/2015/09/republican_presidential_debate_who_won_vote_in_our_poll.html

Koeze, E. (2015, September 16). Most-Attacked Figures. *FiveThirtyEight*. Retrieved from http://fivethirtyeight.com/live-blog/2016-election-second-republican-presidential-debate

Lacey, D. (2015, September 16). Who Won the Second Republican Presidential Debate? *Time*. Retrieved from http://time.com/4037510/poll-second-republican-presidential-debate

Lapinski, J., & Kopicki, A. (2015, September 20). Poll: Carly Fiorina prevails in second debate, Trump still leads GOP. *MSNBC*. Retrieved from http://www.msnbc.com/msnbc/poll-carly-fiorina-prevails-second-debate-trump-still-leads-gop

Libresco, L. (2015b, September 16). Who spoke the most? *FiveThirtyEight*. Retrieved from http://fivethirtyeight.com/live-blog/2016-election-second-republican-presidential-debate

May, G. (2016, August 14). The Presidential Debates Will Almost Surely Decide the Election. *The Daily Beast*. Retrieved from http://www.thedailybeast.com/articles/2016/08/14/the-presidential-debates-will-almost-surely-decide-the-election.html

Perticone, J. (2015, September 17). GOP Candidates All Entered the "Spin Room" After Debate. All Except For One. *Independent Journal Review*. Retrieved from http://www.ijreview.com/2015/09/422944-carly-fiorina-dropped-everyones-jaw-right-debate-ended-total-power-move

Peters, G. T., & Woolley, J. T. (2015, September 16). Presidential Debates. Republican Candidates Debate in Simi Valley, California. Retrieved from http://www.presidency.ucsb.edu/ws/index.php?pid=110756

Schroeder, A. (2016, August 12). Donald Trump Missed the Most Important Fact About Debates. *Time*. Retrieved from http://time.com/4446776/donald-trump-debates

Silver, N. (2015a, September 17). What Went Down In The Second GOP Debate. *FiveThirtyEight*. Retrieved from http://fivethirtyeight.com/live-blog/2016-election-second-republican-presidential-debate

Silver, N. (2015b, September 17). Where does Fiorina go from here? *FiveThirtyEight*. Retrieved from http://fivethirtyeight.com/live-blog/2016-election-second-republican-presidential-debate

Skinner, R. (2015, September 17). Do hate and racism drive support for Donald Trump? *Brookings Institution*. Retrieved from https://www.brookings.edu/2015/09/17/do-hate-and-racism-drive-support-for-donald-trump

Smith, V. J. (2007). Aristotle's Classical Enthymeme and the Visual Argumentation of the Twenty-First Century. *Argumentation & Advocacy*, 43 (3/4), 114–123.

Sprunt, B., & Mutnick, A. (2015, September 16). On The Clock: Trump Gets Most Time In GOP Debate. *National Public Radio*. Retrieved from http://www.npr.org/sections/itsallpolitics/2015/09/16/440827414/on-the-clock-who-spoke-the-longest

Thompson, S. A., & Yeip, R. (2015, October 21). Who Qualified for the Next Republican Debate? *Wall Street Journal*. Retrieved from http://graphics.wsj.com/elections/2016/cnbc-gop-debate-polls

Trump assesses second GOP debate performance. (2015). MSNBC. Retrieved from http://www.msnbc.com/hardball/watch/trump-assesses-second-republican-debate-527049795592

Wall Street Journal. (2015, September 24). Mood of the Electorate. Retrieved from http://graphics.wsj.com/wsjnbcpoll

Wall Street Journal. (2016). 2016 Election Polls. Retrieved from http://graphics.wsj.com/elections/2016/polls

Walsh, K. T. (2015, September 17). Carly Fiorina Gains Stature in Second GOP Debate. *U.S. News & World Report*. Retrieved from http://www.usnews.com/news/blogs/ken-walshs-washington/2015/09/17/carly-fiorina-gains-stature-in-second-gop-debate

CHAPTER THREE

<<<<<<<<<<<<<<<<<<<<<<<<<<>>>>>>>>>>>>>>>>>>>>>>>>>>

GOP Primary Debate #3
Boulder, Colorado, October 28, 2015
Ben Voth

<<<<<<<<<<<<<<<<<<<<<<<<<<>>>>>>>>>>>>>>>>>>>>>>>>>>

On October 28, 2015, the Republican National Committee conducted a Presidential candidate primary debate in collaboration with television news cable network channel CNBC. Despite the long march of a Republican primary that included seventeen candidates and a dozen debates, Boulder does stand out with some rhetorical significance from the other primary debates. This debate is iconic for the sound byte regarding a classic trope of Republican politics: media bias against conservatives. This debate produced one of the more replayed moments of the primary debate season stretching from fall 2015 into early spring 2016. Senator Ted Cruz launched this rhetorical cruise missile in response to a question from CNBC's Carl Quintanilla:

> "Congressional Republicans, Democrats and the White House are about to strike a compromise that would raise the debt limit, prevent a government shutdown and calm financial markets that fear another Washington-created crisis is on the way," Quintanilla said. "Does your opposition to it show that you're not the kind of problem solver American voters want?"

Cruz declined to immediately answer the question and instead addressed the questions that had been asked during the debate.

"The questions that have been asked so far in this debate illustrate why the American people don't trust the media," Cruz said. "This is not a cage match. And you look at the questions: 'Donald Trump, are you a comic book villain?'; 'Ben Carson, can you do math?'; 'John Kasich, will you insult two people over here?'; 'Marco Rubio, why don't you resign?'; 'Jeb Bush, why have your numbers fallen?'" [Emphasis added.]

He then added for emphasis, "How about talking about the substantive issues people care about?"

The debate audience responded to Cruz's attack on the CNBC debate moderators with a strong round of applause.

Cruz cut off Quintanilla when he claimed his budget question was about a substantive issue, pointing out the "contrast" between how moderators treat Democrats versus Republicans during debates.

> "Carl, I'm not finished yet," he said. "The contrast of the Democratic debate, where every fawning question from the media was, 'Which of you is more handsome and wise?'" (Howerton, 2015).

The exchange establishes this early RNC primary debate as one of the more memorable if not more significant of the entire political season for both Republicans and Democrats.

AARON KALL, EDITOR

Rhetorical Significance of Presidential Primary Debates

Since at least 1960, when Kennedy and Nixon debated in the first televised debate, millions of prospective voters have tuned in to gain a relatively unmediated sense of the political options for the presidency (McKinney). By comparison, televised presidential debates currently tend to dwarf the political conventions that take place in August and September. Viewership of the conventions has been declining for some time and contracted considerably in 2012. For 2012, the Democratic and Republican conventions were viewed by less than 20 million people. This is not the case for the televised presidential debates (*Historical TV Ratings,* 2016).

The debates can make a significant difference for the two contestants. Since 1960, Gallup polling indicates noticeable persuasive effects. Only in the 1984 election did the October debates fail to register a change in the polling of the two major candidates (Reagan and Mondale). Poll changes since 1960 range from 12 points for President Bush in 2000 to one point for President Bush Sr. in 1988 (Saad, 2008).

Presidential debates constitute a significant communication opportunity for presidential candidates. Very few communication outlets offer a comparable audience. As a matter of comparison, the *Saturday Night Live* skit about the debates on any following Saturday will likely attract about 3 million viewers. *Saturday Night Live* drew one of its largest viewing audiences in October 2008 when Sarah Palin joined Tina Fey on the show. The Palin SNL attracted 17 million viewers, which is exponentially larger than the average viewership of the NBC comedy show (Holmwood, 2008). Most of the news shows hosted by debate moderators attract between 2 and 8 million viewers at the most.

The Principles of Debate

Presidential debates pose a special analytical problem for academics. Presidential debates are a political communication vehicle offered as an ideal pedagogical for voters. It is important to reflect on the well-established academic ideals of debates. Debates represent an ideal form of communication wherein typically two sides have an equal opportunity to present their viewpoints and a reasonably fair adjudication of those views by a relatively impartial party. The four essential ingredients of a debate according to most studies of the topic are:

1. A topic of controversy-- typically known as the resolution.
2. Two sides to oppose one another on the topic-- typically known as affirmative and negative sides
3. Equal time to speak assigned to both sides.
4. A judge to review and render a decision as to which side won the performed debate.

These four ingredients create a communication context of inherent fairness so that competing ideas on a matter can be reasonably compared. The ideal of debate for purposes of the presidential election is mediated by the respective parties of the DNC and RNC and the media organizations who host the events. Incumbent candidates and challengers are not required by law or statute to participate in these debates. In fact, in 1964, 1968, and 1972 there were no presidential debates. In many states, governors do not participate in debates. In fact, incumbents face a peculiar strategic communication burden in that attending a debate with a new challenger will inherently elevate that challenger both in the public imagination and the polls themselves. Though many were stunned at the loss of President Obama in debate number one during the election of 2012, he followed in a tradition of incumbents stumbling in the first debate. President Bush in 2004 and President Reagan in 1984 both ostensibly lost their first debates while recovering to win re-election. Incumbents face serious risks in agreeing to debate. The recent 2016 season of primary debates was energized by the absence of an incumbent. Everyone was a challenger trying to break into the most powerful political office in the world.

Presidential Primary Debates 2015-2016

Primary debates do not typically attract the large audiences of general Presidential debates that usually take place one month prior to the election. Primary debates take place more than one year in advance, and the prospects for an audience are therefore much reduced. For Republicans, the candidates were so numerous that they were originally divided into two slates of candidates that debated at different times—with the leading candidates performing their debates in the primetime viewing schedule while the "undercard" debate was offered earlier in the evening. Democrats began with five candidates but almost immediately were reduced to two candidates: Bernie Sanders versus Hillary Clinton. The winnowing of the Republican field was much slower and, arguably, hindered by the peculiar dynamics of public preference for outsiders such as Ben Carson and Donald Trump. The conventional leaders of the political packs—Scott Walker and Jeb Bush—were never able to establish themselves through the debate process as true frontrunners.

On October 24, a few days before this debate, the poll leaders as noted by *Real Clear Politics* were: Ben Carson at 28%, Donald Trump at 24%, Marco Rubio at 9.3%, Ted Cruz at 8.7% and Jeb Bush at 5.7% (*Polls: Iowa*, 2016). By November 5, Cruz and Rubio were tied at 12 percent. Carson and Trump were at 26% and 22% respectively. Jeb Bush was fifth with 7%. The polling suggests that the debate performances of Rubio and Cruz did improve their polling positions and provided slightly more support for Cruz. In the long march of polling data, it does appear that this debate of October 28 was an important rhetorical launching point for the Cruz campaign that would ultimately lead to his challenge to the dominance of Donald Trump in 2016 and Cruz defeating Trump in the Iowa caucus (Polls Iowa, 2016). Cruz was a decisive polling candidate from October 28 until January 5, 2016 when he became the polling leader for Republicans. This debate event as located within this polling data suggests that it was an important factor for his campaign.

The RNC primary debates were also distinctive beyond the

large number of candidates. Viewership for these debates was often twice as large as debates held by the DNC. In fact, some commentators complained that DNC debates were scheduled against popular sporting events to discourage viewership (Debenedetti, 2015). The first two Republican primary debates held by CNN and Fox News garnered more than 20 million viewers–which is a staggering number for television viewing, especially for primary debating. Even with smaller networks hosting, such as CNBC, the viewership of the debates broke 14 million (Debenedetti, 2015). The November 14 debate two weeks after the Colorado debate gained 8.5 million viewers for the Democrats. It was not unusual for Democratic party debates to have roughly half the viewers as Republican primary debates and it contained a signal about national enthusiasm for the arguments of each party. Regardless of party, the primary debates represented real money-making opportunities for networks and financially valuable political advertising for candidates. In many respects the debates carried out by the Republicans factored into Donald Trump's no personal cash approach to winning the Republican primary, and it drove the paradoxical outcome whereby the cash-laden front-runner of Jeb Bush was run out of the Republican primary process early. Without the debates, it is unlikely that Jeb Bush would have lost so early and so decisively.

Arguments and Outcomes of Boulder Debate

John Kasich, Mike Huckabee, Jeb Bush, Marco Rubio, Donald Trump, Ben Carson, Carly Fiorina, and Ted Cruz were all on stage at the University of Colorado for the debate on October 28. The conflict between Cruz and the moderators from CNBC came early and led to a marked decline in order for the debate. The transcript shows abundant evidence of cross-talk and the eight Republican candidates gradually united against their journalistic hosts in a manner largely unseen in the primary debates to this point.

A clear dialectic formed between the moderators from CNBC and the candidates. The long-standing complaint among Republicans that the journalists are biased against their party was on vivid display. The loud response of the audience to Cruz's counter-attack suggested the argument had powerful salience. Audience measures for the comment set records for public dial-testing with a score of 98 out of 100 (Stanage, 2015). An additionally striking aspect of the argument by Cruz was the precision of his remarks. He was able to quote verbatim and in order the accusations made in the past three questions by moderators. He also continued to engage in a protracted critique of the forum and process after confronted by moderators and begged for a response to the question provided to him. It is worthwhile to look at the ideological tension between Republicans and the journalistic press corp. One of the other big winners for the night also made a strong attack against the media. Senator Marco Rubio assailed media coverage of the Benghazi hearings regarding Hillary Clinton: "She has her super PAC helping her–the American mainstream media (Jackson, 2015)."

Journalistic Antagonism Toward Republicans and Conservatives

The media plays a powerful role in shaping the potential of a presidential candidate. Theodore H. White wrote in *The Making of the President, 1972*, "The power of the press is a primordial one. It determines what people will think and talk about–an authority that in other nations is reserved for tyrants, priests, parties, and mandarins." The media's role has been met with considerable public frustration. Public antipathy toward journalists and a concurrent lack of trust for journalism has grown for over a decade. The public sense of this painful reality is, arguably, a driving factor in present frustration evident in polling regarding institutions. Put simply, public trust of major cultural institutions is at an all-time low ("Confidence," 2015). When Gallup first began asking about public trust for the television press in 1993, 19% of the public had very high trust in the television press and 16% had very little trust. Today in June of 2016, 8% of the public has very high trust and 38% have very little trust for the television press. Television press are among the least trusted institutions measured in the United States by Gallup and includes institutions such as the military and the church ("Confidence," 2015). It is difficult to overstate the public hostility to journalists and the smaller community of television journalism. The CNBC debate moderators set a high bar in terms of ideological conduct that garnered more negative review of moderators than probably any other primary debate. This made Cruz's comments both timely and salient.

DEBATING THE DONALD

The public believes that the media is profoundly biased, and they believe journalists dramatically distort the information they receive. Those trends have accelerated to unprecedented levels of public anger. The problem of media bias is well documented and detailed in the excellent work by communication professor Jim Kuyper, detailing a similar systemic corruption of the journalistic process that is supposed to interrogate the politically powerful in order to prevent abuses of the weak and vulnerable (Kuyper, 2014). Kuyper traces a similar trend rooted in the 1960s where journalistic assessment of the Vietnam war embodied in the CBS news anchor Walter Cronkite took an ideological turn. Cronkite's misrepresentations of American military success in Vietnam were decisive in rallying anti-war activists toward further engagement in the cause. These interpretations were vital to the Jacobin insurgencies against the Democratic Party convention in 1968 Chicago.

Such trends amplified by journalism schools on college campuses have accentuated the ideological delivery of news in the 21st century. Party affiliation of journalists remains decisively one-sided—favoring the Democrats by more than 3 to1 in almost all newsrooms (Cillizza, 2014). A mutual fantasy between the political party of favor (Democrats) and journalists is that this political collaboration is morally justified as part of a broader agenda of protecting the weak from the ravages of inequality. Donald Trump, who has a long tradition of supporting the Democratic Party, including Hillary Clinton, was helped tremendously in his campaign to be the RNC nominee, against more conservative Republican candidates (Patterson, 2016). These Jacobin-styled arguments seek to displace individual liberty in favor of state-managed equality, convinced journalists to approach their craft with a clearer unrepentant ideology that interrogates one party defending established interests (Republicans) and the opposing party (Democrats) as being an inherent insurgency against those established interests. The public is overwhelmingly convinced that this bias is real and destructive to their trust of the original social contract in the First Amendment.

A powerful example of how far from a free press we have gone can be found in a Republican primary debate of 1996. Not unlike 2016, Republicans had a number of candidates seeking the nomination to run against incumbent president Bill Clinton. Among them was a surprising upstart by the name of Alan Keyes. Keyes is an African-American and in 1996 his oratorical skills were greatly admired and he finished strongly in the Iowa caucus and New Hampshire primary. That set up a televised candidate debate in 1996 at an Atlanta TV station. Keyes was invited to attend by the Atlanta Press Club. About a week before the event, the station had second thoughts about hosting Keyes, but Keyes remain adamant that he had an invitation and other candidates said the original plan should be honored. That set the stage for a rather incredible incident. On the night of the debate, Keyes arrived along with dozens of supporters for the televised debate. As Keyes approached the venue, the station called Atlanta police to the site. In front of television news crews recording the event, Alan Keyes was handcuffed and pushed into the backseat of a police car. He was driven to the edge of Atlanta and released on the top of a parking garage while the television debate went on without him. At no time was Alan Keyes charged with a crime. He was simply handcuffed by officers and forcibly removed from the property of the station and driven away. It sounds like something from a distant authoritarian government. The next day, the Democratic mayor of Atlanta, Bill Campbell, apologized for Keyes' mistreatment, saying "this is not usually how we treat our guests in the city." That was the end of the conflict. No lawsuits were filed. No other apologies were made. One of the nation's first serious African-American presidential candidates was handcuffed in Atlanta and kidnapped from a televised public debate. Imagine for a moment if in 2008, Presidential candidate Barack Obama had shown up for a Democratic primary debate and instead of entering the studio, was met by police officers, forcibly detained, and driven off-site until the debate was over. America's epistemological communities would have rallied Jacobin forces to powerful results–immediately. Epistemological voices would have thundered against the outrageous racial slur inherent in such actions. It is impossible to reconcile the events that happened to Keyes–and still viewable today on YouTube ("Alan Keyes," 2015)–without understanding that the journalistic community believes that the concept of racism is an ideograph. Michael Calvin McGee pioneered this important rhetorical notion suggesting that certain terms exert powerful political influence in society despite their compartmentalized

wording and symbolism (McGee, 1980). Alan Keyes could not be a victim of racism because racism is an ideograph that serves only Jacobin ideological interests. It demonstrates rather forcefully that journalism exists as service for these ideological interests and not for the political interests of individual liberty as embodied in Alan Keyes' free political speech rights and political arguments.

Journalism today continues to serve limited political interests. Fox News is derided as "partisan" by our elite while almost all other news outlets are relatively unchallenged as non-partisan. Fox was not allowed to moderate any of the 2012 Presidential debates. The problems between the Republicans and the media extend back to the rivalry that took down President Nixon in the early 1970s. The salience of this argument shows little signs of abating or declining.

The newest twist was the sharp antagonism between Megyn Kelly and Donald Trump in the first RNC primary debate. Fox stood from its inception as the standard bearer of conservative and Republican politics for television news. The brutal exchanges from the Fox debate were an exigence toward the Colorado debate and created a ripe condition for confrontation with the more traditionally left-leaning CNBC moderator crew. The Harvard Study of news coverage in this election cycle provided this summary:

> "Even if meta-narratives are not as self-fulfilling as Kovach and Rosenstiel suggest, there is no question that journalists create and apply them as a shorthand way to describe presidential candidates. In 2008, for example, journalists early on embraced the idea that

Barack Obama represented hope and change and could deliver it through his charismatic leadership and communication skill. It was a narrative that carried all the way to the November election.

"Whether the meta-narratives that emerged during the 2016 invisible primary will persist is a yet unanswered question but the outlines of these early narratives was unmistakable. Trump was the shoot-from-the-lip bully, given to braggadocio and insulting and outrageous comments. Yet, he also had a finger on the anger felt by many middle- and lower-class white voters. As regards Clinton, she was the candidate best prepared for the presidency as a result of her experience and detailed knowledge of policy issues. But this positive meta-narrative competed with more frequently employed negative ones–that she was difficult to like, overly calculating, and hard to trust. As for Sanders, the storyline was that he means what he says–that he speaks, not from what the polls say is expedient, but from what he believes" (Patterson, 2016).

Speaking Times at the Debate

The opportunity to speak and equal time are important principles in the standard conduct of debates. Televised primary debates suffer from important distortions to this expectation and likely contribute to public frustration about the process. Here are the speaking times for the CNBC debate in Boulder:

Candidate	CNN Debate	CNBC Debate
Trump:	0:18:47	0:09:26
Cruz:	0:10:45	0:07:34
Kasich:	0:09:44	0:09:42
Rubio:	0:11:21	0:10:10
Bush:	0:15:48	0:06:39
Carson:	0:12:56	0:07:02
Christie	0:12:36	0:08:31
Paul:	0:10:28	0:06:15
Fiorina:	0:13:30	0:10:32
Walker:	0:08:29	DNP
Huckabee	0:09:20	0:07:39
Average Airtime Per Candidate	Sept. 15 0:12:09	Oct. 28 0:08:21

Rand Paul had the least amount of speaking time while Rubio and Fiorina had the most speaking time. The differentials are noticeable and highly influenced by the practice of allowing candidates to respond when they are mentioned by name during arguments. Candidates had an average of almost eight and a half minutes of speaking time in the hour and a half debate. Despite a decisive performance, Cruz had an unusually small amount of speaking time. Trump had a high amount but was reigned in considerably from his time domination of the previous debate. There was a 28-minute interval of the debate where Trump said nothing (Earle & Fredericks, 2015). As a point of potential reform, it is important to consider how future debates might more effectively render equal time and opportunity for candidates. By the end of the primary debate season, the average speaking time of Trump (20 minutes) was nearly twice that of other candidates. Cruz came in second with his average of 16 minutes and Rubio in third with a little more than 14 minutes per debate. These averages correlate so strongly with polling positions that it is important to consider how maintaining the fairness principle is necessary for a fair debate. It does seem likely that CNBC sought to dramatically reduce the amount of airtime given to Trump relative to what he received in the previous CNN debate.

Carly Fiorina as Clinton Counterpoint

Carly Fiorina was among the newest outsiders who used the debates for her clear advantage. After her decisive performance in primary debate number one as part of an undercard debate, Fiorina moved up to the major leagues of top candidates. In this debate she continued to be decisive in her rhetorical choices to attack Hillary Clinton more forcefully than other candidates. She also made women an economic issue:

> "Former technology executive Carly Fiorina says it is
> the "height of hypocrisy" for Hillary Rodham Clinton

to talk about being the first woman president when "every single policy" she endorses is "demonstrably bad for women."

Fiorina is joining Texas Sen. Ted Cruz in going after Clinton in the third Republican presidential debate.

Fiorina says 92 percent of the jobs lost during President Barack Obama's first term belonged to women. And Cruz says 3.7 million women went into poverty during Obama's presidency" ("Minute to Minute," 2015).

Fiorina continued to be a positively received debater in the third debate and her stature and polling after the debate reflected this.

Rubio and Bush: The Florida Battle

Bush came rhetorically loaded to attempt a takedown of Senator Marco Rubio. As two big Republican players from Florida, the third debate was the optimum occasion for the presumptive nominee, Jeb Bush, to begin his climb from the polling cellar toward the nomination. Bush planted his rhetorical foot on Rubio by stating that the senator's poor attendance record suggested he had a rather "French" view of what constitutes a work week. Bush's humorous jab did not appear to anticipate a rejoinder. Rubio embarked on passionate critique of Bush's attack that highlighted the desperation of Bush's campaign. Commentators scored the exchange as a victory for Rubio and it was the first major setback to the idea that Bush could systematically climb toward the nomination by picking off the outsider frontrunners.

Polling Results for the Debate

Surveys after the debate suggest that Rubio won the debate. Chris Christie and Ted Cruz were also believed to be strong performers. Among Democrats polled, Rubio and Cruz were thought to be the big winners ("Colorado CNBC," 2015). More decisive were opinions about who was the loser in the debate. There was a strong consensus among Democrats and Republicans that Jeb Bush was the biggest loser in the debate ("Colorado CNBC debates," 2015). That was likely a result of the rapidly escalating expectations that Bush should make a major move soon if he was to become the nominee for the Republican party. Those expectations became more and more difficult to reach with each debate.

The third Republican primary debate was an important argumentative event for the larger campaign. The lack of a breakthrough for Jeb Bush suggested that the conservatives and outsiders were likely to dominate the ongoing campaign. October 28 is a polling marker for Rubio and Cruz who went on a tandem uptick toward leading positions to challenge the ascendancy of Donald Trump. All of the candidates organized around a Republican ideograph of media bias to mount a concerted attack on the CNBC moderators. Ted Cruz's riff on the first three moderator questions became a classic meme for his campaign and overall strength of debate skills. It became a launching point to his long running rivalry toward the conclusion of the campaign where Trump and Cruz fought to the end at Indiana in spring of 2016.

References

Alan Keyes Barred from Presidential Debate and "Kidnapped" by Atlanta Police–1996. (2015). *YouTube*. Retrieved from https://www.youtube.com/watch?v=SehAtMQPNmQ

Cillizza, C. (2014, May 6). Just 7 Percent of Journalists are Republicans. That's Far Fewer than even a Decade Ago. *The Washington Post*. Retrieved from https://www.washingtonpost.com/news/the-fix/wp/2014/05/06/just-7-percent-of-journalists-are-republicans-thats-far-less-than-even-a-decade-ago/

Confidence in Institutions. (2015). *Gallup*. Retrieved from http://www.gallup.com/poll/1597/confidence-institutions.aspx

Debenedetti, G. (2015, November 15). Disappointing debate ratings spark Democratic campaign complaints: The DNC comes under fire for Saturday's low viewership figures. *Politico*. Retrieved from http://www.politico.com/story/2015/11/democratic-debates-cbs-clinton-sanders-omalley-215909

Earle, G., & Fredericks, B. (2015, October 28). Underdogs Come Out of the Woodwork at the Third Republican Debate. *New York Post*. Retrieved from http://nypost.com/2015/10/28/underdogs-come-out-of-the-woodwork-at-third-republican-debate

Historical TV Ratings For Presidential Debates 1960-2008 Presidential Campaigns. Retrieved from http://uspolitics.about.com/od/elections/l/bl_historical_tv_ratings_prez_debates.htm

Holmwood, L. (2008, October 20). Sarah Palin helps Saturday Night Live to best ratings in 14 years. *The Guardian*.

Howerton, J. (2015, October 28). Cruz Unexpectedly Goes Off on CNBC Moderator Over Phrasing of Question. *The Blaze*. Retrieved from http://www.theblaze.com/stories/2015/10/28/ted-cruz-unexpectedly-goes-off-on-cnbc-debate-moderator-over-phrasing-of-question-im-not-finished-yet

Jackson, D. (2015, October 28). Colorado debate: Highlights from Republicans' third faceoff. *USA Today*, Retrieved from http://www.usatoday.com/story/news/2015/10/28/live-republicans-face-off-colorado-debate/74760792

Kuyper, J. (2014). *Partisan Journalism: A History of Media bias in America*. (Lanham, Maryland: Rowman and Littlefield).

McGee, M. C. (1980). The "ideograph": A link between rhetoric and ideology. *Quarterly Journal of Speech,* 66: 1-16.

McKinney, M. (September 2012). Debating Democracy: The History and Effects of the U.S. Presidential Debates. *Spectra*, 48 (3).

Minute to Minute Breakdown of GOP Presidential Debate in Colorado. (2015, October 28). *PBS*, Retrieved from http://www.pbs.org/newshour/rundown/minute-minute-breakdown-gop-presidential-debate-colorado

Patterson, T. E. (2016, June 13). Pre-Primary News Coverage of the 2016 Presidential Race: Trump's Rise, Sanders' Emergence, Clinton's Struggle. Shorenstein Center, Harvard University, Retrieved from http://shorensteincenter.org/pre-primary-news-coverage-2016-trump-clinton-sanders

Polls: Iowa Republican Caucus. (2015, February 1). *Real Clear Politics*. Retrieved from http://www.realclearpolitics.com/epolls/2016/president/ia/iowa_republican_presidential_caucus-3194.html

Saad, L. (2008, September 25). Presidential Debates Rarely Game-Changers; But have moved voter preferences in several elections, *Gallup*, Retrieved from http://www.gallup.com/poll/110674/Presidential-Debates-Rarely-GameChangers.aspx

Stanage, N. (2015, October 28). Crowd Roars as Cruz Attacks the Media. *The Hill*, Retrieved from http://thehill.com/blogs/ballot-box/presidential-races/258476-crowd-roars-as-cruz-attacks-the-media

Voth, B. (2016, March 20). The Real Reason Presidential Debates Have Been So Awful. *Fortune*, Retrieved from http://fortune.com/2016/03/20/presidential-debates-awful

White, T.H. (1973). *The Making of the President,* 1972, New York: Bantam Books, 1973.

CHAPTER FOUR

<<<<<<<<<<<<<<<<<<<O>>>>>>>>>>>>>>>>>>

GOP Primary Debate #4
Milwaukee, Wisconsin, November 10, 2015
Dr. Ryan W. Galloway

<<<<<<<<<<<<<<<<<<<O>>>>>>>>>>>>>>>>>>

On November 10th, 2015, eight Republican presidential candidates squared off in the Milwaukee Theatre in a debate hosted by Fox Business News (Opoien, 2015). While the debate was notable for the exchange, the debate was also notable for what it was not. The Milwaukee debate came after the Boulder, Colorado debate, where the candidates spent much of the evening attacking the moderators. In the Milwaukee debate, by contrast, the moderators played a relatively restrained role, asking few follow-up questions. The Milwaukee debate thus gives a glimpse into the dynamics of the race following the controversial debate in Boulder.

This essay will examine the role of the moderators in the Milwaukee debate. I will argue for a more engaged moderator role, one that holds the candidates accountable for answering the questions posed by the moderator as well as ensuring argumentative clash between the candidates. I will first review the controversy created by the debate in Boulder, to examine the complaints about moderators made in the Boulder debate. Second, I will look at the literature regarding the role of moderators more generally, attempting to help clarify what the proper role of a moderator in a presidential debate should be. Finally, I will analyze the Milwaukee debate, and illustrate where the moderators came up short.

I defend a strong moderator role that asks follow-ups in an effort to get candidates to engage questions directly, as well as draw comparisons between their positions and opponents. While moderators should not be antagonists to the candidates, neither should they be supplicants who allow the candidates to recite their talking points on the issues in the debate. If the debates become merely a stage for candidates to effectively give their stump speeches, the point of having a debate is moot.

Reaction to Boulder Debate

The Boulder debate, held on October 28, 2015, is most known for the reaction the candidates had to the moderators. Michael Falcone of ABC News said that, "the night was defined not by the candidates' attacks on each other, but on the moderators..." (Falcone, 2015). One commentator argued that, "Republican presidential candidates lit into CNBC's moderators at Wednesday night's debate" (Republican presidential candidates battle moderators, 2015). Brent Johnson said, that "the most consistent targets" in the debate were "the anchors who moderated, and the media in general" (Johnson, 2015). Maria Bartiromo of the Fox Business Network accused CNBC's moderators of missing "the mark in the last debate of helping viewers understand where candidates stand on issues" (Tomkiw, 2015). The moderators were accused of trying to get the candidates "to attack each other rather than discuss the issues" (Paul, 2015). The candidates complained about, "loaded questions, a lack of balance, and the moderators' eventual kindergarten-class-like loss of control" (Martosko, et al. 2015). Reince Preibus, the chair of the Republican National Committee was quoted as saying, "It's like they tried to design a Rubik's cube for every question to take the worst element...of what the moderators and what the media should bring to the table (Johnson, 2015)."

However, some defended the moderators, with Brian Steel, CNBC's senior vice president for public relations, arguing that "People who want to be President of the United States should be able to answer tough questions"

(Republican presidential candidates battle moderators, 2015). In addition, some accused the moderators of being too weak, with Chris Tognotti saying that the moderators failed by letting the candidates turn the question back on the moderators allowing the candidates to "wriggle free from a sensitive topic" (Tognotti, 2015). David Horsey of the Los Angeles Times defends a strong moderator role, "[v]oters though, would be less than well-served by a questioner who is no more engaged than the voice on a car's GPS system" (Horsey, 2015). While it may be true that the CNBC moderators were too divisive in the Boulder debate, moderators exercising too much self-restraint may pose problems of their own.

In the wake of the Boulder debate, the campaigns drew up a list of proposed rules, and while the rules fizzled out, it illustrated the need to capitulate to the campaigns in order to keep the debates going (Broadcasting & Cable, 2015, Nov. 16). David Graham pointed out, "plotting fell apart over the simple reality that the candidates are all competing for the same job, and their interests don't merely diverge—they're directly opposed" (Graham, 2015). While the candidates could agree that they did not like the moderators in Boulder, they could not reach a consensus on what exactly they are looking for. I now turn to the scholarly literature on the question of the appropriate role of moderators in presidential debates.

The Role of Moderators

The role of the moderator in a debate is to serve the public interest in getting to the heart of creating an informed citizenry. Jim Lehrer says that the moderator of a presidential debate "is a step and a process that is one of the most important things we do as an American democratic society" (quoted in Morabito, 2013). Hardy & Scheufele note that an informed citizenry is crucial for a representative democracy to be responsible to the needs and wills of the public (2009). Gans writes that "the country's democracy may belong directly or indirectly to its citizens, but the democratic process can only be truly meaningful if these citizens are informed" (Gans, 2003, p. 1). Eveland, McLeod & Nathanson state, "[I]t is important to ensure that the debates provide pertinent information for the general voting public" (1994, 391).

Because Yawn et al. (1998) conclude that voters are forced to "rely on short-term influences–often candidate image" when watching primary debates (Yawn, 1998, 156), moderators play a crucial role in helping the public focus on the issues. According to Hinck, et al (2013) "[m]oderators were found to play a role in shaping the quality of the discourse in debates." The question is then, how should moderators shape the discourse in debates? Keeping the public interest in mind, the role of the moderator should be to ensure that the public is provided relevant information in order to make an informed decision at the ballot box.

That said, scholars generally view moderators in a negative light, with one arguing that moderators ask questions "to make headlines" (Morello, 2005, 213). Hogan (1989) accuses moderators of asking leading and loaded questions. Because moderators' questions can function as an important prompt affecting the content of the debate (Bitzer & Rueter, 1980; McCall, 1984), the role of the moderator should be carefully scrutinized. Silva and Herbeck lament that panelists play an adversarial role, and this diminishes the quality of the debate (Silva & Herbeck, 232).

Jim Lehrer makes the case for a restrained moderator when he argues against moderators "getting too keen on the spotlight," and that "the ability to facilitate a meaningful exchange between the candidates" is the most important role of a moderator (Morabito, 2012). In contrast to average citizens at town hall debates, moderators were seen to "ask more argumentative, accusatory, and leading questions" (Eveland, McLeod, & Nathanson, 1994, 390). Bitzer & Reuter (1980) contend that, "the more appropriate role for panelists is 'that of a gentle Socrates practicing the art of midwife–coaxing from the candidates their best thought through skillful questions and suggestions." Thus, the scholarly consensus seems to be in favor of moderator restraint, and allowing the candidates to flesh out the issues in the debate.

However, moderators also need "to press the candidates to really answer a question–and call them out on it if their opponent doesn't first" (Morabito, 2012). Panetta also warns that a compromised moderator gives the candidate license to ignore questions (Panetta, 2011). Germond & Witcover argue against debates where there is "little continuity or depth of the sort that voters need to get a clear idea of what each of the candidates would actually do to cope with the nation's most pressing problems."

Thus, the question becomes, what makes for an effective moderator? Simply, an effective moderator is one that asks effective questions. For the purposes of this chapter, I define an effective question as Milic (1979) does, one that "reveals the position of a candidate on a given issue, so that the voter may decide whether he wishes to support a candidate with such a view" (189). An effective question is thus issue-oriented, and bolsters an informed citizenry.

Merely allowing candidates to repeat talking points on stage without asking follow-up questions turns the debate into a mere recitation of stump speeches. To facilitate a debate, the moderator must ensure that candidates actually answer the question posed, and not evade the question while referring back to their pre-prepared scripts given on the campaign trail. Ed Panetta says, ""debate is more than a joint press conference" (Panetta, 2011). Lenny Steinhorn of American University was quoted as saying, "[a] debate is not an opportunity for a candidate to memorize their news releases and speak them to the public. It's a chance to get into the complexity of their thinking, how deep they are in their analysis, and how they see the world and whether they are able to walk into the Oval Office..." (Gough, 2008). Debates are a unique opportunity to get into in-depth analysis of the candidates' stances on issues, and should not be undermined by a timid moderator.

Further, moderators must ensure that the debate results in argumentative clash with the ideas of the other candidates, and not merely resulting in side-by-side speeches where each candidate states their point of view. As McCall (1984) writes, "panelists must present their questions in a manner that…prompts the candidates into distinguishing themselves and their ideas from their opposition" (98). A clash of ideas must take place, with candidates illustrating the strength of their own ideas, while attacking the weaknesses of their opponents. While this may lead moderators to be accused of asking leading and loaded questions, the notion of facilitating a debate is different than merely providing a platform for speeches. A debate requires clearly defined issues and argumentative clash.

Analysis of Milwaukee Debate

Unlike the Boulder debate, the Fox Business News moderators were on their best behavior in the Milwaukee debate. Todd & Murray called the moderators' behavior an overcorrection of the previous debate, and argued that Rubio wasn't challenged at all, getting to evade the immigration question and receiving a softball on Hillary Clinton (Todd & Murray, 2015). The Boulder debate acted as a rhetorical constraint on the Milwaukee moderators,

131

who did not want to invoke the ire of the candidates as the Boulder moderators had. Additionally, given that Fox is generally considered to be more ideologically aligned with the Republicans, they did not wish to illustrate animosity toward the candidates.

Much as the McCain campaign placed moderator Gwen Ifill in an adversarial role (Panetta, 2011), the Republican candidates placed the CNBC moderators in an adversarial role in the Boulder debate. Thus, the Fox Business Network moderators started the debate in a compromised position—if they were too aggressive they would risk the wrath of the candidates and have their objectivity questioned. Unlike Ifill, who was turned into an opponent by the attacks, the Fox News moderators were turned into supplicants who only served to leave the Republican candidates' positions unchallenged, failing in the essential role of a moderator to act on behalf of the viewers of the debate. In response, the moderators played a constrained role, largely asking informative questions without much follow-up.

The debate was allegedly about the economy, and the questions were largely about the economy and foreign policy. The opening question of the debate saw Trump divert a question about the minimum wage into one about high taxes. While the moderator did ask for a follow-up about not raising the minimum wage, Trump did not offer any rationale for not raising the minimum wage (Who said what, 2015). The moderators gave him a pass for offering reasons for his opposition, failing the public interest by letting the candidate get away without clarifying his stance on a matter of public interest.

Perhaps more to the point, Fiorina was asked a question that, "Now, in seven years under President Obama, the U.S. has added an average of 107,000 jobs a month. Under President Clinton, the economy added about 240,000 jobs a month. Under George W. Bush, it was only 13,000 a month. If you win the nomination, you'll probably be facing a Democrat named Clinton. How are you going to respond to the claim that Democratic presidents are better at creating jobs than Republicans?" (Who said what, 2015). Fiorina avoided the question arguing, "Yes, problems have gotten much worse under Democrats. But the truth is, this government has been growing bigger and bigger...crushing the engine of economic growth for a very long time" (Who said what, 2015). The moderators asked no follow-up questions, nor did they ask for clarification of the Republicans positions on the state of the economy in general, or how Republicans would respond to Democrats' claims that the economy is simply getting better under Obama. Instead of probing deeper into the questions, the moderators in this debate chose to let the candidates repeat their talking points, failing the public interest in the name of appeasing the candidates.

In another exchange, Trump was asked: "Can we just send 5 million people back with no effect on the economy?" Trump failed to answer the question, arguing that "we're a country of laws. We either have a country or we don't have a country" (Who said what, 2015, Nov. 10). Trump does not speak to the economic effects of his deportation plan, illustrating the failure of the moderator to require the candidates to answer the question presented. While the deportation plan has been a central theme of Trump's campaign, the compromised moderators allow Trump to avoid a direct answer to a question of pertinent national interest.

Later in the debate, Rubio was asked a question about traditional jobs being replaced by robots and responded about how the American economy was in a global competition with developed economies (Who said what, 2015). While the question of the competition between developed economies is certainly a pertinent one, Rubio dodges the question of how low-skilled jobs are being replaced by automation. Rubio was not only given a pass on explaining how his policies would prevent job automation, his answer did not allow for a comparison between candidate positions on this issue.

Rand Paul was asked whether his tax plan would create a near-term budget crisis just as his presidency would be beginning and diverted the question to one about the size of government. While size of government is a central philosophical question for the Republican Party, Paul's answer papered over how his tax plan would risk depriving the government of needed funds. Americans were left to wonder how the math actually added up, with the moderators failing to interject and force Paul to defend his policy to the American people.

In the Milwaukee debate, the moderators played a passive role, offering few follow-ups or almost any attempt to keep the candidates on track. As Molly Ball said, "[t]he moderators aren't giving the candidates much pushback, so they're going to have to take matters into their own hands" (Graham et al, 2015). The debate failed to serve the public interest by not requiring candidates to answer questions directly, instead allowing them to rely on pre-prepared commentary from their campaign speeches. In addition, the candidates were not called upon to contrast their views, leaving the viewer confused as to which economic policy would be most beneficial for the country.

While traditional scholars decry the role of an active moderator, a passive moderator should also be avoided. Presidential debates fundamentally serve the public interest by requiring candidates to engage in in-depth analysis of their issues, and are one of the few formats where candidates are forced to expound on their position beyond the mere talking points one would usually see in a stump speech. While there is concern about panelists becoming pseudo-debaters (see McCall, 1984), compromised moderators also fail to serve the public interest.

The moderators in the Milwaukee debate became apologists for the Republican candidates, offering no resistance to misleading claims or efforts to dodge questions. Follow-up questions were rare, and little effort was made for candidates to distinguish their positions from one another. While some passivity in the face of the outcry in Boulder was warranted, a role where the moderator becomes functionally a timekeeper is one that fails to serve the interests of American democracy.

As the ability to craft arguments under pressure is a skill we would hope for in our presidential candidates, the ability to stand up to an assertive moderator is certainly one we would hope our candidates would have. While moderators can be accused of being too aggressive and asking "gotcha" questions, our presidential contenders will have to face much worse situations when confronting Congressional leaders of another party, or with foreign leaders. While we would hope for a modicum of civility in presidential debates, moderators who stick up for themselves are fundamentally serving the public interest of a well-informed citizenry. As politicians are experts at turning questions back on moderators and giving evasive answers, the public deserves a moderator who will force the candidates' hands and demand answers to issues of pressing national concern.

Assertive moderators serve the public interest in two fundamental ways: they require the candidate to clarify their positions on controversial issues, and they demand comparison and contrast between positions taken by various candidates. As candidates and their teams have incentives to try and manipulate the debate process, we will see if the rules and regulations created in the negotiations between campaigns and candidates serve to bolster or impede the national interest in a fair and vibrant democracy.

References

Bitzer, L.F., & Rueter, T. (1980). *Carter vs. Ford: The counterfeit debates of 1976.* Madison: University of Wisconsin.

Broadcasting & Cable (2015). Debate and switch. Retrieved from http://www.broadcastingcable.com/archive/2015/2015 1116

Eveland, W.P., McLeod, D.M., & Nathanson, A.L. (1994). Reporters vs. undecided voters: An analysis of questions asked during the 1992 presidential debates. *Communication Quarterly,* 42, 390-406.

Falcone, M. (2015, October 29). The note: in case you missed the battle in Boulder. Retrieved from http://abcnews.go.com/Politics/note-case-missed-battle-boulder/story?id=34819790

Gans, H.J. (2003). *Democracy and the news.* New York: Oxford University Press.

Germond, J.W., & Witcover, J. (1992, October 13). This is the wrong debate format. *San Diego Union-Tribune,* B6.

Gough, P. (2008, October 7). NBC: Tom Brokaw ready for debate. *The Hollywood Reporter.* Retrieved from http://www.hollywoodreporter.com/news/nbc-tom-brokaw-ready-debate-20605

Graham, D.A. et al (2015, November 10). Who won the Republican presidential debate. *The Atlantic*. Retrieved from http://www.theatlantic.com/politics/archive/2015/11/republican-debate-fox-business-milwaukee/415284

Hardy, B.W., & Scheufele, D.A. (2009). Presidential campaign dynamics and the ebb and flow of talk as a moderator: Media exposure, knowledge, and political discussion. *Communication Theory, 19,* 89-101.

Hinck, S.S., Hinck, R.S., Dailey, W.O., & Hinck, E.A. (2013). Thou shalt not speak ill of any fellow Republicans? Politeness theory in the 2012 Republican primary debates. *Argumentation & Advocacy, 25,* 259-274.

Hogan, J.M. (1989). Media nihilism and the presidential debates. *Journal of the American Forensic Association, 25,* 220-225.

Horsey, D. (2015, November 2). Republican candidates debate about debates and fail to agree. *Los Angeles Times.* Retrieved from http://www.latimes.com/opinion/topoftheticket/la-na-tt-republican-debate-about-debates-20151102-story.html

Johnson, B. (2015, October 29). Christie, GOP rivals slam moderators, media at debate. Retrieved from http://www.nj.com/politics/index.ssf/2015/10/christie_gop_rivals_slam_moderators_media_at_debat.html

Martosko, D., Schwab, N., Rushing, J.T., & Chambers, F. (2015, October 29). Vicious hits keep coming at CNBC after widely panned Republican debate.

Retrieved from
http://www.dailymail.co.uk/news/article-
3295865/Vicious-hits-coming-CNBC-widely-panned-
Republican-debate-Chris-Christie-accuses-awful-
moderators-showing-bias-Ted-Cruz-claims-
moderators-wanted-elect-Hillary-Clinton.html

McCall, J.M. (1984). The panelists as pseudo-debaters: An
evaluation of the questions and questioners in the
Presidential debates of 1980. *Journal of the American
Forensic Association,* 21, 97-104.

Milic, L.T. (1979). Grilling the pols: Q&A at the debates.
In S. Kraus (Ed.), *The great debates: Carter vs. Ford
1976.* Bloomington, IN: Indiana University Press.

Morabito, A. (2012, September 24). All the President's
moderators. *Broadcasting & Cable,* 12-13.

Morello, J.T. (2005). Questioning the questions: An
examination of the "unpredictable" 2004 Bush-Kerry
town hall debate. *Argumentation & Advocacy,* 41, 211-
224.

Opoien, J. (2015, November 11). Republican presidential
candidates debate in Milwaukee as Scott Walker looks
on. *The Capital Times.* Retrieved from
http://host.madison.com/ct/news/local/govt-and-
politics/election-matters/republican-presidential-
candidates-debate-in-milwaukee-as-scott-walker-
looks/article_bbacc7d2-da68-5f7e-ac63-
06c086989025.html

Panetta, E. (2011). Gwen Ifill: Moderator or opponent in
the 2008 Vice Presidential debate? In F.H. van
Eemeren (Ed.), *Proceedings of the Seventh Conference
of the International Society for the Study of
Argumentation* (1454-1466). Amsterdam NL: SicSat.

Paul, J. (2015, October 28). GOP debate audience slams CNBC moderators' questions. *Denver Post*. Retrieved from http://www.denverpost.com/2015/10/28/gop-debate-audience-slams-cnbc-moderators-questions/

Republican presidential candidates battle moderators, media (2015, Oct. 28). *CNN Wire*. Retrieved from http://kdvr.com/2015/10/28/republican-presidential-candidates-battle-moderators-main-stream-media

Silva, I., & Herbeck, D. (1997). *Conference Proceedings—National Communication Association: Argument in a Time of Change*.

Todd, C., & Murray, M. (2015, November 11). Everything you need to know about last night's GOP debate. Retrieved from http://www.msnbc.com/msnbc/everything-you-need-know-about-last-nights-gop-debate

Tognotti, C. (2015, November 7). 5 lessons the Republican debate moderators can learn from CNBC's utter disaster. *Bustle*. Retrieved from http://www.bustle.com/articles/122303-5-lessons-the-republican-debate-moderators-can-learn-from-cnbcs-utter-disaster

Who said what and what it meant (2015, Nov. 10). *Washington Post*. Retrieved from https://www.washingtonpost.com/news/the-fix/wp/2015/11/10/well-be-annotating-the-gop-debate-here

Yawn, M., Ellsworth, K., Beatty, B., & Kahn, K.F. (1998). How a presidential primary debate changed attitudes of audience members. *Political Behavior, 20,* 155-181.

CHAPTER FIVE

<<<<<<<<<<<<<<<<<<<<O>>>>>>>>>>>>>>>>>>>>

GOP Primary Debate #5
Las Vegas, Nevada, December 15, 2015
Dr. Eric Morris

<<<<<<<<<<<<<<<<<<<<O>>>>>>>>>>>>>>>>>>>>

On November 13, 2015, a series of coordinated attacks in Paris, France killed 130 people. The Islamic State of Iraq and the Levant (ISIL) claimed responsibility. The death toll remains the highest for an attack claimed by ISIL outside of the Middle East. The attack led to reconsideration of immigration policy by several European Union states. Similarly, many in the United States began to link two major issues in the Republican Presidential Primary–the immigration question and the strategy to respond to ISIL (Schreckinger, 2015). Specifically, many candidates used the attack to call attention to the Obama Administration's decision to allow 10,000 Syrian refugees into the United States.

Weeks later, the December 2, 2015, San Bernadino, CA attack increased these concerns. Although the attacks included a United States Citizen and lawful resident who had self-radicalized without direct commands from ISIL, the incident spurred Donald Trump's controversial statement "calling for a total and complete shutdown of Muslims entering the United States" (Trump, 2015) on December 7. Although this proposal was widely attacked from within and outside the Republican primary, and has slowly evolved throughout the campaign, it has maintained significant support in public opinion surveys (Hellmann, 2016).

It should be no surprise, then, that the dispute about whether recent attacks justified a dramatic shift in strategy was the dominant question in the Republican primary debate on December 15, 2015. This debate, sponsored by CNN and conducted in Las Vegas, NV featured nine candidates: Ohio Governor John Kasich, Former Hewlett Packard CEO Carly Fiorina, Florida Senator Marco Rubio, Former Neurosurgeon Ben Carson, Donald Trump, Texas Senator Ted Cruz, Governor Jeb Bush, Governor Chris Christie, and Kentucky Senator Rand Paul. The stage order reflected recent polling, and the top five (Trump, Carson, Cruz, Rubio, and Bush) were center stage and featured prominently in the most significant exchanges. Grouping those on stage as senators (Cruz, Rubio, Paul), governors (Bush, Kasich, Christie), and outsiders (Trump, Carson, Fiorina) also yields insight into the dynamics–it is not surprising that the final three (Trump, Cruz, Kasich) represented each group.

Some debate scholarship views presidential debates as "focal points" in the campaign (Carlin, 1992). According to this perspective, the high viewership and attention on debates reduces polling movement, as if voters are waiting to see if the debate alters their perspective. The debates often 'test' growing perceptions about candidate images and campaign themes, either providing evidence to solidify or refute perceptions of the candidates. Thus, the participants are able to engage in strategic maneuvering to adapt to the larger campaign situation (Morris & Johnson, 2011). After the debate, polling begins to move again– usually in the prior direction, but occasionally in another direction. *Real Clear Politics* polling averages (2016) in late 2015 were consistent with the focal points expectation. Carson peaked in early November near 25%, but then declined steadily with a short stay near 15% in the days before the debate. Trump rose from 25% in early November to 35% in early January, pausing near 30% in the days before the debate. Rubio and Cruz each rose from single digits to around 15% and then paused in the days before the debate. After the debate, Cruz rose toward 20% and Rubio slipped toward 10%. In late 2015, Bush slowly slid from just under 10% to 4%, paused for a few days right before the debate, and recovered to 5% after it. The data is consistent with Trump getting former Carson voters, Cruz getting former Rubio voters, and Bush getting nearly no additional voters after the debate.

This essay seeks to identify critical exchanges in the December 15, 2015, debate, which served as focal points in the pre-Iowa stages of the Republican primary. Six significant exchanges are discussed: Trump's pledge, Cruz's refusal to attack Trump, the Cruz-Rubio dynamic, Bush's direct attacks on Trump, the Nuclear Triad exchange, and the co-option of terminology. Although the debate was no more decisive than other debates or campaign events, Trump's continued polling rise and Rubio's reversal of momentum require explanation. Also, the debate could be viewed as a missed opportunity for certain candidates–in particular, Bush, whose approach was far more aggressive than in some prior debates, and Carson, who failed to reverse his previous polling decline.

Trump's Pledge

After the first Republican primary debate on August 6, 2015, Republican pollster Frank Luntz interviewed a focus group of undecided primary voters (Tani & LoGiurato,

2015). That group responded very negatively to Trump's performance, and particularly his refusal to pledge support for the eventual candidate and rule out an independent bid. Ironically, several of the other candidates who took the pledge have either declined to endorse Trump or have done so with obvious reluctance. This concern did not disappear until the December debate, when Salem Radio's Hugh Hewitt asked the question again:

> HEWITT: My listeners tell me again and again they are worried that Hillary Clinton will win the White House because you'll run as an independent. Are you ready to assure Republicans tonight that you will run as a Republican and abide by the decision of the Republicans?

> TRUMP: I really am. I'll be honest, I really am (Team Fix, 2015).

Trump's answer did not appear to be a capitulation so much as a decision, as neither the question nor the reaction indicated that Trump had significantly changed his position. Thus, while the exchange reassured voters concerned about this question, it did not appear to damage Trump's reputation for saying what he thinks. Certainly none of the other candidates objected, as Trump's pledge potentially benefits them and rejecting it would backfire.

During the fall general election debates, it would not be surprising if Trump answered questions in ways that reversed unpopular positions that he has taken on prior issues–particularly if those positions are not likely to lose him votes from his core supporters. In fact, there is evidence of Trump recalibrating his position on mass deportation, an issue more important to his base than most other issues (Marshall, 2016). Although Secretary Clinton will have angles of attack not available to Republican candidates, these sorts of 'clarifications' are challenging because moderators generally do not "fact-check" candidates in real time during debates. The outcry when Candy Crowley did fact-check Mitt Romney in 2012 (Byers, 2012) suggests that the rare exception proves the rule. It might be possible for Clinton to object during the debate (or her campaign to do so afterward), but that will be challenging if the new position is seen as more moderate than the old position. Trump's opponents should realize that campaigning against his rhetorical excesses and business career might have more durability than campaigning against specific commitments that may be dramatically altered in a debate.

The Cruz Refusal

Trump and Cruz ended up first and second in the eventual delegate count. If they had reached an agreement before the fifth debate to protect each other while narrowing the race, it is hard to imagine they would have done anything differently. Each of them took a pass when CNN Chief Political Correspondent Dana Bash offered the chance for them to directly attack each other (emphasis added):

> BASH: Mr. Trump, just this weekend you said Senator Cruz is not qualified to be president because he doesn't have the right temperament and acted like a maniac when he arrived in the Senate. But last month you said you were open to naming Senator Cruz as your running mate.
>
> TRUMP: I did.
>
> BASH: So why would you be willing to put somebody who's a maniac one heartbeat away from the presidency?
>
> TRUMP: Let me just say that I have gotten to know him over the last three or four days.

He has a wonderful temperament. (LAUGHTER) He's just fine. Don't worry about it.

BASH: Okay. Senator Cruz. Senator Cruz, you have not been willing to attack Mr. Trump in public.

TRUMP: You better not attack . . . (LAUGHTER)

BASH: But you did question his judgment in having control of American's nuclear arsenal during a private meeting with supporters. Why are you willing to say things about him in private and not in public?

CRUZ: Dana, what I said in private is exactly what I'll say here, which is that the judgment that every voter is making of every one of us up here is who has the experience, who has the vision, who has the judgment to be commander in chief. That is the most important decision for the voters to make. That's a standard I'm held to. And it's a standard everyone else is held to. And I will note, you know, in the whole course of this discussion about our foreign policy threats, it actually illustrates the need for clarity of focus. You know, my daughters, Caroline and Catherine, came tonight. They're 7 and 5. And you think about the Los Angeles schools canceling their schools today. And every parent is wondering, how do we keep our kids safe? We need a commander in chief who does what Ronald Reagan did with communism, which is he set out a global strategy to defeat Soviet communism. And he directed all of his . . . (CROSSTALK) I'm answering the question, Dana. He directed all of his forces to defeating communism. One of the things we've seen here is how easy it is for Barack Obama and Hillary Clinton to get distracted from dealing with radical Islamic terrorism. They won't even call it by its name. We need a president who stands up, number one, and says, we will defeat ISIS. And number two, says the greatest national security threat facing America is a nuclear Iran.

BASH: Senator, senator, I just . . .

CRUZ: And we need to be focused on defeating . . .

BASH: Senator, a lot of people have seen . .

.

CRUZ: . . . defeating radical Islamic terrorists.

BASH: . . . a lot of people have seen these comments you made in private. I just want to clarify what you're saying right now is you do believe Mr. Trump has the judgment to be commander in chief?

CRUZ: What I'm saying, Dana, is that is a judgment for every voter to make. What I can tell you is all nine of the people here would make an infinitely better commander in chief than Barack Obama or Hillary Clinton (Team Fix, 2015).

This extended exchange is highly unusual, as primary candidates typically concentrate their energy on those they consider most threatening to their prospects in the primary, and generally retreat from attack only if they calculate they cannot win and are hopeful to be selected as a vice presidential candidate.

It makes sense that each would prefer the other as the final opponent. Since Cruz had alienated many in the Republican establishment, being paired against an even more objectionable choice was the only way he would receive begrudging support from Republican elites (he did). That same elite alienation would make Cruz the best possible opponent from Trump's perspective. Finally, Cruz had certainly observed that Trump primarily attacks those who attack him directly, and decided it was better to wait until the field narrowed.

This exchange doesn't have obvious parallels to general election debates, which typically have only two candidates. It is notable that Trump declined late spring debates that might have paired him one-on-one against Cruz (Riddell, 2016). Trump benefited from a large stage, where he could seem presidential while standing as the front-runner with well-qualified candidates, but avoid detailed discussions that might reveal limitations in his understanding of public policy. An opponent able to pull Trump away from his core issues (immigration, ISIS) into other questions (agriculture, health care, global poverty) that voters care about might succeed in generating a "Stockdale moment" (Yousefzadeh, 2005) in a general election debate.

The Cruz-Rubio Dynamic

Cruz might have foregone opportunities to directly attack Trump, but there was no similar restraint between Cruz and Rubio. Since both had been rising in the polls and had similar qualifications (Senator), they may have calculated that attacking each other was the best near- term strategy. There were detailed disputes over the opponents' positions on Libya, surveillance, and particularly immigration. Both candidates could be seen as trying to co-opt some of Trump's appeal as an immigration hardliner. Each attempted to cast doubt on the others' hardline statements, as seen in this segment:

BASH: Senator Cruz?

RUBIO: No, no, give him time.

CRUZ: In Florida promising to . . . (CROSSTALK)

RUBIO: Ted, do you . . .

CRUZ: go in the fight against amnesty . . .

RUBIO: Did Ted Cruz fight to support legalizing people that are in this country illegally?

CRUZ: He campaigned promising to lead the fight against amnesty.

FIORINA: Ladies and gentleman, this is why the American people are standing up.

BASH: Senator Cruz, can you answer that question please?

RUBIO: Does Ted Cruz rule out ever legalizing people that are in this country now?

BASH: Senator Cruz?

CRUZ: I have never supported a legalization . . .

RUBIO: Would you rule it out?

CRUZ: I have never supported legalization, and I do not intend to support legalization. Let me tell you how you do this, what you do is you enforce the law.. (CROSSTALK)

FIORINA: This is why the nation is fed up .
. .

BASH: One at a time please.

CRUZ: Watt you do is enforcement the law .
. .

FIORINA: We have been talking about this .
. .

BASH: Ms. Fiorina, please wait your turn, we're going to get to you.

FIORINA: Sorry, but you haven't gotten to me. This is why . . .

CRUZ: What you do . . .

BASH: Senator Cruz go ahead.

FIORINA: the people are fed up with the political class (Team Fix, 2015).

This particular exchange helped Fiorina more than Rubio or Cruz. This was not the only exchange about the details of policy difference and actual votes in the Senate. Others involved Rand Paul's take on government surveillance. In every case, the discussion of extremely important minutiae created moments where those out of the race could attack the Senators collectively in order to highlight executive experience. Christie was particularly direct:

> "Listen, I want to talk to the audience at home for a second. If your eyes are glazing over like mine, this is what it's like to be on the floor of the United States Senate. I mean, endless debates about how many angels on the head of a pin from people who've never had to make a consequential decision in an executive position" (Team Fix, 2015).

Trump's approach in these parts of the debate was to stay out of it completely. The larger dynamic was not only a problem for the three Senators, but really for everyone viewed as an establishment politician–including Christie, Bush, and Kasich. Again, the number of candidates continually played to Trump's advantage, allowing his to save mental energy for occasional injection or answers to direct questions.

Bush's Direct Attacks on Trump

Despite superior fundraising, Bush was a distant fifth in the polls coming into December and needed to dramatically alter the dynamic of the race. Conversely, candidates vying for second place could afford to attack each other and worry about Trump later. At the time, conventional wisdom assumed that the Republican establishment would unify around a mainstream candidate after the first few primaries. There was an eventual rally effect around Cruz, but not until months later when Trump's delegate lead was overwhelming.

Bush tried at least four approaches to land a major blow against Trump, but post-debate polling suggested he did not succeed with either. First, his opening remarks referred to Trump as the "chaos candidate"–a term he used twice early, but did not revisit.

> "We need to embed our forces–our troops inside the Iraqi military. We need to arm directly the Kurds. And all of that has to be done in concert with the Arab nations. And if we're going to ban all Muslims, how are we going to get them to be part of a coalition to destroy ISIS? The Kurds are the greatest fighting force and our strongest allies. They're Muslim. Look, this is not a serious proposal. In fact, it will push the Muslim world, the Arab world away from us at a

time when we need to reengage with them to be able to create a strategy to destroy ISIS. So Donald, you know, is great at–at the one-liners, but he's a chaos candidate. And he'd be a chaos president. He would not be the commander in chief we need to keep our country safe" (Team Fix, 2015).

Second, Bush suggested on fifteen different occasions (including the quote above) that we need a serious candidate for president, and that Trump was not a serious candidate and lacked serious proposals. Third, Bush (and Trump) ignored the moderators and rules for three direct exchanges with talk-overs. Finally, Bush got significant applause for coming back at Trump with this line at the beginning of the first exchange: "Donald, you're not going to be able to insult your way to the presidency. That's not going to happen." However, Bush attempted to use the same line near the end of the second exchange, and did not get the final word. That time, Trump recovered, setting up Fiorina to get the last word:

BUSH: You're never going to be president of the United States by insulting your way to the presidency.

TRUMP: Well, let's see. I'm at 42, and you're at 3. So, so far, I'm doing better.

BUSH: Doesn't matter. Doesn't matter.

TRUMP: So far, I'm doing better. You know, you started off over here, Jeb. You're moving over further and further. Pretty soon you're going to be off the end. . . .

FIORINA: This doesn't do a thing to solve the problems (Team Fix, 2015).

It's unlikely that Bush could have reversed the dynamic of the race with a different one-liner, but it is important to determine why these exchanges were not effective in raising new doubts about Trump. First, he attacked Trump's outsider status. Primary voters were not looking to dismiss outsider candidates categorically–at one point, different outsiders (Trump, Carson, and Fiorina) represented more than 50% in polling. Second, the strongest insider by polling, Cruz, took a pass when offered a chance to comment on Trump's judgment. Third, Trump may simply be better with impromptu one-liners than many candidates. At one point, he dismissed Bush saying "I know you're trying to build up your energy, Jeb, but it's not working very well" (Team Fix, 2015). The better strategy might be to avoid one-liners in situations where Trump could respond immediately and respect the time rules.

Nuclear Triad Exchange

One missed opportunity for Trump's opponents was Trump's complete misunderstanding of a question related to the nuclear triad (submarines, missiles, and long range bombers). Trump appeared to be unfamiliar with the terminology, and interpreted the question as relating to nuclear proliferation by others instead of the nuclear posture of the United States.

> HEWITT: Mr. Trump . . . (APPLAUSE) . . . Dr. Carson just referenced the single most important job of the president, the command, the control and the care of our nuclear forces. And he mentioned the triad. The B-52s are older than I am. The missiles are old. The submarines are aging out. It's an executive order. It's a commander-in-chief decision. What's your priority among our nuclear triad?

TRUMP: Well, first of all, I think we need somebody absolutely that we can trust, who is totally responsible; who really knows what he or she is doing. That is so powerful and so important. And one of the things that I'm frankly most proud of is that in 2003, 2004, I was totally against going into Iraq because you're going to destabilize the Middle East. I called it. I called it very strongly. And it was very important.

But we have to be extremely vigilant and extremely careful when it comes to nuclear. Nuclear changes the whole ball game. Frankly, I would have said get out of Syria; get out–if we didn't have the power of weaponry today. The power is so massive that we can't just leave areas that 50 years ago or 75 years ago we wouldn't care. It was hand-to-hand combat.

The biggest problem this world has today is not President Obama with global warming, which is inconceivable, this is what he's saying. The biggest problem we have is nuclear–<u>nuclear proliferation</u> and having some maniac, having some madman go out and get a nuclear weapon. That's in my opinion, that is the single biggest problem that our country faces right now.

HEWITT: Of the three legs of the triad, though, do you have a priority? I want to go to Senator Rubio after that and ask him.

TRUMP: I think -- I think, <u>for me, nuclear is just the power</u>, the devastation is very important to me.

There may be long term negative effects from this exchange. Many Republicans who oppose Trump have suggested they don't trust his judgment in international security, particularly in relation to U.S. nuclear weapons. However, Rubio followed up by describing the triad without directly attacking Trump's understanding of the issue. Even when moderators attempted to return to the nuclear temperament question, the question involved a reference to Senator Cruz and Trump ignored the nuclear part and spoke positively about Cruz instead.

The temptation from the previous exchanges is to assume that Trump comes off poorly for his lack of knowledge. That might be true for those familiar with nuclear strategy, but there is a strategy in Trump's approach as well. Instead of attempting to grapple with questions outside of his comfort zone, Trump seeks to interpret questions in ways that authorize him to speak closer to his comfort zone. Trump is more comfortable expressing concern over nuclear proliferation than explaining his nuclear doctrine, so the question is interpreted accordingly. Trump is more confident speaking about Cruz's temperament than his own, and so he selects the part of the question he will answer. Those moderating general election debates would do better to ask Trump simple, direct questions instead of complex questions that give him more options to change the topic. An opponent can note when Trump has avoided a question, but voters usually don't impose much of a penalty for occasionally changing the subject.

Co-Option of Terminology

When rhetoric critics discuss language choices, they sometimes speak of particular word choices as "fantasy themes" (Bormann, 1972), which refer away from the immediate situation. Situations where multiple people grab a hold of the same terminology and use it for their own purposes are called fantasy chains, and signal that there is particular power in the terminology. Although most interactions in a political debate could be understood with fantasy theme terminology, three from this debate were salient.

First, as mentioned above, Bush used variations of the word "serious" fifteen times to suggest that Trump was not a serious candidate with serious proposals. This line of attack has significant potential, as it might loosely describe why Trump has still, in August 2016, been unable to consolidate some traditional Republican voters. However, Bush's terminology did not chain out dramatically – Rubio used variants of the word four times, and Fiorina and Paul each did so once. It could be argued that Bush was no longer a "serious" candidate at the time of the debate, since he was polling around 5% despite significant fundraising and name recognition. Perhaps if more serious candidates such as Cruz had co-opted the terminology, it could have posed a problem to Trump.

Second, Trump had repeatedly simplified his campaign message as "winning." He used the term interchangeably to describe his campaign and also America's desire to "win" as a country. Nearly every candidate found an opportunity to use a variant of the term to describe their policies or position, whether in relating to the campaign, ISIS, or more generally. Both Trump and Cruz used variants at least five times each. It would appear that Trump's message was "winning" (in multiple senses), as other candidates sensed the power of the term and attempted to tap into it.

Finally, Cruz used variations of the term "radical Islam" thirteen times, and made specific note of Obama's unwillingness to use the term. This terminology chained out with all of the leading candidates using it at least once. Of those on the ends (polling the lowest), only Rand Paul used it, but that may reflect limited speaking time. In taking credit for emphasizing the terminology, one could say that Cruz had a significant rhetorical impact on the primary, and Trump used the term again in his acceptance speech.

The general election debates will provide new opportunities, although many unique terms from the debates (such as chaos candidate) do not chain out. At a minimum, Trump's opponents should expect to hear variations of winning and radical Islam, as well as other commonplace terminology from his stump speeches. Suggesting that Trump is not a serious candidate could have some utility in peeling away Republicans uncomfortable with him as their candidate. However, Trump is aware of the power of language to chain out– hence his consistent use of terms such as "Crooked Hillary" or "Lyin' Ted." His use of the term "political correctness" to dismiss a wide range of attacks is another example.

Debating effectively against Trump requires selection of a few key terms that reflect voter discomfort with his candidacy, and the ability to use those terms several times during the debate. For example, the word bankrupt might be used more effectively to describe his proposals, as it reminds voters that some of Trump's businesses have declared bankruptcy without making the election a referendum on whether Trump was successful in business.

Although the fifth debate did predate poll movements from Rubio to Cruz, the larger swing from Carson to Trump was well-established prior to the debate, and continued after the pre-debate pause. Although the fifth debate did not fundamentally alter Trump's trajectory toward the nomination, it represents missed opportunities for the other leading candidates and demonstrates how Trump was able to maintain momentum by staying above the fray while others jockeyed for long term viability. It also demonstrated that, regardless of public policy expertise, Trump has the verbal dexterity to answer complex questions selectively, and pivot away from topics beyond his comfort zone.

The focal points approach and the experience of the fifth debate suggest several strategies for general election debates involving Trump. At time of writing, the electoral dynamic is favorable for Secretary Clinton, but the debates provide Trump an opportunity to alter the dynamic either by her image of preparedness or appearing more presidential than in previous appearances.

Thus, a strategy to keep the debate mundane might be effective. By focusing policy discussion away from Trump's preferred issues (China, Russia, ISIS, immigration, guns, NAFTA, police safety, and outsourcing of jobs), he might reveal gaps in understanding more damaging than the nuclear triad. Issues important to some voters such as agriculture subsidies and exports, environmental issues besides global warming, infrastructure funding, global poverty, rapidly expanding renewable energy sectors, and perhaps financial regulation of the insurance sector.

Just as some terminology chained out from the December 15 debate, anyone debating against Trump might benefit from careful terminology choices. The phrase "casino capitalism" was used against Romney in 2012 but is probably more appropriate in 2016. Describing some Trump policy proposals as "bankrupt" could remind voters of Trump's bankruptcies, but make him appear defensive if he brings them up in response. Similarly, Trump is likely to use the term "political correctness" to dismiss objections to his offensive comments, so a couple of retorts that will dismiss that term without descending into personal attacks would be helpful.

Finally, Trump effectively avoided conflict with Cruz in the fifth debate by strategically complimenting him. There could be chances to compliment Trump in ways that might undermine him. First, Trump is good at interpersonal comebacks–so complimenting his skill as a television entertainer might be more effective than getting into a spiral of attacks. Second, Trump has gone farther than most outsiders would, and complimenting him on tapping into discontent might take the edge off of that discontent. Finally, congratulating Trump for seeing the light on any issue where he is attempting to pivot away from earlier statements might draw attention to the shift more effectively than criticizing the shift. If properly executed, none of these approaches need to validate Trump as presidential. Instead, they would elevate the debate from the politics of interpersonal combat that served Trump effectively from time to time in the primaries.

References

Bormann, E. G. (1972). Fantasy and rhetorical vision: The rhetorical criticism of social reality. *Quarterly Journal of Speech*, 58(4), 396-407.

Byers, M. D. (2012, October 17). Crowley fact-checks. *Politico*. Retrieved from http://www.politico.com/story/2012/10/seeking-control-crowley-fact-checks-mitt-082512

Carlin, D. P. (1992). Presidential debates as focal points for campaign arguments. *Political Communication*, 9(4), 251-265.

Hellmann, J. (2016, June 16). Poll: Americans split on Trump's proposed Muslim ban. *The Hill*. Retrieved from http://thehill.com/blogs/ballot-box/presidential-races/283789-poll-americans-split-on-trumps-muslim-ban-proposal

Marshall, J. (2016, August 24). Dazed and Confused. *Talking Points Memo*. Retrieved from http://talkingpointsmemo.com/edblog/dazed-and-confused

Morris, E., and Johnson, J. M. (2011). Strategic maneuvering in the 2008 presidential debates. *American Behavioral Scientist*, 55(3), 284-306.

Real Clear Politics (2016). 2016 Republican Presidential Nomination. Retrieved from http://www.realclearpolitics.com/epolls/2016/president/us/2016_republican_presidential_nomination-3823.html

Riddell, K. (2016, April 21). Why Donald Trump should debate Ted Cruz. *Washington Times.* Retrieved from http://www.washingtontimes.com/news/2016/apr/21/why-donald-trump-should-debate-ted-cruz/

Schreckinger, B. (2015, November 15). GOP candidates link Paris attacks to immigration: Trump, Cruz and others say their rhetoric on border security and Syrian refugees has been vindicated. *Politico.* Retrieved from http://www.politico.com/story/2015/11/paris-attacks-republicans-immigration-trump-cruz-215895

Tani, M., & LoGiurato, B. (2015, August 6). A Fox News focus group just torched Donald Trump after the debate. *Business Insider.* Retrieved from http://www.businessinsider.com/donald-trump-fox-news-focus-group-debate-frank-luntz-2015-8

Team Fix. (2015, December 15). 5th Republican debate transcript, annotated: Who said what and what it meant. *Washington Post.* Retrieved from https://www.washingtonpost.com/news/the-fix/wp/2015/12/15/who-said-what-and-what-it-meant-the-fifth-gop-debate-annotated/

Trump, D. J. (2015, December 7). Donald Trump Statement on Preventing Muslim Immigration. Retrieved from https://www.donaldjtrump.com/press-releases/donald-j.-trump-statement-on-preventing-muslim-immigration

Yousefzadeh, P. (2005, June 28). *A Belated Tribute and Apology to a Hero: Adm. Jim Stockdale.* Retrieved

from
http://www.military.com/NewContent/0,13190,Defens
ewatch_072805_Yousefzadeh,00.html

CHAPTER SIX

<<<<<<<<<<<<<<<<<<<<O>>>>>>>>>>>>>>>>>

GOP Primary Debate #6
North Charleston, South Carolina, January 14,
2016
Aaron Kall

<<<<<<<<<<<<<<<<<<O>>>>>>>>>>>>>>>>>

Following a month away from the debate stage because of
the winter break, seven Republican presidential candidates
descended on North Charleston, South Carolina for a two-
hour debate hosted by Fox Business Network. Maria
Bartiromo and Neil Cavuto had previously moderated the
November Milwaukee debate and received some mild
praise following the CNBC debacle in Boulder. The slate of
candidates consisted of former Florida Governor Jeb Bush,
Dr. Ben Carson, New Jersey Governor Chris Christie,
Texas Senator Ted Cruz, Ohio Governor John Kasich,
Florida Senator Marco Rubio, and frontrunner Donald
Trump. Seven participants constituted the smallest field to
date, which ensured additional airtime for the candidates
and more substantive exchanges. This was the first of two
Republican debates scheduled in South Carolina, as several
participants would return for the Greenville debate on
February 13 the week before the state's primary. The fact

that South Carolina was the only state to host two GOP debates illustrates its critical importance to the race.

Although it had been a month since the last debate in Las Vegas, the campaigns were quite active during the holiday season and the polls were holding steady. Trump maintained a comfortable lead in national polls and more than doubled Rubio's support in New Hampshire. He remained in a dead-heat with Cruz in Iowa, where voting would commence in about two weeks. Earlier in the race, Trump and Cruz enjoyed a cordial relationship despite their constant battle on the trail. They teamed up to rally against the Iran nuclear deal on Capitol Hill in September and mostly avoided attacking each other on the debate stage and elsewhere. Some even wondered: Could this be evidence of a potential Trump-Cruz ticket down the road? (Pappas, 2016). Their relationship took a turn for the worse as Cruz ascended in Iowa polls. In early January during an interview with *The Washington Post*, Trump questioned the legality of Cruz's Canadian birthplace and the conflict between the two candidates quickly escalated. Trump, hoping to eat into the senator's support in Iowa, repeatedly questioned whether Cruz was a natural born citizen (Lee, 2016). Cruz accused Trump of jumping the shark and the citizenship feud appropriately came to a head early in the North Charleston debate.

Moderator Cavuto afforded Cruz the opportunity to defend his presidential eligibility, as he was born in Canada to an American mother. Cruz's background as an attorney and constitutional scholar enabled him to present a persuasive case during the debate. He discussed the applicable situations of John McCain and George Romney, who had both previously run for president while experiencing similar eligibility concerns. Soon it was Trump's turn to counter and he noted several scholars who questioned Cruz's eligibility to be president, including Harvard Law School's Laurence Tribe, a former professor of Cruz's. Trump's argument was pretty weak on the legal merits and precedent, but his goal was to simply instill uncertainty surrounding Cruz's candidacy. Trump swung for the fences while on stage:

> "Here's the problem. We're running. We're running. He does great. I win. I choose him as my vice presidential candidate, and the Democrats sue because we can't take him along for the ride. I don't like that. OK? [*laughter*] The fact is–and if for some reason

he beats the rest of the field, he beats the rest of the field [*inaudible*]. See, they don't like that. They don't like that. [*audience booing*] No, they don't like he beats the rest of the field, because they want me. [*laughter*] But– if for some reason, Neil, he beats the rest of the field, I already know the Democrats are going to be bringing a suit. You have a big lawsuit over your head while you're running. And if you become the nominee, who the hell knows if you can even serve in office? So you should go out, get a declaratory judgment, let the courts decide. And you shouldn't have mentioned the polls because I would have been much...[*cross talk*] (Peters & Woolley, 2016)."

The famously litigious Trump assured the audience he wouldn't file a lawsuit over Cruz's eligibility, but unscrupulous Democrats may have other ideas. Mentioning Cruz as a potential vice-presidential candidate was also a deft political move and display of strength by the frontrunner. In the end, the citizenship battle during the debate was largely a draw and served as an appetizer for the New York values exchange later in the evening. The controversy regarding Cruz's eligibility to be president is quite reminiscent of Trump's obsession with President Obama's birth certificate during the run-up to the 2012 election. This issue has not received much attention during the present cycle, but could be featured prominently in the general election debates given North Charleston and moderator discretion.

Cruz was not the first politician Trump accused of potentially being ineligible to be president. While flirting with entering the 2012 race, Trump arrived in New Hampshire and flashed a wide smile as he took credit for the release of President Obama's long-form birth certificate (Zeleny, 2011). This was the culmination of months of work on an issue that simultaneously boosted Trump's standing among Republican primary voters. He had spent several months questioning the president's birthplace, religion, and academic performance. Trump offered a substantial financial reward for dirt on his past and reportedly sent investigators to President Obama's home state of Hawaii in search of any impropriety (Howard, 2016). He wasn't the only person consumed with this conspiracy theory, but Trump offered mainstream credibility to those who were incorrectly convinced President Obama was born outside the United States. This line of inquiry offered Trump a political platform, but ultimately he decided against running for president in 2012 and the issue returned to the backburner. Executives at NBC privately called on Trump to tone down his remarks, fearing they would hurt ratings of "The Apprentice" (Parker & Eder, 2016). The subject would reemerge after Trump formally declared his candidacy last June, but has mostly remained absent from the campaign trail and debate stage.

Despite being presented with the opportunity, Trump has avoided discussing his fascination and history surrounding President Obama's birth certificate. He was recently asked about it by ABC 6 local Philadelphia reporter Matt O'Donnell, to which Trump replied, "I told you, I don't talk about it anymore." He declined comment to *The New York Times* in July, but in a CNN interview around the same time said he would love to talk about the subject (Stelter, 2016). Although Trump may be avoiding direct engagement, surrogates like former campaign manager Corey Lewandowski, continue to publicly fan the flames. In his role as paid commentator on CNN in early August, Lewandowski asked if Obama got accepted to Harvard University Law School as a U.S. citizen or whether he was brought into the school as a citizen from another country (Corasaniti, 2016). Some of Trump's rhetoric on the campaign trail is eerily reminiscent of the birtherism controversy from the last cycle. During a campaign rally in Sunrise, Florida, on August 10, Trump referred to the president as "Barack Hussein Obama". Following the Orlando nightclub shooting in June, he called into *Fox & Friends* to insinuate that President Obama may get the ideology of radical Islam "better than anybody understands." Some critics interpreted Trump's rhetoric surrounding the Orlando shooting to be edging closer to his 2011 embrace of the birther movement (Stelter, 2016). His slippery slope return to the dark side could be complicating critical minority outreach efforts, which are now front and center of the campaign.

As part of Trump's general election pivot, he's engaging in a more explicit effort to reach African-American voters. Two recent NBC News battleground state polls had him registering zero percent support from such voters (Howard, 2016). In early September Trump visited Great Faith Ministries in Detroit after accepting an invitation from Bishop Wayne Jackson. His reception was somewhat mixed, as numerous vocal protesters were nearby and a prominent fixture of the media coverage. Part of the problem plaguing Trump's outreach efforts is his unwillingness to address the central issue which propelled him into politics (Resnick, G., & Chapman, M., 2016). In order to complete a successful pivot and accrue tangible polling results, a mea culpa may be required. The venue for this could be the campaign trail or more likely a debate stage.

Though Trump has been hesitant to overtly delve into birtherism, Clinton has been less reserved. In her first joint campaign appearance with President Obama in July, she described the president as "someone who has never forgotten where he came from." She then needled Trump and reminded him that Obama's birthplace is Hawaii. The general election debate moderators have a tremendous amount of autonomy and there is nothing preventing Lester Holt or the others from exploring this issue in greater depth. Trump could continue to stonewall the line of inquiry or could take the high road by apologizing. This could make him appear magnanimous and possibly earn the respect of voters who still hold a grudge over the way he attempted to delegitimize the country's first African-American president. Clinton would be wise to connect birtherism to a pattern of other questionable Trump actions, including alleged claims of housing discrimination.

Following the exchange over Cruz's eligibility to be president, the topic changed to gun control. The tragedies in Paris and San Bernadino were still fresh in the minds of the candidates and public, which elevated the importance of this particular subject. Moderator Bartiromo asked Trump if there were any circumstances that should limit gun sales of any kind in America. His response was pretty direct and unequivocal:

> "No. I am a 2nd amendment person. If we had guns in California on the other side where the bullets went in the different direction, you wouldn't have 14 or 15 people dead right now. If even in Paris, if they had guns on the other side, going in the opposite direction, you wouldn't have 130 people plus dead. So the answer is no and what Jeb said is absolutely correct. We have a huge mental health problem in this country. We're closing hospitals, we're closing wards, we're closing so many because the states want to save money. We have to get back into looking at what's causing it. The guns don't pull the trigger. It's the people that pull the trigger and we have to find out what is going

on. [*applause*] We have to protect our 2nd amendment and you cannot do this and certainly what Barack Obama was doing with the executive order. He doesn't want to get people together, the old-fashioned way, where you get Congress. You get the Congress, you get the Senate, you get together, you do legislation. He just writes out an executive order. Not supposed to happen that way [*applause*]" (Peters & Woolley, 2016).

Trump has been a pretty consistent supporter of the 2nd Amendment and this wasn't the first time the issue came up during the debates. In Boulder he said that gun-free zones are "a catastrophe and offer target practice for the sickos and mentally ill." Later in the Detroit debate, Trump would similarly argue there should be no restrictions on the 2nd Amendment and that he no longer supported a ban on assault weapons. Gun control was a frequent topic of conversation in both the Republican and Democratic primary debates. Clinton and Senator Sanders frequently did battle over previous records and the proper solutions going forward. Both presidential candidates should be well prepared for this during the general election debates. They will be arguing about a signature hot-button issue in front of a much different electorate from the primaries.

During a gun control debate, Clinton needs to distinguish her position from Trump's characterization. On the campaign trail and during debates, Trump has implied that she would fundamentally eliminate the 2nd amendment via the combination of executive action and the appointment of liberal justices to the Supreme Court. While Clinton is certainly to the left of Trump on gun control, her position is not as radical as Trump describes and she's done a pretty decent job of elucidating this point during the campaign. Clinton would be well-served to point out Trump's evolving positions regarding this issue. In 2012 he tweeted that President Obama had "spoken for me and every American" during his Newtown vigil for the shooting victims of that horrendous massacre. In Trump's 2000 book, *The America We Deserve,* he supported the 1994 federal assault weapons ban (Krieg, 2016). In June Trump suggested patrons at the Pulse nightclub in Orlando could have prevented or mitigated the attack had they been armed. He quickly backtracked from this position after receiving intense pressure from the National Rifle Association. Following the tragedies in Paris, San Bernadino, and Orlando, public support for stricter gun laws has been on the rise, which could bolster Clinton's policy proposals during the debates. Support for tighter gun control laws increased 9 percentage points after the Orlando attack and around 90 percent favor background checks and other measures recently debated in the Senate (Agiesta, J., & LoBianco, T., 2016). Voter intensity may be on the side of the NRA, but from a pure numbers perspective, Clinton could benefit from this issue during the general election debates if handled adroitly.

Immediately following this discussion of gun control, moderator Bartiromo pivoted to a discussion about New York values. Two days prior to the debate, Cruz appeared on the *Howie Carr Show* and said Trump "embodies New York values." With upcoming contests in Iowa and South Carolina, this was a calculated attack designed to drum up support from his core supporters. Being from New York herself, Bartiromo asked for a more detailed explanation of the phrase. Cruz described the values as socially liberal or pro-abortion and pro-gay-marriage. He brought up Trump's infamous appearance on *Meet the Press* in 1999, where he espoused liberal positions on numerous social issues. Cruz closed, remarking that "not a lot of conservatives come out of Manhattan."

Since Cruz had telegraphed his New York values attack publicly just days earlier, Trump was ready with an epic retort:

> "So conservatives actually do come out of
> Manhattan, including William F. Buckley
> and others, just so you understand.
> [*applause*] And just so—if I could, because
> he insulted a lot of people. I've had more
> calls on that statement that Ted made – New
> York is a great place. It's got great people,
> it's got loving people, wonderful people.
> When the World Trade Center came down, I
> saw something that no place on Earth could
> have handled more beautifully, more
> humanely than New York. You had two one
> hundred...[*applause*] ...you had two 110-
> story buildings come crashing down. I saw
> them come down. Thousands of people
> killed, and the cleanup started the next day,
> and it was the most horrific cleanup,
> probably in the history of doing this, and in
> construction. I was down there, and I've
> never seen anything like it. And the people
> in New York fought and fought and fought,

and we saw more death, and even the smell of death—nobody understood it. And it was with us for months, the smell, the air." And we rebuilt downtown Manhattan, and everybody in the world watched and everybody in the world loved New York and loved New Yorkers. And I have to tell you, that was a very insulting statement that Ted made. [*applause*]" (Peters & Woolley, 2016).

Although Trump's New York values material was likely canned, his example of William F. Buckley as a Manhattan conservative demonstrates quick thinking and reflexes that are essential in high-stakes debates. The moderator being from New York was coincidental, but certainly played to Trump's advantage. Trump and Clinton New York residencies could add an interesting dynamic to their debates. The moderators are likely to select some New York-centric topics even though the state is unlikely to be competitive in the general election. Clinton would be smart to study the Trump flip-flop video montage to which Cruz referred. Some major issues on which he's changed positions include: the Iraq War, criminalizing abortion, and raising the minimum wage. John Kerry and Mitt Romney were vulnerable to similar charges in earlier debates and Trump has a long and inconsistent record that could be difficult to coherently defend during a 90-minute debate with only one opponent.

Toward the end of the debate, moderator Bartiromo asked Trump about the running and responsibility of his business if he were elected president. He proudly responded:

> "Well, it's an interesting question because I'm very proud of my company. As you too know, I know I built a very great company. But if I become president, I couldn't care less about my company. It's peanuts. I want to use that same up here, whatever it may be to make America rich again and to make America great again. I have Ivanka, and Eric and Don sitting there. Run the company kids, have a good time. I'm going to do it for America. So I would — I would be willing to do that." (Peters & Woolley, 2016).

Clinton's favorability ratings have significantly declined recently because of controversies surrounding her private e-mail server and the Clinton Foundation. In

187

response to these recent revelations, President Clinton announced his involvement with the foundation will cease if his wife is elected president, but their daughter will continue working with it (Ali, 2016). The Clinton Foundation will surely come up during the general election debates and Clinton should rightly point out the foundation's succession plan is nearly identical to Trump's plans, even though she has received a great deal more scrutiny.

Trump devoted his entire closing statement to criticizing the Iran nuclear deal,

> "I stood yesterday with 75 construction workers. They're tough, they're strong, they're great people. Half of them had tears pouring down their face. They were watching the humiliation of our young ten sailors, sitting on the floor with their knees in a begging position, their hands up. And Iranian wise guys having guns to their heads. It was a terrible sight. A terrible sight. And the only reason we got them back is because we owed them with a stupid deal, $150 billion. If I'm president, there won't be

stupid deals anymore. We will make America great again. We will win on everything we do." (Peters & Woolley, 2016).

Trump has been a consistent and ferocious critic of an international agreement he disdains. Recent revelations only give him additional ammunition heading into the fall debates. The Institute for Science and International Security alleges the U.S. and its negotiating partners in secret allowed Iran to evade some restrictions in order to meet the economic sanctions relief deadline (Landay, 2016). Clinton was Secretary State during secret talks with Iran, but had left office prior to the beginning of formal negotiations. Despite this nuance, Trump will make an effort to connect Clinton with the unpopular deal. A Pew Research Center poll from last fall found just 21 percent of the American public supported the Iran nuclear deal while nearly half of the country disapproved (Pew Research Center, 2015). Iran presents Trump with a golden opportunity, but he should be careful about overplaying his hand. He has a history of committing Iran-related gaffes, including being mistaken about seeing video footage of a $400 million cash for prisoner exchange in early August.

The North Charleston debate ended up being quite a memorable affair for many reasons. Trump boycotted the next event in Des Moines and didn't debate again until February 6 in Manchester. He lost the Iowa caucus to Ted Cruz, but followed with resounding wins in New Hampshire, Nevada, and South Carolina. Since there were only seven candidates on stage, everyone benefited from additional speaking time. Cruz emerged the leader with 17:28 of airtime followed by Trump at 16:39 (Shain, 2016). The citizenship eligibility exchange resulted in a draw, but most media commentators felt Trump had the better overall night because of the New York values exchange and did nothing to jeopardize his frontrunner status. A Google snap poll showed viewers believed Trump won the night with 37.3 percent to Cruz's 26.6 percent (Holland & Oliphant, 2016). Since the event was broadcast on *Fox Business Network*, its ratings were a little underwhelming. The North Charleston debate drew about 11 million viewers, which was a smaller audience than any of the season's GOP debates. (Kissell, 2016). Trump may have experienced his strongest performance to date, but he must mature and reach a different level altogether prior to his upcoming showdowns with Clinton.

References

Agiesta, J., & LoBianco, T. (2016, June 20). Poll: Gun control support spikes after shooting. *CNN*. Retrieved from http://www.cnn.com/2016/06/20/politics/cnn-gun-poll

Ali, S. (2016, September 1). The Clinton Foundation controversy. *The Express Tribune*. Retrieved from http://tribune.com.pk/story/1174346/clinton-foundation-controversy

Corasaniti (2016, August 3). Corey Lewandowski, Former Trump Campaign Manager, Dives Back Into 'Birtherism'. *The New York Times*. Retrieved from http://www.nytimes.com/2016/08/04/us/politics/corey-lewandowski-obama-birther.html

Holland, S., & Oliphant, J. (2016, January 16). Friendly no more: Trump, Cruz erupt in bitter fight at Republican debate. *Reuters*. Retrieved from http://www.reuters.com/article/us-usa-election-idUSKCN0US18M

Howard, A. (2016, July 28). 'Birtherism' Is Back and That May Be Bad News For Trump. *NBC News*. Retrieved from http://www.nbcnews.com/news/us-news/birtherism-back-may-be-bad-news-trump-n618731

Kissell, R. (2016, January 15). GOP Debate Ratings: Fox Business Network Draws 11 Million Viewers. *Variety*. Retrieved from http://variety.com/2016/tv/news/ratings-gop-debate-fox-business-network-11-million-1201680815

Krieg, G. (2016, June 20). The times Trump changed his positions on guns. *CNN*. Retrieved from http://www.cnn.com/2016/06/20/politics/donald-trump-gun-positions-nra-orlando

Landay, J. (2016, September 1). U.S., others agreed 'secret' exemptions for Iran after nuclear deal: think tank. *Reuters.* Retrieved from http://www.reuters.com/article/us-iran-nuclear-exemptions-exclusive-idUSKCN1173LA

Lee, M.J. (2016, January 15). GOP debate: Trump-Cruz 'bromance' is over. *CNN*. Retrieved from http://www.cnn.com/2016/01/14/politics/republican-debate-2016-highlights

Pappas, A. (2016, January 18). A Timeline Of Donald Trump And Ted Cruz's Deteriorating Bromance. *The Daily Caller*. Retrieved from http://dailycaller.com/2016/01/18/a-timeline-of-donald-trump-and-ted-cruzs-deteriorating-bromance

Parker, A., & Eder, S. (2016, July 2). Inside the Six Weeks Donald Trump Was a Nonstop 'Birther'. *The New York Times*. Retrieved from http://www.nytimes.com/2016/07/03/us/politics/donald-trump-birther-obama.html

Peters, G. T., & Woolley, J. T. (2016, January 14). Presidential Debates. Republican Candidates Debate in North Charleston, SC. Retrieved from http://www.presidency.ucsb.edu/ws/index.php?pid=111395

Pew Research Center (2015, September 8). Support for Iran Agreement Fails. Retrieved from http://www.people-press.org/2015/09/08/support-for-iran-nuclear-agreement-falls

Resnick, G., & Chapman, M. (2016, September 3). Donald Trump, The Birther, Goes To a Black Church in

Detroit. *The Daily Beast*. Retrieved from http://www.thedailybeast.com/articles/2016/09/03/don ald-trump-the-birther-goes-to-a-black-church-in-detroit.html

Shain, A. (2016, January 14). GOP candidates spar in SC presidential debate. *The State*. Retrieved from http://www.thestate.com/news/politics-government/politics-columns-blogs/the-buzz/article54821895.html

Stelter, B. (2016, July 3). Donald Trump 'would love to' talk about birtherism. Here's why he doesn't. *CNN Money*. Retrieved from http://money.cnn.com/2016/07/03/media/donald-trump-obama-birtherism

Zeleny, J. (2011, April 27). Trump Takes Credit for Release of Obama Birth Certificate. *The New York Times*. Retrieved from http://thecaucus.blogs.nytimes.com/2011/04/27/trump-takes-credit-for-release-of-obamas-long-form-birth-certificate

CHAPTER SEVEN

<<<<<<<<<<<<<<<<<<<<<<<O>>>>>>>>>>>>>>>>>>>>>>

GOP Primary Debate #7
Des Moines, Iowa, January 28, 2016
Aaron Kall

<<<<<<<<<<<<<<<<<<<<<<<O>>>>>>>>>>>>>>>>>>>>>>

The Trump campaign had a tremendous amount of momentum in January of 2016 and the wind was at its back for a variety of reasons. The candidate's debate performance in North Charleston, South Carolina on January 14 was seen as his best performance of the campaign (Diamond, 2016). Trump was delving into the birtherism issue again by challenging Senator Ted Cruz's eligibility to be elected President. During the North Charleston debate, Trump deftly defended New York values by talking about the city's response and heroism in the aftermath of attacks on the World Trade Center in 2001. National polls released in late January from CNN/ORC and Washington Post-ABC News showed Trump hovering around the 40 percent mark for the first time, which doubled the support of Cruz, who stood in second place (Agiesta, 2016; Balz & Clement, 2016). Two state polls from this time period similarly showed a Trump advantage over Cruz in Iowa, with a cushion of seven points (Dinan,

2016; Hook, 2016). In addition to the positive polling data, the frontrunner racked up several high-profile endorsements in January that could potentially garner a lot of political mileage. Trump received endorsements from the trio of Liberty University President Jerry Falwell Jr., former Alaska Governor Sarah Palin, and Arizona Sheriff Joe Arpaio. Despite all of these positive developments, Trump decided to publicly challenge the parameters of the January 28 debate in Des Moines. This power play was completely unnecessary and culminated in a week of distraction and campaign heartache.

It's worth going back several months to fully understand the genesis of the Des Moines debate dispute. Fox News hosted the first Republican primary debate on August 6, 2015, in Cleveland, which was moderated by Chris Wallace, Bret Baier, and Megyn Kelly. Kelly immediately asked Trump about previous statements and tweets that were disparaging of women. He took exception to this line of questioning in real-time and repeatedly criticized Kelly in the aftermath of the debate. Trump appeared on *CNN Tonight* with Don Lemon the next evening and escalated the feud with Kelly by calling her a lightweight and overrated. He infamously commented, "You can see there was blood coming out of her eyes, blood coming out of her wherever" (Transcript, 2015). During this interview Trump also hinted he may not agree to participate in another debate that involved Fox News. In spite of the controversy with moderator Kelly, the public perceived Trump as the runaway winner of the Cleveland debate. Online polls conducted by *Drudge Report*, *Time Magazine*, and *Slate Magazine* all showed a convincing victory for the businessman (Voorhees, 2015). While the Trump-Kelly feud attracted a tremendous amount of media attention, the end result turned out fine for the campaign and there was little reason to think any lingering animosity would spillover to the second debate hosted by Fox News over five months later. Trump did threaten to skip CNN debates in September and December unless they donated $5 million dollars to his preferred charity, but this ended up being a hollow ultimatum (Gold, 2015). The events in the week preceding the Des Moines debate quickly spiraled into a point of no return for the campaign.

The Trump campaign spent the weekend prior to the Thursday Des Moines debate trying to work the referees. Campaign manager Corey Lewandowski allegedly threatened that Kelly would receive another rough treatment from Trump if she served as moderator again (Rucker & Balz & Johnson, 2016). Trump appeared on

CNN's *The Situation Room with Wolf Blitzer* on Monday evening and it appeared things were still on track for Thursday night. Trump said that he would probably attend the debate, but Kelly hadn't treated him fairly earlier and the decision wasn't 100 percent (Transcript, 2016). Trump was betting that his celebrity status and ability to attract a large television audience for the event would give the campaign leverage and get Kelly excluded from the event. The Fox News debate in Cleveland was watched by 24 million viewers, making it the highest-rated primary debate in television history (Stelter, 2015). Fox News and its president Roger Ailes elevated the fight on Tuesday. He not only affirmed that Kelly would remain on as moderator, but also issued a statement mocking Trump's leadership abilities and temperament. In the end, Lewandowski told reporters after a press conference in Iowa that Trump wouldn't be attending the Des Moines debate and the decision was final. The Fox News statement was officially cited as the reason for cancelling his participation in the event. Trump said, "I was all set to do the debate, I came here to do the debate. When they sent out the wise-guy press release done by some PR person along with Roger Ailes, I said: 'Bye bye, OK" (Holland & Gibson, 2016). Both Trump and Lewandowski predicted poor ratings for the debate and a loss in advertising revenue for Fox News due to the absence of the frontrunner. The campaign was now scrambling to develop some counterprogramming in the form of a Special Event for Wounded Warriors & Veterans.

After the initial shock of Trump's decision to skip the Des Moines debate subsided, political and media reaction to the move was somewhat mixed. Trump had run an unconventional campaign to date and this was seen as another confounding decision that could go against the political grain and potentially pay big dividends. He quickly commandeered the news cycle and all the attention the week before the Iowa caucus remained on Trump. Surrogates remained privately skeptical of the unorthodox play, but put on a poker face and hoped for the best. The campaign predicted voters would see Trump's decision as an example of the bold and unforgiving attitude Trump promised to bring into the Oval Office (Diamond, 2016). Others feared this could be the first major unforced error of the campaign. It had survived disparaging the military service of war hero John McCain and threatening to shoot someone on Fifth Avenue in New York, but this seemed different. Skipping the debate risked irrevocably damaging the Trump brand, while permitting his opponents additional airtime and the opportunity to grab the spotlight. Trump was undercutting his own appeal and wouldn't be able to suck up all the oxygen on the debate stage (Tures, 2016). Carly Fiorina and Chris Christie had gained considerable political mileage by attacking Trump in previous undercard debates. These indictments were especially effective because Trump wasn't present to defend himself and successfully counterpunch, which is one of his greatest strengths. On the stump and in previous debates, Trump had talked tough about dealing with leaders from China, Mexico, and Russia. If Trump was afraid to take questions from Megyn Kelly in a two-hour debate, how could he effectively grapple with someone like Vladimir Putin (Kall, 2016)? Finally, the debate controversy undermined Trump as a shrewd dealmaker. He gambled that Fox News would cave to his demands and side with him over Kelly. This was clearly a major miscalculation and potential indictment of his negotiating skills as president.

Despite Trump's absence, the Fox News debate in Des Moines was underway at 8 p.m. Central Time on Thursday as scheduled. The Baier, Kelly, and Wallace trio of moderators presided and seven candidates participated: former Florida Governor Jeb Bush, Dr. Ben Carson, New Jersey Governor Chris Christie, Texas Senator Ted Cruz,

Ohio Governor John Kasich, Kentucky Senator Rand Paul, and Florida Senator Marco Rubio. Kelly immediately began the evening by addressing the elephant not in the room tonight, Donald Trump. Cruz fielded the question and made a naked political appeal to his supporters. Overall, Trump wasn't a major focus of debate that night. His name was mentioned a total of thirteen times: five times by the moderators, four times by Bush, and twice by Rubio and Cruz (Peters & Woolley, 2016). Bush playfully referred to Trump as a little teddy bear and mocked his absence from the debate. While Trump wasn't a major player at the Iowa Events Center, he was causing quite a stir three miles down the road at Drake University.

The Trump campaign had hastily organized a one hour event to benefit military vetarans that would start at the exact same time of the debate. CNN and MSNBC covered the event live and even with last-minute planning a capacity crowd of 700 people attended (Gibson, 2016). Trump mentioned he would prefer to be five minutes away participating in the debate and that Fox News had recently treated him nicely in hopes of altering his decision. He gave a shortened version of his stump speech about the Iran deal, free trade, and immigration. Trump announced during the event over $6 million dollars had been raised for veterans through his personal donation and those of other rich friends. Some of the donors were personally in attendance and he allowed them to be recognized and make short speeches. It was revealed several months later the event netted closer to $4.5 million for the charities and Trump didn't send his $1 million check to the Marine Corps-Law Enforcement Foundation until May (Fahrenthold, 2016).

Fresh off the undercard debate, former Arkansas Governor Mike Huckabee and former Pennsylvania Senator Rick Santorum arrived at the event and were permitted to give short speeches on stage. While speaking, Santorum awkwardly spoke from the left side of the stage so he wouldn't be recorded in front of the Trump campaign sign emblazened on the podium. After a brief concluding presentation by a military veteran the event had commenced. Trump likened the night to the Academy Awards, but it was far from it. The major questions going forward concerned how the two competing events were perceived and whether Trump would face any political repercussions from Iowa voters. The answer to these questions would quickly become apparent.

Immediately following the conclusion of the dueling events, there was an intense scrutiny on television viewership numbers and advertising revuene as it related to Fox News' bottom line. According to the Nielsen ratings, more than 12.4 million people tuned in to watch the Des Moines debate. CNN and MSNBC reportedly earned about a quarter of the Fox News ratings with their live coverage of Trump's veterans event (Rhodan, 2016). While a 12.4 rating for a primary debate is solid, it paled in comparison to ratings from earlier Republican primary debates carried on Fox News and CNN. Trump campaign manager Corey Lewandowski's prediction of only a few million viewers for the debate had proven wildly off the mark. Trump claimed his inclusion would have doubled ratings, but there is obviously no way to verify this bold prediction. There is no doubt some multitasking occurred from technologically savy viewers on that Thursday night. Some were likely watching the debate on a big screen while keeping an eye on the Trump event on their smart phones (Stelter, 2016). Even though the ratings for Fox News were lower sans Trump, they apparently didn't suffer any financial penalty in his absence. Much of their advertising deals didn't carry a ratings guarantee and spots sold after Trump bowed out went for roughly $200,000, which remained a premium rate for a debate (Vranica & Flint, 2016). The war between Fox *News* and Trump surrounding the Des Moines debate was entertaining television, but didn't negatively impact their bottom line or reputation. They exercised loyalty to Megyn Kelly and stood their ground during negotiations with a shrewd businessman. The aftermath of the controvery turned out fine for Fox News, but its impact on frontrunner Trump was far more uncertain as voting was only a few days away.

The instant media analysis following Thursday night's events was positive for Trump. His number one threat Cruz had a lackluster debate performance because he was under a microscope and attracted circular fire that would have otherwise been reserved for Trump. His interruptions of moderator Chris Wallace weren't successful like earlier actions in the CNBC Boulder debate and Des Moines may have been Cruz's worst debate performance of the cycle (Todd, Murray & Dann, 2016). The Fox News moderators were also fact-checking in realtime, which Trump was able to avoid for the time being. This tactic would re-emerge again in the Detroit debate in March. Even though Trump chose not to participate in the debate, his alternative event still kept him relevant to the media narrative. The lead story on all the Thursday evening Des Moines newcasts remained Trump (Harwood, 2016). First impressions are often incorrect and many of these snapshot prognostications would later prove wrong for a variety of reasons. There was one final piece of news that provided a complacent campaign with some additional optimism.

The final Bloomberg Politics/Des Moines Register Iowa Poll before the February Caucus was released on Saturday evening. The survey covered Tuesday through Friday and showed Trump at 28 percent with a five point lead over Cruz (McCormick, 2016). While several polling firms were surveying Iowa in the lead up to election day, this was generally considered the most reliable one and was exclusive to the *Des Moines Register* for almost 75 years. It's often referred to as the gold standard of polling because of its sterling reputation for accuracy (Des Moines Register, 2016). Given the poll's positive track record, the Trump campaign had to feel pretty good about their chances in Iowa over the weekend. Tuesday night would yield a different story and soul-searching regarding the debate decision.

After all the votes in Iowa were tallied, Cruz surprisingly emerged victorious with 27.65 percent of the vote. Trump eeked out a dissapointing second place finish at 24.31 percent and finished only about one point ahead of Rubio. Cruz provided a body blow to Trump, delivering him an unexpected smackdown (Jacobs, 2016). An autopsy of Trump's stinging defeat was immediately conducted. There were non-debated issues that were certainly cause for concern. Evangelicals make up a large portion of Republican caucus voters and Trump's earlier liberal positions could have been problematic. Cruz has a strong connection with this important voting bloc and a superior ground game as well. Trump was self-reflective about the defeat and immediately identified the debate as a major contributing factor. On the Tuesday night *Hannity* show he admitted that skipping the event helped his opponents and that some Iowans were dissapointed he didn't present his case to them. Rather than sulk about the setback, he expressed no hard feelings and took the second place finish in stride. Trump promised to return to Iowa during the general election and even talked about buying a farm there one day because of his love for the state (Johnson, 2016). While several factors played a role in Trump's unexpected runner-up finish, it's worth examining in further detail the reasons the debate boycott was so damaging to his brand and closing argument to Iowa voters.

Though Trump enjoyed a lead in most January polls and the last one taken before voting day, he ended up getting passed by Cruz in Iowa at the finish line. Since the Des Moines debate was only five days before the caucus, it marked the perfect opportunity for the candidates to present their closing arguments and make favorable impressions on undecided voters. By skipping the debate, Trump blew this opportune moment and paid the ultimate political price. Iowa entrance poll surveys showed that Rubio won 30 percent and Cruz won 25 percent of the Republican voters that decided in the days between the debate and the caucus. Conversely, Trump only won 14 percent of these voters (Stelter, 2016). Late-deciding voters were offended by the Trump snub and viewed it as a personal affront. In addition to missing the opportunity to present a compelling closing argument, Trump's absence from the debate allowed his opponents additional airtime and they took advantage of this golden opportunity. Rubio and Cruz both had more than 13 minutes during the Des Moines debate to state their respective cases and uncommitted voters liked what they heard. Rubio especially capitalized, which helped contribute to his strong third place showing (Kall, 2016). Anecdotal evidence from both campaign canvassing and a Frank Luntz focus group of two dozen Iowa Republican voters bolsters this theory. Trump had acrued so much goodwill from being a strait shooter, as opposed to a candidate that engages in political games. While the decision may have been well-intentioned, it clearly was a gamble that failed to pay off with Iowa voters.

Although it's easy to pile on Trump for his unsuccessful boycott of the Des Moines debate, it's important to put this controversy in a larger context. He is neither the first nor last political candidate that will boycott a debate. History is rife with numerous examples of such action. No presidential election debates were held in the years 1964, 1968, and 1972. The second presidential debate and vice-presidential debate in 1980 was canceled because of a dispute regarding the inclusion of third-party candiate John Anderson. In 2000, George W. Bush skipped the first two Republican primary debates. In 1996 Bob Dole bypassed a South Carolina Republican debate in favor of returning to Washington, D.C. to engage in budget negotiations. The most appropriate analogy to Trump is frontrunner Ronald Reagan skipping the *Des Moines Register* debate in 1980 because of performance concerns. Iowans were insulted by this decision and Reagan lost the caucus to George H.W. Bush (Rhodan, 2016). Trump would have been wise to keep this fact in mind, which could have prevented history from repeating itself. The error in judgment didn't end up being fatal to the longterm prospects of either candidate. They both experienced resounding wins in New Hampshire and eventually clinched the Republican nomination.

While Trump did participate in eleven Republican primary debates, his boycott in Iowa was not unique. At a press conference shortly after the Miami debate in early March, he complained about repetitive debate questions and said that television networks benefit from the events more than the candidates. The writing was on the wall that Trump preferred not to particpate in any additional debates, even if they were scheduled and sanctioned by the Republican National Committee. On March 16, a debate in Salt Lake City ahead of the Utah caucus was canceled after Trump announced he wouldn't attend. He claimed to have only recently learned of the debate and previously made plans to address the American Israel Public Affairs Committee's annual conference in Washington, D.C. Ted Cruz in turn denounced the decision and gave Trump the nickname "Ducking Donald" (Jackson, 2016). Cruz challenged Trump to additional debates in Wisconsin, New York, Pennsylvania, and Indiana. Trump politely declined all such invitations. In late May during an appearance on

Jimmy Kimmel Live, Trump agreed in principle to debate Vermont Senator Bernie Sanders in California if the proceeds went to charity. Sanders accepted the challenge immediately on Twitter, but Trump reneged on the promise a day later. Trump has also floated the idea of skipping general election debates if they run opposite National Football League games because of audience size concerns. It's never a good idea to try and guess what Trump will do, but it's a safe bet that he will attend and try to make up the current deficit he faces against Clinton in national and swing state polls.

The decision to miss the Des Moines debate was short-sighted, but didn't result in any longterm damage to the Trump campaign. He rebounded withimpressive victories in New Hampshire, South Carolina, and Nevada. Trump even made amends with Megyn Kelly, who co-moderated the Detroit Republican debate in early March. He later participated in Kelly's first prime-time special on May 17, which drew 4.8 million viewers (Battaglio, 2016). Iowa voters have also seemed to forgive Trump for his debate boycott. He and Clinton are currently locked in a statistical tie in the state (Nelson, 2016). The American public can be very forgiving of politicians, especially when it seems they have generally learned from their mistakes. Trump may attempt to negotiate the most favorable terms for the general election debates in the fall with Clinton, but he's witnessed firsthand the negative ramifications that can result from non-participation. There is little doubt that he will be at Hofstra University in New York on September 26 and a good portion of the American public will be attentatively watching to see what happens.

References

Agiesta, J. (2016, January 26). CNN/ORC Poll: Donald Trump dominates GOP field at 41%. *CNN*. Retrieved from http://www.cnn.com/2016/01/26/politics/donald-trump-ted-cruz-polling

Balz, D. & Clement S. (2016, January 26). As first voting nears, Trump seems stronger. *Washington Post,* Retrieved from https://www.washingtonpost.com/politics/as-first-voting-nears-trump-seems-stronger/2016/01/25/349439d4-c392-11e5-a4aa-f25866ba0dc6_story.html

Battaglio, S. (2016, May 18). Megyn Kelly's interview with Donald Trump draws 4.8 million viewers on Fox. *Los Angeles Times*. Retrieved from http://www.latimes.com/entertainment/envelope/cotown/la-et-ct-megyn-kelly-trump-ratings-20160518-snap-story.html

Des Moines Register (2016, January 30). Final Iowa Poll released. Retrieved from http://www.desmoinesregister.com/story/news/election

s/presidential/caucus/2016/01/27/final-iowa-poll-before-caucuses-released-saturday/79411100

Diamond, J. (2016, January 15). GOP debate winners and losers. *CNN*. Retrieved from http://www.cnn.com/2016/01/15/politics/republican-debate-2016-winners-losers

Diamond, J. (2016, January 28). Skipping debate, Donald Trump gambles with Iowa. *CNN*. Retrieved from http://www.cnn.com/2016/01/27/politics/donald-trump-iowa-debate-2016-election

Dinan, C. (2016, January 25). Trump Widens Lead Over Cruz In New Iowa Poll. *Talking Points Memo*. Retrieved from http://talkingpointsmemo.com/polltracker/arg-jan-21-24-trump-lead-widens

Donald Trump Live on 'CNN Tonight.' (2015, August 8). *CNN*. Retrieved from http://www.cnn.com/TRANSCRIPTS/1508/08/cnnt.01.html

Donald Trump Live on 'The Situation Room.' (2016, January 25). *CNN*. Retrieved from http://transcripts.cnn.com/TRANSCRIPTS/1601/25/sitroom.02.html

Fahrenthold, D. (2016, May 21). Trump said he raised $6 million for veterans. Now his campaign says it was less. *Washington Post*. Retrieved from https://www.washingtonpost.com/politics/trump-said-he-raised-6-million-for-vets-now-his-campaign-says-it-was-less/2016/05/20/871127a8-1d1f-11e6-b6e0-c53b7ef63b45_story.html

Gibson, G. (2016, January 29). Trump draws full house at own event as he snubs Fox News debate. *Reuters*.

Retrieved from http://www.reuters.com/article/us-usa-election-trump-idUSKCN0V705T

Gold, H. (2015, December 1). Trump threatens to boycott CNN debate, demands $5 million. *Politico.* Retrieved from http://www.politico.com/blogs/on-media/2015/12/donald-trump-threatens-to-boycott-cnn-debate-again-216302

Harwood, J. (2016, January 29). An absent Trump won this debate: Why? *CNBC.* Retrieved from http://www.cnbc.com/2016/01/29/an-absent-trump-won-this-debate-why.html

Holland, S., & Gibson, G. (2016, January 27). Trump pulls out of Republican debate in Iowa. *Reuters.* Retrieved from http://www.reuters.com/article/us-usa-election-idUSKCN0V502J

Hook, J. (2016, January 28). Donald Trump Solidifies Lead Over GOP Rivals in First States to Vote. *Wall Street Journal.* Retrieved from http://www.wsj.com/articles/donald-trump-solidifies-lead-over-gop-rivals-in-first-states-to-vote-1453978800

Jackson, D. (2016, March 16). Monday Republican debate in Utah canceled. *USA Today.* Retrieved from http://www.usatoday.com/story/news/politics/onpolitics/2016/03/16/donald-trump-debate-salt-lake-city-john-kasich-ted-cruz/81853066

Jacobs, J. (2016, February 2). Cruz wins GOP caucuses, beating Trump. *Des Moines Register.* Retrieved from http://www.desmoinesregister.com/story/news/elections/presidential/caucus/2016/02/01/republican-ted-cruz-wins-iowa-caucuses/79625866

Kall, A. (2016, February 2). Debate controversy trumps the Donald in Iowa. *Des Moines Register*. Retrieved from http://www.desmoinesregister.com/story/opinion/colu mnists/caucus/2016/02/02/debate-controversy-trumps-donald-iowa/79717400

Kall, A. (2016, January 27). Debate snub is "huuge" self-inflicted error by Trump. *Des Moines Register*. Retrieved from http://www.desmoinesregister.com/story/opinion/colu mnists/caucus/2016/01/27/debate-snub-huuge-self-inflicted-error-trump/79430754

McCormick, J. (2016, January 30). Trump Overtakes Cruz in Final Iowa Poll Before Caucuses. *Bloomberg Politics*. Retrieved from http://www.bloomberg.com/politics/articles/2016-01-30/des-moines-register-bloomberg-politics-iowa-poll-republicans

Nelson, L. (2016, August 11). Poll: Clinton and Trump in dead heat in Iowa. *Politico*. Retrieved from http://www.politico.com/blogs/swing-states-2016-election/2016/08/poll-trump-clinton-iowa-226917

Peters, G. T., & Woolley, J. T. (2016, January 28). Presidential Debates. Republican Candidates Debate in Des Moines, IA. Retrieved from http://www.presidency.ucsb.edu/ws/index.php?pid=11 1412

Rhodan, M. (2016, January 29). Republican Debate Beats Trump Rally in Ratings Battle. *Time* Magazine. Retrieved from http://time.com/4199653/republican-debate-trump-rally-ratings

Rucker, P., Balz, D., & Johnson, J. (2016, January 26). Trump says he won't participate in GOP debate on Fox News. *Washington Post*. Retrieved from https://www.washingtonpost.com/politics/trump-says-he-wont-participate-in-gop-debate-on-fox-news/2016/01/26/58fa0b2e-c490-11e5-a4aa-f25866ba0dc6_story.html

Stelter, B. (2016, February 2). Did Trump's debate snub hurt him? Fox News commentators say it did. *CNN Money*. Retrieved from http://money.cnn.com/2016/02/02/media/donald-trump-fox-news-iowa-caucuses

Stelter, B. (2015, August 7). Fox's GOP debate had record 24 million viewers. *CNN Money*. Retrieved from http://money.cnn.com/2015/08/07/media/gop-debate-fox-news-ratings

Stelter, B. (2016, January 29). Who won the ratings race: Fox News or Donald Trump? *CNN Money*. Retrieved from http://money.cnn.com/2016/01/29/media/republican-debate-ratings-donald-trump/index.html?iid=hp-stack-dom

Todd, C., Murray, M., & Dann, C. (2016, January 29). First Read: Why Donald Trump Won the Debate Without Showing Up. *NBC News*. Retrieved from http://www.nbcnews.com/meet-the-press/first-read-why-donald-trump-won-debate-without-showing-n506786

Tures, J. (2016, January 27). How Skipping the Debate Could Cost Trump Badly. *Huffington Post*. Retrieved from http://www.huffingtonpost.com/john-a-tures/how-skipping-the-debate-c_b_9095074.html

Voorhees, J. (2015, August 7). Did Trump Actually Win the Debate? How to Understand All Those Instant Polls That Say Yes. *Slate Magazine*. Retrieved from http://www.slate.com/blogs/the_slatest/2015/08/07/did

_trump_win_or_lose_the_fox_news_debate_the_instan
t_polls_and_ratings.html

Vranica, S., & Flint, J. (2016, January 28). A GOP Debate
Without Donald Trump Likely Won't Crimp Fox's
Wallet. *Wall Street Journal.* Retrieved from
http://www.wsj.com/articles/a-gop-debate-without-
donald-trump-likely-wont-crimp-foxs-wallet-
1454012960

CHAPTER EIGHT

<<<<<<<<<<<<<<<<<<<<◇>>>>>>>>>>>>>>>>>>>>

GOP Primary Debate #8
Manchester, New Hampshire, February 6, 2016
Dr. Brett Bricker and Dr. Sarah Topp

<<<<<<<<<<<<<<<<<<<<◇>>>>>>>>>>>>>>>>>>>>

After skipping the debate in Des Moines, and taking second in the Iowa caucus behind Ted Cruz, Trump came into New Hampshire behind in the delegate race. With only twenty-three delegates at stake, New Hampshire may seem of limited mathematical significance, but because of the symbolic importance of New Hampshire, much was at stake. With an early spot in the presidential nominating calendar, a sound victory in New Hampshire can help a candidate "get a jolt that will help carry the campaign through the next primaries" (Cook, 2016, para. 6). Conversely, a poor performance in New Hampshire may pose the risk of dismantling the momentum of a front-runner: "a favorite that does poorly in New Hampshire may see his or her lead begin to crumble" (para. 6). With Trump leading in almost every New Hampshire poll taken in the eight months prior to the primary, Trump needed not just to win a plurality of the vote, but to maintain substantial distance between himself and other contenders in order to meet the expectations of the primary (Silver, 2016). Nate Silver, an election statistician, argued that if Trump finished with a "vote share in the mid-to-high 30s" it would "erase many of our doubts about Trump's ceiling and make him look formidable in South Caroline and beyond" (Silver, 2016, para. 9).

Despite performing very well in pre-primary polling, Trump left Iowa for New Hampshire with some uncertainty. Peter Grier (2016), writing for the *Christian Science Monitor* in the run-up to the primary, speculated that there were "warning signs" that "the Trump phenomenon may have peaked" and that Trump was "vulnerable to a rival or rivals who can consolidate on anti-Trump sentiment" (para. 5). Moreover, because the New Hampshire primary is notoriously dominated by late-deciders, the debate, which took place just days before the primary, was potentially transformative (Feldman, 2016). Understanding the importance of New Hampshire, and recognizing that his refusal to participate in the Iowa debate may have cost him the caucus, Trump tossed his hat into the Manchester, New Hampshire debate (Diamond, 2016).

Eighth in the GOP series, the February 6, ABC News debate was the first without an undercard in the 2016 debate series. To qualify, contestants had to have placed among the top three in the Iowa GOP caucuses earlier in the week or be ranked in the top six of New Hampshire or national GOP polls recognized by ABC News. Two candidates, Carly Fiorina and former Virginia Governor Jim Gilmore, failed to make the cut, while seven candidates polled strongly enough to qualify.

With 13.2 million viewers, the debate was among the highest-rated GOP debates of 2016 (Stelter, 2016). Moderated by ABC *World News Tonight* anchor David Muir and ABC Chief Global Affairs Correspondent Martha Raddatz, the debate began with what some called "an embarrassing flub" (Stelter, para. 6) and others deemed a "train wreck" (Gold, 2016, para. 1), when several candidates did not hear their names announced and stood awkwardly backstage, but still on camera.

Once introductions were corrected, Trump, the front-runner, was situated at center stage, flanked on his right by Marco Rubio, Jeb Bush and John Kasich and Ted Cruz, Ben Carson and Chris Christie on his left. During the course of the two-hour debate, moderators' questions covered a variety of topics, including Trump's temperament, Cruz's deceitful robocalls, eminent domain,

North Korea, immigration, health care, conservatism, taxes, terrorism, Libya, torture, policing, candidate electability, and abortion. Like other debates each question was directed toward a particular candidate, who was given 60 seconds to answer. If he invoked another candidate's name, that individual was given 30 seconds to respond. The debate concluded with all candidates giving a closing statement. By the time closing statements ended, pundits were already weighing in on the night's winners and losers.

Determining the winner or loser of any single primary debate is a difficult task; however, quantitative and qualitative metrics provide some insight into the public's perception of Trump's performance. Three reputable polling sources questioned potential voters before and after the debate, each showing gains for Trump over that period of time. *Morning Consult* had Trump with 38% of the vote just following the Iowa caucus, and found Trump with 44% of the vote in a poll taken just four days after the debate (Wilson, 2016, table 1). *Ipsos/Reuters* (2016) found similar gains for Trump in polls taken over the same interval (Ipsos Public Affairs, p. 7, 9); and, *Quinnipiac* (2016) found an eight percent gain for Trump between February 4th and 10th. These polls suggest that Trump's position improved because of his performance in the debate.

More supporting evidence can be found in the Google Consumer Surveys poll conducted midway through the debate, which found that a plurality of respondents believed Trump was winning the debate (Silver, 2016). Through *Google Consumer Surveys*, researchers create multi-question surveys, but each respondent is only asked a small sample of those questions. The survey then infers demographic data based on embedded content like the IP address or the DoubleClick cookie (McDonald, Mohebbi & Slatkin, 2012). Although this method is unique, it is empirically a valid tool for predicting election outcomes and has been tested across multiple disciplines (Silver, 2012; Callegaro et al., 2014).

Despite these quantitative signals of success, not everyone was impressed with Trump's performance. David Graham (2016), a political analyst at *The Atlantic*, claimed that Trump "stumbled," "hit rough patches," and was largely a "non-factor" (para. 1, 2, 11). John Fund (2016), a Fox News analyst, argued that the debate exposed Trump as a "bully boy" and that this realization should force him to rethink his debate approach as "many people [see him] as a bully and not just an effective deal maker" (para. 10). To these analysts, Trump's aggressive tone and temperament were clouding his message and turning voters against him.

As is clear from this diverse commentary, Trump had some wins and some losses in the debate. He partially won because the debate helped propel him to a large victory in New Hampshire. He met expectations, and carried solid momentum into the following races. Significant real-time and delayed polling data support the claim that the debate as a whole improved his likelihood of victory. Additionally, he dodged potential landmines by keeping his answers short and largely staying below the radar of the personal attacks levied by the other candidates. However, he suffered losses as well. The debate may also have solidified the negative perception of Trump as a bully, and as lacking presidential temperament.

This debate provides clues into why Trump is a successful debater, and illuminates some possible weaknesses that can be exploited by a savvy opponent. In what follows, we outline the primary takeaways from the Manchester debate for which close observers of the presidential debates will want to watch.

Trump Bends Reality to His Advantage

In Manchester, Trump tended to argue with little regard for reality. Although it is impossible to tell whether Trump was lying, or misspeaking, or possibly mistaking himself, his repeated disregard for the truth is worth documenting. In one appeal to presidential temperament, Trump stated his lone reluctance to enter Iraq: "I'm the only one up here…that said…'Don't go, don't do it, you're going to destabilize the Middle East.'" This argument was repeated throughout the primaries as a way to undermine the argument that Trump, as president, would have an itchy trigger finger. His statement implies that Trump forewarned against the invasion from the get-go. However, the evidence for this is non-existent. His only two public statements regarding the war in Iraq, prior to the invasion, were about the stock market–one saying that the fighting would hurt the market, the other stating the exact opposite (Kessler & Lee, 2016). Trump's opposition to the war became public around August of 2004, over one year after the invasion began and there is "no evidence of Trump opposing the Iraq war prior to it beginning" (Legum, 2016, para. 3). Because of Clinton's vote in support of the authorization of use of force in Iraq, we can expect this issue to re-emerge in the presidential debates.

A second lie can be found in the heated exchange between Jeb Bush and Trump regarding eminent domain. In this exchange, Bush attacked Trump for using eminent domain for private purposes:

> BUSH: …what Donald Trump did was use eminent domain to try to take the property of an elderly woman on the strip in Atlantic City. That is not public purpose, that is down right wrong."
>
> (APPLAUSE)
>
> And here's the problem with that. The problem was, it was to tear down–it was to tear down–it was to tear down the house . . .
>
> The moderators gave Trump 30 seconds to respond:
>
> TRUMP: Let me talk. Quiet. A lot of times…
>
> (BOOING)
>
> …that's all of his [Bush's] donors and special interests out there.
>
> (BOOING)

So–it's what it is. That's what–and by the way, let me just tell you, we needed tickets. You can't get them. You know who has the tickets for the–I'm talking about, to the television audience? Donors, special interests, the people that are putting up the money.

(BOOING)

That's who it is. The RNC told us. We have all donors in the audience. And the reason they're not loving me . . .

(BOOING)

. . . the reason they're not- excuse me. The reason they're not loving me is, I don't want their money. I'm going to do the right thing for the American public. I don't want their money. I don't need their money. And I'm the only one up here that can say that.

Unfortunately for Trump, and for an audience that may have liked to hear a more coherent response on eminent domain, his criticism of the RNC ticket sales is unfounded. The RNC gave equal allotment of tickets to each candidate.

The largest single bloc in attendance was two hundred students from the host college, St. Anselm, in Manchester. Only seventy-five RNC donors were in attendance, which was less than ten percent of the crowd (Kiely et al, 2016).

A third falsehood can be found in the economic discussion midway through the debate. As Trump often does, he touted the benefits of his tax plan, arguing that he will bring jobs back on shore by cutting taxes. In this appeal, he falsely claimed, "We're [USA is] the highest taxed country in the world." Based on every potential metric of evaluating tax rates, this claim is false. The top income tax rate in the United States is in the lowest third according to multiple economic and tax advisory surveys; taxes account for a relatively small amount of US GDP; and, taxes per capita are in the middle of the pack (Fiske and Jacobson, 2015). The most comprehensive measurements of US tax rates "show the U.S. either is in the middle of the pack or on the lighter end of taxation compared with other advanced industrialized nations" (Fiske and Jacobson, 2015, para. 21).

There are other statements, like Trump's claim that China has "absolute control" of North Korea, that make clear Trump is willing to play fast and loose with the facts.

This has been documented throughout this campaign. A *Politifact* (2015) article found that seventy-six percent of his rated statements were mostly false, false or "pants on fire" (a euphemism to describe a statement so far from fact it can only be assumed to be a lie) (Holan & Qiu). This approach will undoubtedly influence the presidential debates.

Thus far, Trump's lies have had little consequence. Every lie is documented, fact-checked and then publicized. The media ostracizes him, calls him un-presidential and spends quite a bit of time and attention picking through the falsehoods that permeate Trump's discourse. However, even as this media barrage has picked up, Republicans have *twice* as much confidence in Trump's honesty as Democrats do in Clinton's honesty, according to a May 2016 *Rasmussen* poll of 1,000 likely voters. There are several explanations for this phenomenon. Republican voters are less likely to frequent liberal websites, which most heavily document Trump's lies. Moreover, Trump appeals to an anti-establishment voter base that may view all politicians as liars, so the truth-tests of Trump only confirm a suspicion they have of all politicians. It's also quite likely that Trump's attack on the media as deceitful plants a kernel of doubt among potential voters that it may be just as likely that the media is lying about him lying. For a potential voter already inclined to support Trump, it only takes a hint of suspicion to trigger their anti-media biases.

However, Trump's lies may catch up to him against a well-prepared debate opponent. Clinton, knowing Trump's likelihood to disregard reality, will surely show up with clear documentation of Trump's previous stances and commitments. She may quote him verbatim, or rely on the moderators to remind Trump when he is contradicting previous statements or straying too far from reality. Because the presidential debates will be between two contestants, there will be more depth to responses and greater opportunities for back-and-forth. This may play to Clinton's advantage as she will be able to call Trump out directly for his lies, and he will be forced to explain himself on that particular subject. Too often in primary debates, each speaker gets a limited time to speak on each subject, so it is much more difficult to dig deeply to uncover a lie. One final advantage for Clinton is that much of the audience will be uncertain voters or independents, who may be more likely to be turned off by dishonesty than a devout Republican seeking evidence confirming their existing pro-conservative biases.

Trump Evades Detail and Has Predictable Platitudes

It is not uncommon for candidates to dodge answering questions that require commitment to specific policies, but Trump has developed an approach almost entirely vacant of meaningful policy discussion, preferring instead a smattering of trite clichés. Criticized throughout the primaries for this rhetorical move, Trump did little in this debate to prove his critics wrong.

One recurrent platitude to which Trump returned is tied to his campaign slogan of making America great again. For example, as Ted Cruz was answering a question about comments he made attacking Trump's temperament, Trump interrupted, saying:

> TRUMP: First of all, I respect what Ted just said, but if you noticed, he didn't answer your question. And that's what's going to happen–OK.
>
> (APPLAUSE)
>
> That's what's going to happen with our enemies and the people we compete against. We're going to win with Trump. We're going to win. We don't win anymore. Our

country doesn't win anymore. We're going
to win with Trump. And people back down
with Trump. And that's what I like and
that's what the country is going to like.

Although heavy on appeals to patriotism and ego, his
reliance on this platitude is light on policy. Trump fails to
clarify how he will fulfill his campaign promise, skipping
any mention of what policies would help America become
great again.

Of course, to make America great again implies it is no
longer so. Trump also relied on tropes of America's fall
from grace under Obama's leadership. In response to a
question about whether he would implement a redline on
North Korea, Trump started by saying, "Marco said earlier
… President Obama knows exactly what he's doing, like
we have this president that really knows. I disagree . . . I
think we have a president who … is totally incompetent,
and he doesn't know what he's doing. (APPLAUSE) …
And our country is going to hell … "

Importantly, Trump didn't mention North Korea until
pressed again by Martha Raddatz, the moderator, at which
point, he said:

TRUMP: We have–tremendous–has been just sucked out of our country by China. China says they don't have that good of control over North Korea. They have tremendous control. I deal with the Chinese all of the time. I do tremendous–the largest bank in the world is in one of my buildings in Manhattan.

I deal with them. They tell me. They have total, absolute control, practically, of North Korea. They are sucking trillions of dollars out of our country–they're rebuilding China with the money they take out of our country. I would get on with China, let China solve that problem.

(BELL RINGS)

They can do it quickly and surgically. That's what we should do with North Korea.

Nearly incoherent, and lacking specifics of how he would pressure China and what he would propose China should do to influence North Korea, he claims his encounters with Chinese bank tenants has prepared him to deal with one of the largest issues facing America.

Notably, Trump's policy on North Korean proliferation rests on a third platitude as well: his business acumen. Seeking to position himself as a non-establishment candidate, Trump has worked on honing his image as successful businessman capable of breaking gridlock and passing policies in Washington. As a businessman, he claims he can make things happen in Washington. Why? Because he is a good deal maker:

> TRUMP: [A] good deal maker will make great deals, but we'll do it the way our founders thought it should be done. People get together, they make deals. Ronald Reagan did it with Tip O'Neil very successfully, you didn't hear so much about executive orders, if you heard about it at all. You have to be able to get a consensus.
>
> Now, the real person like it was mentioned about the deal with Iran, how bad a deal is that? It doesn't get any more amateurish than that. A good deal maker would never make a deal like that. With Congress, you

have to get everybody in a room, and you have to get them to agree. But, you have to get them to agree what you want, and that's part of being a deal maker. You can't leave the White House, go to Hawaii and play golf for three weeks and be a real deal maker. It doesn't work that way. You have to get people in, grab them, hug them, kiss them, and get the deal done. But, it's got to be the deal that you want.

Introducing Conservative touchstones and again relying on patriotic appeals, Trump bypasses specific mention of how a consensus could be built or why he would be more successful than any existing politician.

Trump has also sought to position himself as the jobs president. Bringing jobs back to the U.S. by ending corporate inversion has become a subset of his business-experience platitude. When asked *how* he would fulfill his jobs promise, Trump responded, "I will bring jobs back from China. I will bring jobs back from Japan. I will bring jobs back from Mexico…" The most specific he ever gets is to say, "We're not going to lose ["great companies"] anymore because we're going to have a tax structure that is going to keep them in our country." What that tax structure looks like and how he will get it done are open questions.

The same detail vacuum holds true when he discusses his "policy" for health care. Making clear he will repeal Obamacare, he left listeners guessing what he supports:

> TRUMP: We are going to replace Obamacare with something so much better. And there are so many examples of it.... We're going to take out the artificial boundaries, the artificial lines. We're going to get a plan where people compete, free enterprise. They compete. So much better.... In addition to that, you have the health care savings plans, which are excellent.
>
> What I do say is, there will be a certain number of people that will be on the street dying and as a Republican, I don't want that to happen. We're going to take care of people that are dying on the street because there will be a group of people that are not going to be able to even think in terms of private or anything else and we're going to take care of those people.

And I think everybody on this stage would have to agree . . .(BELL RINGS) . . .you're not going to let people die, sitting in the middle of a street in any city in this country.

Rather than identifying a specific policy, Trump positioned himself in support of something better than the Affordable Care Act (aka Obamacare) and against people dying in the streets. This position, while politically safe and noncontroversial to a GOP audience, is wholly bereft of specifics.

In the primaries, reliance on pathos-driven platitudes without policy detail has served Trump well. Emotive appeals have allowed him to bring in a base of Republican voters who felt disenfranchised by the establishment, while still capturing enough of the GOP mainstream to secure the nomination.

It is possible, however, that Clinton will be able to take advantage of the policy void during the general election debates. Known as a policy wonk, Clinton's detailed policy discussions could act as a foil to Trump's incoherent answers. Similarly, she can use her background as Secretary of State, Senator and even First Lady as a trump card, contrasting her extensive experience with his rawness.

That said, Clinton should be wary of becoming too reliant on policy detail. Precisely because Trump's appeal tends to be driven by "emotional contagion" (Koerth-Baker, 2016, para. 5), it would be a mistake for Clinton to cede pathos-driven appeals to Trump. If Clinton gets too deep in the policy weeds she may fail to attract important voter segments who may be motivated more by fear, insecurity, or patriotism than in-the-weeds policy discussions. Finding a way to wed pathos with policy will be key.

Trump is Willing to Alienate the Immediate Audience

In most debate settings, the immediate audience matters. High school and college debaters try to convince a judge to circle their name on the ballot, and congressional debates are an attempt to persuade the audience to support a particular stance on statutes, resolutions or amendments. However, this is less true in presidential debates. The immediate audience represents a small sliver of the overall voting population, so their opinion on the debate matters much less than the broader reception throughout the country. Trump recognizes this, and makes argumentative choices based on this understanding.

In Manchester, Trump had two direct, and negative, interactions with the immediate audience. The first involved Trump's response to audience laughter after he claimed he was going to replace Obamacare with "something so much better." As they laugh, he aggressively retorted, "And I will tell you, part of the reason we have some people laughing, because you have insurance people that take care of everybody up here."

In this exchange, Trump directly responded with an ad hominem attack on the audience, accusing them of being bought off by the insurance industry. Whether Trump was right or wrong is unclear. What is clear is that Trump felt no regard to coddle the immediate audience that didn't appreciate his response. Instead, Trump went on the attack, caring little about alienating the potential voters in the room.

The second exchange was described in the 'lying' section above, where Trump said the audience was "full of donors" in response to booing him over his exchange with Bush over eminent domain. In this attack, he was willing to lie about the immediate audience, knowing they were not all donors, because he knew there would be little ramification and the audience at home would not be able to discern reality from Trump's imagination.

Although this strategy of antagonizing the immediate audience may lose him an academic debate, or a debate on the Senate floor, it is a savvy argumentative approach for winning a primary or an election. In each debate, Trump has millions of viewers at home that know very little about the audience present at the debate. By labeling the immediate audience as "donors" or representatives from the insurance industry, Trump is able to evade negative consequences from booing or audience laughter. In a sense, the fact that the audience does not like Trump can even play to his advantage as an anti-establishment, self-funded, candidate. A member of the television audience may be even more willing to support Trump if the donors and D.C. big wigs are not lined up to support him.

In the presidential debates, Trump may name, or label, the audience in other ways that advantage him. He may describe them composed of Hillary-backed bankers, the liberal media or some other term that effectively connotes negativity to his followers. Whether he can use this to appeal to court undecideds or independents will be the key factor in determining whether this strategy will succeed.

The February 6 debate in Manchester may have contributed to Trump's victory in the New Hampshire primary three days later. Trump made a number of rhetorical choices that appealed to voters. It seems likely he will continue to rely on similar strategies into the general election cycle. As such, analyzing his tactics can help provide insight for how Hillary Clinton can most effectively counter him.

To defeat Trump, Clinton must firmly take Trump to task for his ethical and political vices: lying and evasion, trite platitudes, and his mislabeling of the immediate audience. Although these tactics can be intimidating and difficult to refute, Clinton and her strategists must prepare with these talking points in mind.

Regarding Trump's lies and inconsistencies, Clinton might consider finding direct quotes from Trump, and hammering out his inconsistencies until his flip-flops become obvious. Because he is willing to deny his own previous statements, or lie about the context in which they were stated, Clinton will not only need to develop her own position on issues, but also pin Trump down to his positions as well. In preparation to defeat Trump's vague and trite platitudes, Clinton should be willing to directly question Trump's answers, even if it provides Trump additional speaking time. For example, she may ask exactly how he plans to prevent unnecessary deaths on the street, while gutting government-subsidized health care. Thus far, Trump has gotten away with vague policy positions because his opponents have been too focused on maximizing their own speaking time, instead of letting Trump dig his own grave. Additionally, Clinton must have her policy positions forthright and detailed. Otherwise, she risks falling prey to the same criticism that she, and the moderators, will likely make of Trump. Finally, when Trump mislabels the immediate audience, Clinton must identify this as a smokescreen that he uses to build his credibility and write-off legitimate audience criticism.

In the end, Clinton can benefit from analysis of the New Hampshire debate to fortify her strategy as she prepares to show voters, especially the undecided, exactly what they will be getting in a President Trump. No doubt, she will be well-prepared.

References

Callegaro, M., Villar, A., Yeager, D., & Krosnick, J. A. (2014). A critical review of studies investigating the quality of data obtained with online panels based on probability and nonprobability samples. In M. Callegaro, R. Baker, J. D. Bethlehem, A. S. Göritz, J.

A. Krosnick, & P. J. Lavrakas (Eds.), Online panel research: A data quality perspective (pp. 23–54). New York, NY: Wiley.

Cook, L. (2016, February 2). Why New Hampshire matters in presidential elections. *U.S. News & World Report*. Retrieved from http://www.usnews.com/news/blogs/data-mine/2016/02/02/why-new-hampshire-matters-in-presidential-elections

Diamond, J. (2016, February 3). Trump says skipping debate might have cost him in Iowa. *CNN*. Retrieved from http://www.cnn.com/2016/02/02/politics/donald-trump-iowa-new-hampshire

Feldmann, L. (2016, February 9). New Hampshire primary: Why late deciders rule. *Christian Science Monitor*. Retrieved from http://www.csmonitor.com/USA/Politics/2016/0209/New-Hampshire-primary-why-late-deciders-rule

Fiske, W., & Jacobson, L. (2015, October 20). Trump says U.S. has 'highest tax rate anywhere in the world'. *Politifact*. Retrieved from http://www.politifact.com/virginia/statements/2015/oct/20/donald-trump/trump-says-us-has-highest-tax-rate-anywhere-world

Fund, J. (2016, February 7). Rubio stumbles, then stabilizes. Trump stays out front at GOP debate in New Hampshire. *Fox News*. Retrieved from http://www.foxnews.com/opinion/2016/02/07/rubio-stumbles-then-stabilizes-trump-stays-out-front-at-gop-debate-in-new-hampshire.html

Gold, H. (2016, February 6). GOP debate begins with introduction train wreck. *Politico*. Retrieved from http://www.politico.com/blogs/new-hampshire-primary-2016-live-updates/2016/02/gop-debate-abc-rocky-introduction-218870

Graham, D. (2016, February 6). A rough night for the frontrunners. *The Atlantic*. Retrieved from http://www.theatlantic.com/politics/archive/2016/02/the-republicans-reset-in-new-hampshire/460260

Grier, P. (2016, February 9). If Donald Trump wins New Hampshire, here's what happens next. *Christian Science Monitor*. Retrieved from http://www.csmonitor.com/USA/Politics/Decoder/2016/0209/If-Donald-Trump-wins-New-Hampshire-here-s-what-happens-next

Holan, A., & Qiu, L. (2015, December 21). 2015 Lie of the Year: the campaign misstatements of Donald Trump. *Politifact*. Retrieved from http://www.politifact.com/truth-o-meter/article/2015/dec/21/2015-lie-year-donald-trump-campaign-misstatements

Ipsos Public Affairs (2016). Reuters tracking. *Huffington Post*. Retrieved from http://big.assets.huffingtonpost.com/2016ReutersTracking.pdf

Kessler, G., & Lee, M. (2016, February 7). Fact checking the 8th GOP presidential debate. *New Haven Register*. Retrieved from http://www.nhregister.com/government-and-politics/20160207/fact-checking-the-8th-gop-presidential-debate

Kiely, E., Jackson, B., Robertson, L., Farley, R., & Gore, D. (2016, February 7). Fact check: the eighth Republican debate. *USA Today*. Retrieved from http://www.usatoday.com/story/news/politics/elections

/2016/02/07/fact-check-eighth-republican-debate/79950654

Koerth-Baker, M. (2016, March 15). Donald Trump incites crowds – and his crowds incite him. *FiveThirtyEight*. Retrieved from http://fivethirtyeight.com/features/donald-trump-incites-his-crowds-and-his-crowds-incite-him

Legum, J. (2016, June 2). Did CNN finally call out Donald Trump for lying? (They did.). *Think Progress*. Retrieved from http://thinkprogress.org/politics/2016/06/02/3784234/screenshot-provides-glimmer-hope-media-coverage-donald-trump

McDonald, P., Mohebbi, M., & Slatkin, B. (2012). Comparing Google consumer surveys to existing probability and non-probability based Internet surveys. *Google Insights*. Retrieved from http://www.google.com/insights/consumersurveys/static/consumer_surveys_whitepaper.pdf

New York Times (2016, February 6). Transcript of Republican presidential debate. *New York Times*. Retrieved from http://www.nytimes.com/2016/02/07/us/politics/transcript-of-the-republican-presidential-debate-in-new-hampshire.html

Quinnipiac (2016, February 17). Trump surges to 2-1 lead among Republicans nationwide, Quinnipiac University national poll finds. Retrieved from https://www.qu.edu/news-and-events/quinnipiac-university-poll/national/release-detail?ReleaseID=2323

Rasmussen Reports (2016, June 1). How do voters weigh Clinton's honesty vs. Trump's? Retrieved from http://www.rasmussenreports.com/public_content/polit

ics/elections/election_2016/how_do_voters_weigh_cli
nton_s_honesty_vs_trump_s

Silver, N. (2011, November 6). Which polls fared best (and worst) in the 2012 presidential race. *FiveThirtyEight*. Retrieved from http://fivethirtyeight.blogs.nytimes.com//2012/11/10/which-polls-fared-best-and-worst-in-the-2012-presidential-race

Silver, N. (2016, February 7). We thought Marco Rubio lost the debate, but New Hampshire might think differently. *FiveThirtyEight*. Retrieved from http://fivethirtyeight.com/features/we-thought-marco-rubio-lost-the-debate-but-new-hampshire-might-think-differently

Silver, N. (2016, February 9). What's at stake in the New Hampshire republican primary? *FiveThirtyEight*. Retrieved from http://fivethirtyeight.com/features/whats-at-stake-in-new-hampshires-republican-primary

Stelter, B. (2016, March 4). Fox's Republican debate is highest rated of 2016. *CNN Money.* Retrieved from http://money.cnn.com/2016/03/04/media/fox-news-gop-debate-ratings

Wilson, R. (2016, February 12). Poll: Wins push Trump, Sanders to new heights. *Morning Consult*. Retrieved from https://morningconsult.com/2016/02/12/donald-trump-bernie-sanders-national-polling

CHAPTER NINE

<<<<<<<<<<<<<<<<<<<O>>>>>>>>>>>>>>>>>>

GOP Primary Debate #9
Greenville, South Carolina, February 13, 2016
Dr. William Mosley-Jensen

<<<<<<<<<<<<<<<<<<<O>>>>>>>>>>>>>>>>>>

On February 13, 2016 the ninth Republican presidential primary debate took place in Greenville, South Carolina. The debate featured six candidates, Jeb Bush, Ben Carson, Ted Cruz, John Kasich, Marco Rubio, and Donald Trump. The debate was moderated by CBS News "Face the Nation" host John Dickerson. He was joined by two panelists, Major Garrett, the Chief White House Correspondent for CBS News, and Kimberley Strassel, member of the editorial board of the Wall Street Journal. The format of the debate was a classic question and answer format, with a candidate allotted one minute to respond to a direct question, 30 seconds for a follow-up and 30 seconds to rebut an attack by one of their five opponents.

This debate stands out for three reasons. First, it represented Jeb Bush's last-ditch effort to stay in the campaign race. His pivotal moments in the debate came as he defended his brother's record on terrorism, and shifting the blame to Bill Clinton. Second, a major theme of the evening was "lying," namely who has been doing the most of it, and how important a consideration that should be. Third and finally, there is widespread GOP consensus to continue an obstructionist stance on nominating a successor to Justice Antonin Scalia. This debate demonstrates that there are issues around which Donald Trump must be careful (criticizing George W. Bush's handling of terrorism), issues that arouse Republican unity (SCOTUS nominations), and common talking points he turns to when attacked (calling his opponent a "liar").

This debate also foreshadows some themes that might resurface in the general election. While looking forward to Trump's debates against Hillary Clinton may seem like prognostication, there are some predictions that are likely to hold. First, Trump is likely to stick to general statements, rather than engaging in the specifics of policy proposals. This is in contrast to Clinton, who prefers to grapple with the particulars, often invoking statistics and studies in her discussions, prompting some to refer to her as a policy "wonk." Second, Trump focuses on his business acumen and deal-making skills. When pressed on *how* he intends to govern, he presents himself as the consummate businessman, persuading his opponents and rallying allies.

Third, Trump doesn't mind playing dirty and attacking an individual's personal life and decisions. Clinton's long history of public service and highly scrutinized private life provides Trump with lots of ammunition in this arena. Fourth, Trump has an aggressive debating style. He frequently interrupts his opponents, and shows little respect for their answers or credibility. Whether he moderates his approach when debating Clinton remains to be seen, but it seems unlikely he will treat her any differently than he did his Republican challengers during the primary process.

Main Themes

The main themes of the ninth Republican Primary debate on February 13, 2016 were multiple and diverse. They included: the death of Antonin Scalia and Supreme Court appointees, foreign policy threats, government spending, immigration, and the importance of political consistency. Each of these issues saw specific questions directed towards specific candidates, with follow-up questions and a lengthy discussion of the issues between the candidates. With the field narrowed to a competitive six candidates, each individual was trying to distinguish themselves from the others, making for a lively and engaging hour and a half. Donald Trump dictated much of the tone for the evening, with opening questions directed at him on all five of the issues.

Supreme Court Justice Antonin Scalia died the morning of the debate from natural causes (Martin & Contreras, 2016). As a longstanding justice in good health, the 79 year-old's passing was sudden and unexpected. Even before Scalia's death the 2016 presidential election was ripe for controversy over Court appointees, with some commentators suggesting that the next president would appoint up to four justices, including a replacement for Scalia (Shabad, 2016). Liberal justices Ruth Bader Ginsburg and Stephen Breyer, as well as the moderate Anthony Kennedy will all be aging significantly as the next president assumes office, at 83, 78 and 80 years of age respectively. The oldest justice to have served was Oliver Wendell Holmes, Jr., serving between 1902 and 1932 and retiring at the age of 90 (Shabad, 2016).

The suddenness of Scalia's passing the morning of the debate thrust the issue into this Republican primary debate. Moderator John Dickerson led a moment of silence for Scalia before the debate began, and started his line of questioning by asking Trump whether he would nominate a justice with 11 months left in his term. Trump indicated that he would try, but that the Republican Senate had a duty to block any nominee that President Barack Obama might put forth (Peters & Woolley, 2016). Consensus emerged early on this issue with Kasich, Carson, and Rubio all calling for the President to forgo nominating a replacement for Scalia. Bush and Cruz both underscored the importance of the election for preventing the Court from moving further to the left, with Cruz in particular emphasizing that point (Peters & Woolley, 2016).

The debate then moved to national security, which featured a clash between Jeb Bush and Trump on the issue of Syria and over former President George W. Bush's handling of the War on Terrorism. This segment was prefaced by Dickerson with a call for specifics in the foreign policy realm. He began by directing a query first at Donald Trump, asking what three questions he would have for his national security advisors, were he to be elected president. Trump responded: "[w]hat we want to do, when we want to do it, and how hard do we want to hit?" (Trump, 2016), before going on to discuss the threat that the Islamic State poses and then suggesting that it was a mistake to attack Iraq in 2003. Dickerson then asked Carson and Rubio why they were qualified to make decisions in a crisis, before focusing on the issue of Syria and Russia's backing of Assad. In responding to Dickerson,

Jeb decried Trump's proposed plan of working with Russia, indicating that Putin's policy in Syria exacerbates tensions and increases terrorist threats, making them an inappropriate partner in the region (Peters & Woolley, 2016). Trump responded by arguing for a renewed focus on ISIS, and vaguely argued that two wars were too expensive, going slightly overtime in his response. Bush was then offered time for a response, but Trump repeatedly interrupted his attempts to convey an argument, even overriding the moderator Dickerson's attempts to control the debate (Peters & Woolley, 2016).

Trump's spat with Jeb escalated over the issue of Iraq. Moderator Dickerson asked Trump about a 2008 interview where he said that George W. Bush should be impeached over getting the U.S. involved in Iraq, and inquired whether Trump still holds that belief. Trump prevaricated in his response, obliquely referring to Jeb Bush's announcement and his defense of his brother George, and then ultimately indicated that the war in Iraq was a big mistake, in part because no weapons of mass destruction were found (Peters & Woolley, 2016). Former Governor Bush responded by defending his family's record in politics, including his father and brother, arguing that George W. Bush established a security apparatus after 9/11 that kept the country safe. Trump interrupted Jeb five times during this one-minute response, including during his defense of his mother, Barbara Bush (CBSN, 2016). Kasich and Rubio were brought into the discussion, with the former defending Collin Powell's arguments for Iraq's possession of weapons of mass destruction and the latter defending the war as promoting democracy and American values. Trump interrupted Rubio twice, and during the exchange Jeb jumped in to rescind an invitation for Trump to attend a rally in Charleston featuring former President George W. Bush (Peters & Woolley, 2016).

Following the discussion of Iraq, the issue of government spending was brought forward with questions from Kimberley Strassel. Strassel addressed Trump first, asking about his plan to leave entitlements untouched and noting that economic growth would need to be between 7.7 and 9 percent to achieve his proposals. She challenged him to provide specifics about how he would accomplish what he promised. Trump responded by arguing that he would "save Social Security" by eliminating fraud and abuse (Trump, 2016) and bring back $2.5 trillion in capital that has been offshored by corporations and individuals. Then, Cruz discussed his flat tax proposal and Rubio defended his high rate on top earners (35 percent) as a way to boost the

Child Tax Credit. Kasich defended his expansion of Medicare from Jeb Bush's attacks, specifically the charge that it was an expansion of government. He pointed out that Ronald Reagan expanded Medicare five times (Peters & Woolley, 2016).

Immigration took center stage after the discussion of government spending, with moderator Dickerson asking Trump what policy he would propose to provide a "humane solution" to the immigration crisis in the United States (Peters & Woolley, 2016). Trump reiterated his policy of creating a stronger border, noting that he would build a wall and that "the wall will be paid for by Mexico" (Trump, 2016). Rubio and Cruz noted the importance of being clear on the issue, with each accusing the other of being more friendly towards undocumented immigrants in the past and both promising to undo President Barack Obama's executive orders allowing deferred action on deportation proceedings for qualified applicants. Jeb Bush defended his position that "compassion" is important in making immigration decisions, and attacked Trump's previous rhetoric on the issue which incorrectly asserted that most undocumented migrants where "rapists" (Peters & Woolley, 2016). Trump responded by supporting Rubio and Cruz's strength on the issue and leveled a sweeping indictment of Jeb's general "weakness" on immigration (Trump, 2016).

The last main theme of the night was the issue of the candidates' governing style and the importance of remaining steadfast. After wrapping up the immigration debate, Major Garrett asked Trump about a promise to impose up to a 35% tax or tariff on companies that attempt to offshore jobs from the U.S. Garrett specifically wondered how Trump viewed the power of the presidency such that something like that was even possible (Peters & Woolley, 2016). Trump responded by suggesting that he would be a "deal-maker" and "build consensus" with Congress to undo various trade pacts, etc. that he views as "no good for us and no good for our workers" (Trump, 2016). Dickerson then asked Trump to explain how he has changed his opinions over time, and why that flexibility should be considered an attribute, rather than a character flaw (Peters & Woolley, 2016). Trump replied that he was similar to Ronald Reagan, in that he had evolved over time on many issues and that age and wisdom had made him more conservative (Trump, 2016). In response, Cruz attacked Trump as a supporter of Planned Parenthood, a charge that caused Trump to refer to Cruz as "worse than Jeb Bush" and the "single biggest liar" (Trump, 2016).

Trump's Strategy

Trump had an overriding strategy going into the debate–put the nail in the coffin for Jeb Bush's nomination hopes, and in doing so demonstrate his strength and leadership in the GOP nomination race. His method of approach was to be a persistent thorn in Jeb's side, and also to undermine the Bush name generally. This created distance between Trump and the more traditional Republicans running in the race, emphasizing that he represented a "break" from the standard politician and the standard campaign. This strategy thus had a short and long-term goal for Trump, politically slay a once powerful rival for the nomination and signal to the audience that the GOP standard-bearers were part of the political past, whereas he represented the future of the party and presidential politics.

The debate occurred one week before the South Carolina primary, which was a crucial moment for former Governor Jeb Bush's campaign. The primary was to be Bush's last stand after finishing sixth in the Iowa caucus and fourth in New Hampshire, all after entering the campaign as the clear front-runner and raising over $100 million in the first six months of 2015 (Cillizza, 2016). Greenville, SC was a strategic location given its status as the county seat for Greenville County, the largest (by population) in South Carolina, and also one of the wealthiest metropolitan areas in the state (GADC, 2016). The debate and the primary were not fated to go Jeb's way, as he suspended his campaign after finishing fourth in the voting there (Lee & Killough, 2016).

Trump took advantage of the "make or break" character of the debate for Jeb Bush by ratcheting up the pressure on him, hoping to reveal the weakness he saw in Bush to a wider audience. Debates provide a key source of information for voters on the candidates' capacity to lead, as they provide a relational interaction, with the candidates confronting each other directly. This confrontation can bring out the best or worst in a candidate, and demonstrates key information about their core personality, potentially swaying voters to support or oppose them (Dailey, Hinck, & Hinck, 2008). Trump attacked Bush on two fronts, one substantively, and one stylistically. Trump sought to take down the Bush name by focusing on what he viewed as an error in judgment from former President George W. Bush in the attack on Iraq, and argued that Bush lied about the presence of weapons of mass destruction (Trump, 2016). Trump employed an aggressive style in the ensuing exchange, interrupting Jeb multiple times, repeating this practice from an earlier exchange on Trump's proposed overtures towards Putin (CBSN, 2016).

Trump's aggressive style was present throughout much of the debate, and Bush was not the only target of Trump's denigrating approach. During a back-and-forth with Ted Cruz on whether or not Trump supported planned parenthood, Trump referred to Cruz as "a nasty guy" (Trump, 2016). While a typical presidential debate is about crafting a vision of the candidate as a reasonable individual who appears engaged, learned, and quick on their feet (Dailey et al., 2008), Trump violates those expectations with regularity. Although there can be liabilities associated with appearing too aggressive, as that can demonstrate that an individual is unhinged, or de-motivate supporters, a demonstration of controlled assertiveness can increase the perception that someone has good leadership qualities (Pelletier, 2010).

Trump has two go-to approaches when defending himself from attack, the first is to call his opponent a liar, and the second is to make comparisons between himself and hallowed Republican icons, such as Ronald Reagan. In the exchange with Ted Cruz over Planned Parenthood, Trump accused Cruz of lying about his statements, and does so again when discussing whether or not he went bankrupt (Peters & Woolley, 2016). Cruz remarked on this tendency of Trump's noting that "Donald has this weird pattern, when you point to his own record, he screams, 'Liar, liar, liar'" (Cruz, 2016). Despite Cruz's statement about Trump, the branding of an opponent as a liar has the potential to undermine their credibility, and in turn effect the audience perception of that individual. Personal attacks (or *ad hominem*) can be very effective, despite being a logical fallacy. In particular, when the attack is connected with a broader rhetorical or argumentative strategy, then they can contribute to an overall assessment of a candidate's strength or weakness (Macagno, 2013). In this case, it is easy to see that Trump is connecting his overall indictment of politicians as untrustworthy because they are "bought and paid for" to the specifics of Cruz's attack.

Each candidate (except Ben Carson) made reference to former President Ronald Reagan in some way during the debate. Cruz alluded to the famous "A Time for Choosing" address, Bush referred to him as one of his "heroes," Kasich likened his Medicaid expansion to Reagan's similar policy and Rubio provided a long soliloquy on Regan's governing success (Peters & Woolley, 2016). Trump engaged in the "race to Reagan" strategy with no small degree of skill, fielding a specific question about his statements that he has made a similar political journey to that of the Great Communicator. Trump explained that like Reagan he began his political life as a liberal, but has through experience become more conservative. This echoes the message of the "A Time for Choosing" address that Cruz also alluded to. Reagan has become the contemporary conservative icon, replacing figures such as Abraham Lincoln and Teddy Roosevelt because his rhetoric and policy advocacy more closely aligns with the current Republican discourse (Longley, Mayer, Schaller, & Sloan, 2015). If Trump can successfully paint himself as an outsider who gradually embraced the conservative vision for America, then he perhaps he can tap into the mythos surrounding the 40th President of the United States.

Media Commentary

The media commentary of the debate focused on the acrimony of the exchanges between Trump and Bush, the immigration discussion between Rubio and Cruz, and the conservatism of Trump. There was no consensus of who won the debate, or who might have improved their position, but there were common themes reported. A number of media outlets reported on the tone of the evening highlighting the division and infighting as the overall vibe of the debate (Costa & Rucker, 2016; Healy, 2016; Woolf,

Jacobs, & Smith, 2016). The only candidates that were deemed to be above the fray were Ben Carson and John Kasich, who both attacked the vitriol of the debate as unproductive and potentially damaging to the GOP (Costa & Rucker, 2016). As the last debate to feature Jeb Bush and Ben Carson, it was a memorable and lively exchange, or as a live commentary of the debate referred to it: "a mess... a glorious, totally engrossing, chaotic mess" (Woolf et al., 2016).

The showdown between Trump and Bush was a key feature of media reaction to the debate. Several outlets noted that it was important for Bush to do well in the South Carolina primary to resuscitate his campaign, and that Trump could gather momentum with a win there (Costa & Rucker, 2016; Healy, 2016). The antagonism in the debate began when Bush strongly criticized Trump's proposal to work with Putin on resolving the Syrian crisis. Bush called Trump's idea "absolutely ludicrous" (Peters & Woolley, 2016). The differences were more than simply over matters of policy, however, as Trump decided to attack the Bush legacy, a move that some analysts felt could work against Trump's chances in South Carolina (Healy, 2016). Others noted that many voters even within the GOP are war weary and the message might resonate with them (Costa &

Rucker, 2016). The Trump-Bush exchanges also highlight the differences between the establishment candidates and the outsider candidates, as George W. Bush remains popular with mainstream GOP positions.

Immigration was noted as an important point of discussion, but one that failed to garner positive attention for the GOP. Cruz and Rubio's exchange was a highlight of the media coverage. News outlets noted that Rubio went out of his way to attack Cruz as being weaker on immigration than he is (perhaps as a strategy to demonstrate his own strength) (Healy, 2016). Additionally, the backhanded remark by Rubio questioning Cruz's capacity to speak Spanish was widely reported (Costa & Rucker, 2016; Healy, 2016). No commentator reported that the party made progress on the issue and one analyst with The Guardian bluntly called the immigration questions the "'let's alienate all non-white' voters portion of the debate" (Woolf et al., 2016).

The uncertain nature of Trump's conservatism was another point of agreement amongst commentators. Some media outlets noted that the debate could call into question Trump's conservative beliefs, as he disagreed with Jeb on George W. Bush's legacy, including specifically charging the Bush administration with fabricating evidence of weapons of mass destruction (Balz, 2016; McCormick, 2016). Todd Harris, one of Rubio's advisors, was quoted after the debate as saying that Trump was "at war with the Republican Party" and experienced pollster GOP advisor Frank Luntz thought the Republican Party likely lost votes after the heated and personal exchange (Costa & Rucker, 2016). Trump's lead in South Carolina polls in the run-up to the debate made him a target for the other candidates, and they sought to score points on any issue they could land a hit (Mehta, Bierman, & Halper, 2016). As some noted, Trump also went out of his way to distinguish himself from traditional Republicans, including on issues of such as eminent domain and criticizing Chief Justice John Roberts (Balz, 2016).

Looking Forward

Although making predictions about the character of the general election is always fraught with danger, there are a few lessons that this debate provides for assessing future debates involving Donald Trump. First, he prefers to stick to general statements. Second, he highlights his businesses successes and negotiating skills. Third, he isn't afraid of ad hominem attacks or attacks against an individual's family connections. Fourth and finally, he has an aggressive and intentionally disruptive style at times, interrupting his opponent frequently. While these things may not be a feature of every debate that Trump has with the former Senator and Secretary of State Hillary Clinton, they are likely enough possibilities.

Trump prefers to speak in generalities and with vague statements about how he will accomplish certain things. For example, when discussing government spending, Kimberly Strassel pressed him for details about how he would save money and he was unable to provide any specifics (Peters & Woolley, 2016). In the exchange with Jeb Bush over Syria, Trump preferred to remain vague about how he would work with Putin on resolving the crisis, rather than dig into specifics. He appeals to general sentiments well, as in his closing speech he repeated the oft-heard line that "[w]e don't win anymore" and that he would "make our country great" (Peters & Woolley, 2016). In a debate against Hillary Clinton, who prefers to deal with concrete facts and specifics, it will be interesting to see how his style matches up with her expertise, especially in the realm of foreign policy. Voters could be swayed by his appeals to simply "hire the best people," or they could feel more confident in the leadership skills and knowledge of Clinton.

Trump is focused on his skills as a negotiator and "deal-maker." When asked to expound on the specifics for something he has promised to do, but which is outside of the scope of presidential power–or seems unlikely–he defaults to his business successes. His auto-biography, *The Art of the Deal*, is chock full of examples of the deals that he has made (Trump & Schwartz, 2009). He seems genuinely pleased with himself in this capacity, and consistently refers to negotiating a "good deal" as a skill that he possesses. This is also an area that he leverages in a variety of argumentative situations, including when pressed about the specifics of presidential authority (noting he would simply negotiate with Congress) or in foreign policy crises (where he suggests we just need to sit down with other powerful countries, such as Russia). While Clinton doesn't have the business experience that Trump can point to, she does have practical experience in foreign diplomacy and in congressional politics. If she can successfully describe a meaningful difference between business negotiations and international and political consensus building, then many of Trump's talking points could easily be ineffective.

Trump isn't afraid to stoop to using ad hominem attacks or attacks against the family members of his opponents. His chief assault against Jeb Bush was his association with George W. Bush and the failed war in Iraq. When Jeb pointed out the low tactics of attacking someone's family, including their father and mother, Trump simply double-downed on the assault, suggesting that if Jeb's mother was so awesome then "maybe she should run" (Trump, 2016). As someone who has long been in public life, and who is married to Bill Clinton, former Senator and Secretary of State Hillary Clinton may be vulnerable in this area. Though many of the key talking points in the primary are unlikely to be deployed by Trump (such as the self-funding of his campaign or opposition to super PACs) there are issues around which he could focus. In particular, Trump has already begun to refer to Hillary as "crooked Hillary," suggesting that his line of attack will be on her credibility and potential corruptibility. He will likely revisit the email security issue with more energy than Bernie Sanders did in the Democratic primary race, as that demonstrates his point about Hillary's trustworthiness.

Trump engages in hostile and aggressive debate tactics. During the course of the ninth Republican debate in Greenville, SC he consistently interrupted his opponents, in particular when they were attempting to make a point about his politics or statements made. He interrupted Ted Cruz to call him a "liar" (Trump, 2016) when Cruz pointed out that he had defended Planned Parenthood in the past. He also referred to him as a "nasty guy" (Trump, 2016) in that exchange. Trump interrupted Jeb Bush in the span of a minute while the former Governor was attempting to defend his brother's administration (CBSN, 2016). As a seasoned politician, and effective debater, Hillary is unlikely to be phased by this behavior. Many of her own primary debates against Bernie Sanders became somewhat heated, with each interrupting the other. There is the possibility that Hillary's aggression might be viewed differently in this context because she is a female candidate however. While research conflicts on the perceptions of gender differences, in general societal expectations of women posit that they be weaker and more subservient in their presentation (Reid, Keerie, & Palomares, 2003). If Hillary violates those norms, some sub-groups (such as white males) might backlash against her while other groups (such as women) might more strongly support her. Although it will be a fine line for Hillary to walk, it isn't a new challenge for her, only for the electorate, which has not had to evaluate a female presidential candidate from a major party in any previous election.

References

Balz, D. (2016, February 13). Trump amplifies personal attacks, and S.C. voters will tell us whether it worked. *The Washington Post*. Retrieved from https://www.washingtonpost.com/politics/trump-amplifies-personal-attacks-and-sc-voters-will-tell-us-if-it-worked/2016/02/13/f3b496fc-d1f1-11e5-abc9-ea152f0b9561_story.html

CBSN. (2016). *Full CBS News South Carolina Republican Debate*. Retrieved from https://www.youtube.com/watch?v=Un3OhYs-tCE

Cillizza, C. (2016, February 17). Why South Carolina is Jeb Bush's last stand in the 2016 race. *The Washington Post*. Retrieved from https://www.washingtonpost.com/news/the-fix/wp/2016/02/17/south-carolina-is-jeb-bushs-last-chance-in-the-2016-race-period

Costa, R., & Rucker, P. (2016, February 15). Bitter debate shows fraying GOP consensus on core beliefs. *The Washington Post*.

Cruz, T. (2016). Republican Candidates Debate in Greenville, South Carolina. *The American Presidency Project*. Retrieved from http://www.presidency.ucsb.edu/ws/index.php?pid=111500

Dailey, W. O., Hinck, E. A., & Hinck, S. S. (2008). *Politeness in presidential debates: Shaping political face in campaign debates from 1960 to 2004*: Rowman & Littlefield.

GADC. (2016). Demographics. Retrieved from
http://www.greenvilleeconomicdevelopment.com/dem
ographics.php

Healy, P. (2016, February 13). In Republican debate, Jeb
Bush Attacks Donald Trump. *The New York Times*.
Retrieved from
http://www.nytimes.com/2016/02/14/us/politics/republ
ican-debate.html

Lee, M., & Killough, A. (2016, February 21). Jeb Bush
suspends his campaign. *CNN Politics*. Retrieved from
http://www.cnn.com/2016/02/20/politics/jeb-bush-
drops-out-2016

Longley, K., Mayer, J., Schaller, M., & Sloan, J. W.
(2015). *Deconstructing Reagan: Conservative
Mythology and America's Fortieth President*:
Routledge.

Macagno, F. (2013). Strategies of character attack.
Argumentation, 27(4), 369-401.

Martin, G., & Contreras, G. (2016, February 16). U.S.
Supreme Court Justice Antonin Scalia found dead at
West Texas ranch. *My San Antonio*. Retrieved from
http://www.mysanantonio.com/news/us-
world/article/Senior-Associate-Justice-Antonin-Scalia-
found-6828930.php

McCormick, J. (2016, February 13). Republican Debate
Turns Ugly Over Foreign Policy, Bush, Borders.
Bloomberg Politics. Retrieved from
http://www.bloomberg.com/politics/articles/2016-02-
14/republican-presidential-debate-starts-in-shadow-of-
scalia-death

Mehta, S., Bierman, N., & Halper, E. (2016, February 14).
A bitter brawl at GOP debate: As the battle between

party establishment and outsiders comes to a head, candidates turn to insults. *Los Angeles Times*.

Pelletier, K. L. (2010). Leader toxicity: An empirical investigation of toxic behavior and rhetoric. *Leadership,* 6(4), 373-389.

Peters, G., & Woolley, J. T. (2016). Republican Candidates Debate in Greenville, South Carolina. *The American Presidency Project.* Retrieved from http://www.presidency.ucsb.edu/ws/?pid=111500

Reid, S. A., Keerie, N., & Palomares, N. A. (2003). Language, gender salience, and social influence. *Journal of Language and Social Psychology,* 22(2), 210-233.

Shabad, R. (2016, January 5). How could the next president reshape the Supreme Court? *CBS News*. Retrieved from http://www.cbsnews.com/news/the-next-president-could-reshape-the-supreme-court

Trump, D. J. (2016). Republican Candidates Debate in Greenville, South Carolina. *The American Presidency Project.* Retrieved from http://www.presidency.ucsb.edu/ws/index.php?pid=111500

Trump, D. J., & Schwartz, T. (2009). *Trump: The Art of the Deal*: Ballantine Books.

Woolf, N., Jacobs, B., & Smith, D. (2016, February 13). Republican debate: Trump v Bush and Cruz v Rubio as tempers flare - as it happened. *The Guardian*. Retrieved from https://www.theguardian.com/us-news/live/2016/feb/13/cbs-republican-debate-south-carolina-live-coverage-antonin-scalia-donald-trump-ted-cruz

CHAPTER TEN

<<<<<<<<<<<<<<<<<<<<<<◇>>>>>>>>>>>>>>>>>>>>>

GOP Primary Debate #10
Houston, Texas, February 25, 2016
Kurt Fifelski

<<<<<<<<<<<<<<<<<<<<<<◇>>>>>>>>>>>>>>>>>>>>>

With 595 delegates up for grabs on Super Tuesday, the February 25th Republican debate at the University of Houston offered Donald Trump a chance to continue his recent hot streak that included winning the South Carolina primary in a convincing fashion. Knowing that Trump could all but put the race away, Marco Rubio put on the debate performance of the primary season landing blow-after-blow with sharp one-liners and still managing to develop a pragmatic, yet persuasive, platform. Ultimately Rubio's performance came too late as he dropped out of the election a mere three weeks later, but he did demonstrate sound debate skills by treating the debate as a game that requires offense and defense, making arguments that Trump was unprepared to deal with, and by mitigating the tricks Trump had at his disposal. Rubio's strategy kept Trump on the defensive throughout the night, resulting in possibly his worst debate performance in the primaries. If he had developed these tactics earlier and honed them through the framework of policy debate, Rubio could have found himself staying competitive later into the primary season or even winning the nomination. With the expertise of a debate coach and Rubio's performance in Houston in mind, this chapter describes how one can continually out-debate Trump.

Because of attrition and CNN's requirements, only John Kasich, Ben Carson, and Ted Cruz joined Trump, Rubio, and moderator Wolf Blitzer. Despite speaking for nearly one-third of the 90-minute debate (Spunt, 2016), Trump was seemingly plaintive throughout the night; according to one metric Trump rebutted 19 attacks by his opponents while only answering 16 questions, a far different ratio than what his opponents had to deal with (Libresco & Koeze, 2016). The debate broached a number of topics, including immigration, healthcare, and foreign policy. Throughout the evening Trump's opponents took turns attacking: Rubio and Kasich focused on Trump as a policymaker; Cruz went after him for not being a true conservative; and Carson was there too, quickly realizing his status as an "also ran." While Rubio's debate skills were on full display, Cruz's inability to know when to hold back meant that the attack was largely mooted, letting Trump off the hook multiple times.

Like most debates, Trump made a series of incomplete arguments by asserting he could get things done with little-to-no rationale as to why, or in debate nomenclature, he had a claim without a warrant. In previous debates, Trump had gotten away with it, exemplified by the number of times Jeb Bush tried to center the conversation on policy, routinely failing because Trump's interruptions and insults knocked him off his game. Where Bush failed, Rubio succeeded because he was not only willing to stand up for himself, but seemed delighted to hammer away at Trump. Typically, Trump avoids debates by being the loudest person in the room and whittling away at his opponents, but by maintaining ethos Rubio had the chance to change the terms of the debate.

In addition to ethos, Rubio exemplified how to successfully debate against Trump by framing how the audience should evaluate arguments; he did this by focusing on the offensive and defensive utility of different positions, prioritizing those that helped him and avoiding issues that hindered him. Where many candidates would say what Trump wanted to achieve was bad (offense), Rubio took the easier route that proved Trump incapable of achieving all of his grandiose claims (defense). This strategy allowed Rubio to prove he had a well-thought-out platform, putting the burden on his opponents to attack his policies rather than his personality.

Rubio showed early on in the debate that he was familiar with a few common, yet effective, debate tricks. First by labeling arguments in just a few words, he created taglines, which are a strong tool when dealing with the time constraints of a debate because they help the audience draw a conclusion about an argument despite having incomplete information. For instance, Rubio highlighted the strategic use of taglines while Trump was discussing his views on immigration policy. Knowing that he would be unable to fully warrant the argument that Trump regularly hires immigrant labor for his resorts and buildings, Rubio provided the audience with the tactful line of, "Again, go online and Google it. Donald Trump, Polish workers. You'll see it." Because his campaign had already done the search, Rubio knew that the top Google hits for *Trump Polish Workers* were two New York Times articles entitled "After 15 Years in Court, Workers' Lawsuit Against Trump Faces Yet Another Delay" (1998) and "Trump Says He Didn't Know He Employed Illegal Aliens" (1990).

Now Trump was not just debating against the four other people on the stage, but against the perceptions of the

14.5 million people watching the debate (Stelter, 2016). This is proven by the fact that in the hour after Rubio provided the audience with search terms, the search *Trump Polish Workers* was not only trending, but the search of "Polish workers" had increased by 700 percent (Google Trends, 2016). Just as important, Rubio only had to recite the three-word tagline "Trump Polish workers" to conjure up a reminder to the audience that there was tension in Trump's immigration platform, which he did later in the debate when Trump called him a liar.

Throughout the exchange, Rubio displayed the strategic thought of a debater, proving his opponent's position is laden with contradictions. By evidencing that Trump regularly uses migrant labor, Rubio called into question how much Trump can be trusted, especially in regards to his fidelity towards closing America's borders. This was not the only time Rubio went after Trump's capacity to return America to greatness by employing Americans. While Trump was being cavalier about starting a trade war with Mexico because it would bring jobs back to America, Rubio quipped, "...about the trade war–I don't understand, because your ties and the clothes you make is made in Mexico and in China. So you're gonna be starting a trade war against your own ties and your own suits…Why don't you make them in America?"

Over the next thirty seconds, Trump tried to explain why currency devaluation meant that he was justified in having clothes made abroad, but Rubio was unrelenting responding four times to Trump, "Well, make them in America." To the layperson, this attack might seem offensive, but in debate, this is use of defense because Rubio proved that there was an irreconcilable flaw in Trump's position. Offense, in this case, would mean defending free trade and impacting what a trade war would do to the economy and America's capacity to negotiate globally. Knowing that he could get away without taking a position on trade and providing his campaign flexibility come the November election, it was strategic for Rubio to prove the flaws with Trump's stance rather than developing his own.

Trump was successful at avoiding policy confrontation during the primary by being vague on most issues. Typically Trump relied largely on bravado to deflect criticism rather than engaging in debates about the specifics of his platform. For the most part, in previous debates, Trump's opponents in the past had let him get away with this, his campaign was able to predict criticism and formulate response within days, or even hours, after he faced new policy arguments. A glaring instance of this is how Trump was able to get away without knowing what the nuclear triad was at the Las Vegas debate. A seasoned debater would have gone after Trump as being incompetent and reckless, willing to take over the world's most powerful military despite not knowing how it functions. While Rubio explained the basic tenets of the nuclear triad at the Las Vegas debate, he hardly took advantage of Trump's vagueness. A novice debate mind might think it is smart to be vague, but ultimately it is a risky move. The less a debater is willing to defend, the weaker their position to an extent that it can result in a massive loss of ethos. Because many debates are constrained by time, debaters can find themselves spending an inordinate amount of time saying what their position is not, rather than using it as a point of strength to go after their opponents.

Rubio came into Houston prepared to capitalize on Trump's willingness to avoid specifics and prevented him from formulating a justification for having an undeveloped response by staying on the attack. The best example of this is when Trump said he would incentivize competition in the insurance market by removing "the lines" between states as an alternative to the Affordable Care Act (ACA) and then went on to criticize the insurance companies and discuss how he is self-funding his campaign. As a reminder of his experience and credibility, Rubio quickly retorted with analysis of healthcare law and then centered the debate on Trump, asking, "What is your plan? I understand the lines around the state, whatever that means. This is not a game where you draw maps…What is your plan, Mr. Trump?"

As Trump responded with ad homs, Rubio remained persistent, asking about the plan, forcing Trump to talk in circles about the lines. Trump then tried to change the subject by attacking Rubio's strength as a debater, but Marco was ready with the line of the night, "He says five things. Everyone's dumb, he's gonna make America great again, we're going to win, win, win, he's winning in the polls and the lines around the state." The crowd erupted.

Within a few minutes after the exchange, Cruz built on Rubio's attack pointing out some of Trump's ideological contradictions in regards to healthcare. By reminding the audience that Trump had recanted support for the liberal healthcare policy and Planned Parenthood throughout the campaign, Cruz made the argument that Trump's vagueness may very well result in the status quo, in this case the ACA and federal funding of Planned Parenthood. Cruz's attack was twofold. The first layer of offensive involved discussing Trump's history of statements in favor of liberal healthcare and support for Planned Parenthood, in doing so, Cruz established that the most concrete views Trump had were in support of the status quo. The second layer of offensive used the strategy of asking Trump a series of questions, which quickly went awry for Cruz.

An experienced debater knows it is most strategic to ask questions when they know what the response will be, something that Cruz either forgot or just was not taught while he was a debater at Princeton or a student at Harvard Law School. His questioning of Trump started well when he asked a few true or false questions, but he opened the door for Trump when he asked, "Did you say if you want people to die on the streets, if you don't support socialized health care, you have no heart?" For the first time in a few minutes, Trump pivoted from defense to offense with his reply of, "Correct. I will not let people die on the streets if I'm president." Until Blitzer intervened, Trump continued to respond to every question with quips about how unethical it is to let people die in the streets, completely mitigating Cruz's attack and portions of Rubio's.

A debate between well-prepared opponents should resemble a chess match, with each argument contributing to part of a larger strategy. Through research and preparation, the sage debater should know not only what their opponent's strengths and weaknesses are, but also what their next move will be. They should know how and when to ask questions, directing their opponent to an answer that reveals weakness rather than providing them with a chance to develop their point. While both debaters succeeded in putting Trump on the defensive during the healthcare portion of the debate, Rubio was more effective at playing the game of debate than Cruz because Rubio continued to put Trump on the defensive by focusing on weaknesses, "the lines," rather than letting him make offensive statements like, "we're not going to let them die in the streets."

By forcing Trump to talk about his alternative to the ACA, Rubio demonstrated the utility new arguments have in debates but also the skill of making an opponent eat their own words. Candidates come into debates prepared to defend against arguments they have already had to deal with and often find themselves caught off guard when they first have to deal with arguments they have not thoroughly analyzed. Having taken on the nickname "choke artist"

280

from Trump because he was caught repeating himself in a previous debate, Rubio knew about this all too well. However, when Trump was talking in circles about "the lines," Rubio was ready to embarrass Trump. Rubio zinged, "Now he's repeating himself." "Talk about repeating. I watched him repeat himself five times four weeks ago," Trump retorted. Ultimately, Rubio would win this battle of ethos, getting a massive applause when he chided, "I saw you repeat yourself five times five seconds ago." In this attack, Rubio not only diminished Trump's ethos, he also helped mitigate the embarrassment he faced in the last debate at the hands of Chris Christie, having repeated himself over-and-over.

This was not the only time Trump got caught off guard. While the candidates were discussing Supreme Court nominees, Cruz went after Trump's capacity of getting a conservative on the bench because he would rather quickly strike a deal with Democrats than remain faithful to conservative principles. Cruz's attack was easily sidestepped by Trump as he made an appeal to pragmatics, pointing out that there is no use in filibustering nominees when it is possible to compromise and get something done. Those who study Trump will find this tactic familiar. While many candidates will deal with unvetted arguments by discussing how conservative or liberal they are, Trump tends to insult his opponents or talk about how successful he was as a businessperson.

One such instance occurred in Houston when conservative radio personality Hugh Hewitt questioned Trump about releasing his tax returns, which Trump had said on Hewitt's show a year earlier he was willing to do. Hewitt asked if Trump was still committed to the statement made on the radio to show, to which Trump responded with an attack about the ratings of Hewitt's show in an attempt to avoid the question. The amount of Trump's personal wealth is something that has gotten Trump off-script many times and likely will in the future. Knowing that the general electorate is concerned with Trump's demeanor (Hartig, Lapinksi, & Psyllos, 2016), he would be smart to tone down the attack when he faces similar questions in the general election debates; personal attacks on a moderator like Gwen Ifill regarding tax returns will only fuel the argument that Trump lacks the temperament to lead. Luckily, for Hillary Clinton's campaign, Trump has yet to release his tax returns, making him the first presidential nominee not to do so since 1976 (Rapperport, 2016).

Paying heed to the tricks in Trump's arsenal, Rubio took a different approach when criticizing Trump as a negotiator. Continuing to be vague, Trump refused to take a stern stance on what should be done in regards to Israel and Palestine. Trump said that his position was irrelevant because all that mattered was his tact as a negotiator, saying that he was the only one on stage capable of reaching a settlement. When it was his turn to respond to the prompt, Rubio took a firm stance in support of Israel mentioning that a deal between Israel and Palestine is not feasible because the Palestinian Authority will walk away from negotiating in the future, just like they had in the past. Rather than attack the idea of negotiations, as Cruz did when talking about nominees for the Court, Rubio pointed out that making deals on real estate in the United States was a far cry from reaching a settlement with a terrorist group like Hamas.

Rubio's criticism of Trump's skills as a negotiator were more poignant than Cruz's for two reasons. First, Cruz went after Trump from an ideological position by saying negotiating is abhorrent if the end result is anything other than strictly conservative. By framing the alternative to negotiating as a failure because nothing gets done, Trump was able to make the case for a more pragmatic approach when making Court appointments. Rather than focusing on ideology and criticizing negotiating as a tool, Rubio was pragmatic by pointing out that the ability to negotiate real estate deals and dealing with terrorists are not analogous. Value claims about the need to be ideologically pure, while useful early in the primaries, are not nearly as effective as describing how a particular framework of approaching policies will work in highly specified scenarios.

Second, and just as important is how the arguments about negotiating were deployed. Cruz introduced the criticism of making deals with Democrats as an offensive position without any prompting on the subject from Trump. Doing so allowed Trump to spin the new argument in his favor and go on the offensive, which he did by pointing out that Cruz's unwillingness to compromise would get nothing done. By waiting for Trump to use his negotiating skills to deflect a question, Rubio put the onus on Trump to prove he was not operating under a fallacy of false equivalence. While Rubio's approach was defensive, it proved that Trump had no solution to the conflict between Israel and Palestine.

Rubio quietly developed a platform throughout the night, taking positions on almost every prompt the candidates were given with little impediment. Certainly, this can be attributed to all of the candidates trying to compare their positions to Trump, but Rubio also benefitted because every time Trump had a chance to speak he had to from a point of defense. With precise detail, Rubio explained how he would practically phase out the Deferred Action on Childhood Arrivals (DACA) and only had to deal with allegations that he is a liar because his position on ethanol subsidies had changed earlier in the primaries. While Trump was babbling about lines Rubio enunciated his alternative to the ACA as healthcare savings, describing how his policy would impact different groups of Americans. The theme was sustained as the night went on and those who watched the debate would likely say that Kasich was the only candidate on stage who did a better of job of explaining how his platform functioned than Rubio. Kasich, however, had little opposition to deal with during the debate because he had been largely written off.

In hindsight, Rubio should have approached the earlier debates with the strategy of pinning Trump down to specifics. Others, most notably Bush, had tried to keep the conversation centered on the merits of Trump's platform but failed because he was able to sidestep the attacks through bravado and insults. Rubio should have succeeded in pinning down Trump by framing his arguments through an offense/defense paradigm, knowing how to preempt Trump's responses, and by making a series of new arguments for which Trump was unprepared to deal. Unfortunately for both Rubio and debate nerds, his campaign failed to identify what made their approach to this debate effective before the next debate, innovating their attack to be about Trump's hand size rather than his policies.

Until Trump can nuance his debate strategy to discuss policy or avoid it all together, Trump should be concerned about what will happen in a one-on-one debate against someone who knows the process of policy making. Having many candidates on stage, Trump can use the weaknesses of others to help mitigate criticism, something Cruz helped with a number of times in Houston. Despite being a champion parliamentary debater at Princeton, Cruz lacked some of the fundamental skills a successful debater should have. Cruz helped Trump on more than one occasion by framing arguments poorly and letting Trump find the wiggle room necessary to develop offense or completely mitigate the attack by changing the subject. In addition, by interrupting Rubio or bandwagoning on his attacks, Cruz's ill-timed and poorly prepared arguments helped Trump center the debate away from his weaknesses.

While pundits will remember the Houston debate because of the series of verbal brawls, which more resembled a food fight than Carson's fruit salad of life, Clinton's campaign will pay heed to it as a teaching tool as they prepare for the debates in the fall. Knowing that Trump's weakness lies in policy expertise, Clinton will want to frame arguments through offense and defense, stay innovative with arguments that Trump cannot predict, and, most importantly, keep the debate focused on policy by preempting his attempt to change the course of the debate. Solely keeping debates focused on the merits of policy might not defeat the enigma that is Donald Trump on the debate stage, but they will be necessary in the larger of scheme of things. Thankfully, for those who have to debate Trump, they have Rubio's performance in Houston as a case study of how to get the job done.

References

Baquet, D. (1990, July 13). Trump Says He Didn't Know He Employed Illegal Aliens. *New York Times.*

Google Trends. (2016, February 26). @Google Trends. *Twitter.* Retrieved from https://twitter.com/GoogleTrends/status/703225164201263104

Hartig, H., Lapinksi, J., & Psyllos, S. (2016, August 18). Poll: Clinton Maintains Big Lead as Voters Doubt Trump's Temperament. *NBC News*. Retrieved from http://www.nbcnews.com/politics/2016-election/poll-clinton-maintains-big-lead-voters-doubt-trump-s-temperament-n631351

Libresco, L., & Koeze, E. (2016, February 25). Trump Was the Center of Attention Tonight. *FiveThirtyEight*. Retrieved from: http://fivethirtyeight.com/live-blog/cnn-republican-debate-live-coverage/? -livepress-update-15794072

Raab, S. (1998, June 14). After 15 Years in Court, Workers' Lawsuit Against Trump Faces Yet Another Delay. *New York Times.*

Rapperport, A. (2016, May 11). Donald Trump Breaks With Recent History by Not Releasing Tax Returns. *New York Times*. Retrieved from http://www.nytimes.com/politics/first-draft/2016/05/11/donald-trump-breaks-with-recent-history-by-not-releasing-tax-returns/?_r=0

Spunt, B. (2016, February 25). On The Clock: Trump Dominated Debate In Speaking Time. *National Public Radio*. Retrieved from http://www.npr.org/2016/02/25/468156547/on-the-clock-which-candidate-is-speaking-the-most-in-tonights-debate

Stelter, B. (2016, February 26). GOP jabfest drew 14.5 million, biggest debate audience since December. *CNN*. Retrieved from http://money.cnn.com/2016/02/26/media/republican-debate-cnn-telemundo-ratings

CHAPTER ELEVEN

<<<<<<<<<<<<<<<<<<<<<<<<<>>>>>>>>>>>>>>>>>>>>>>>>>

GOP Primary Debate #11
Detroit, Michigan, March 3, 2016
Dr. Kelly Michael Young

<<<<<<<<<<<<<<<<<<<<<<<<<>>>>>>>>>>>>>>>>>>>>>>>>>

The March 3, 2016 Republican debate in Detroit, Michigan, hosted by Fox News and Facebook, was fascinating in large part due to the context that Donald Trump faced entering the debate. While Trump was the clear frontrunner for the GOP nomination after winning seven of the Super Tuesday contests and maintaining a strong lead in national polls, the Never Trump movement and a number of negative news stories called into question his viability as a general election candidate (Lee, 2016). For example, on the same day as the Detroit debate, 2012 GOP presidential candidate Mitt Romney gave a damning anti-Trump speech in which he called Trump a "phony, a fraud," and a candidate who engages in "absurd and third-grade theatrics" (O'Keefe, 2016). Romney's speech gave credibility to an anti-Trump movement that led to a tentative—and ultimately failed—agreement in which Senator Ted Cruz, Ohio Governor John Kasich, and Senator Marco Rubio would not campaign against each other in key primary states in an attempt to trigger a contested convention. Representing perhaps the apex of anxiety about Trump actually winning the nomination, the debate featured Cruz and Rubio repeatedly calling into question Trump's ability to present himself as "presidential." In addition, a series of negative news stories about issues such as Trump's unwillingness to denounce overtly racist supporters such a former Grand Wizard of the Ku Klux Klan David Duke, his alleged softening of his anti-immigrant stance during off-the-record comments to the *New York Times* editorial board, and his flip-flops on other issues pestered Trump before the debate (Jeffers, 2016).

Yet, despite all these challenges to Trump's credibility as a presidential candidate, Trump survived what many commentators called a raucous and ugly debate (e.g., Graham, 2016; Lee, 2016). He endured by keeping media attention locked on him and by making his opponents' perform worse than him (Graham, 2016). Rather than move away from the theatrics that Romney criticized, Trump responded with more dramatic attacks, like repeatedly calling Rubio "little Marco" and escalating to the point that Trump referenced the size of his own phallus as argument. While this type of performance would normally sabotage a candidate's intrinsic ethos–credibility determined during a communicative exchange (Benoit & Benoit, 2008), this performance did not harm Trump's popularity. I argue this occurs for two reasons. First, Trump benefits greatly from a common marketing adage that "all attention is good attention." Despite a rough performance at times, Trump dominated the focus of the debate, particularly with his frequent references to his previous primary victories, standings in recent polls and personal attacks and tit-for-tat exchanges with Rubio. Second, this debate highlighted the fundamental problem with the Never Trump movement and corresponding debate strategy: it depended entirely on a traditional understanding of political credibility. Throughout the primary season and especially in the Detroit debate, Trump demonstrated that his credibility was anchored in his celebrity status and his ability to identify as an anti-establishment candidate.

In the chapter that follows, I first explore the primary themes raised in the Detroit debate. Second, I examine Trump's strategy and performance in the debate, specifically analyzing two tactics: 1) the personal attacks on Cruz and Rubio that often escalated into blow-for-blow exchanges with Rubio; and 2) Trump's habitual references to opinion polls and his primary victories. In evaluating these maneuvers, I assess Cruz, Rubio, and Trump's arguments in relation to how they impacted the candidates' credibility. Third, I review various evaluations of Trump's performance from media outlets, political commentators, and snap opinion polls, noting that Trump's performance was heavily criticized by analysts but most agreed that Rubio's performance was far worse. Lastly, I consider how the themes of the debate and Trump's strategy and tactics suggest how Trump may approach the general election debates with former Secretary of State Hillary Clinton and how she should respond.

Given the difficult media cycle for Trump that preceded the March 3 debate and the intensity of the previous debate in Houston, the Detroit debate was focused largely on Trump. The main themes of the evening were: Trump's character and temperament and his inconsistent policy and public statements. There was some policy issue discussion concerning anti-ISIS strategy, foreign policy, infrastructure funding, religious liberty, the Second Amendment, and unemployment that will be referenced throughout this discussion. However, the vast majority of the debate focused on Trump.

Presidential Character and Temperament

Perhaps the most significant theme of the evening was that Trump lacked credibility as a presidential candidate. Communication studies and political science research outlines a number of factors that impact voters' perceptions of credibility. Donald Kinder (1986) notes that candidates' ethos is evaluated in four areas: 1) competence (e.g., expertise, knowledge, and intelligence); 2) character (e.g., honesty, morality, trustworthiness); 3) empathy (e.g., caring and understanding); and 4) leadership (e.g., decisiveness, dependability, and strength). Additionally, William and Pamela Benoit (2008) maintain that perceptions of credibility develop in two ways. First, speakers' ethos is perceived based on their prior reputation, which is their extrinsic credibility. Second, speakers' credibility also is assessed during a speech or debate performance, which is their intrinsic credibility. During the Detroit debate, a considerable amount of time was spent examining Trump's presidential character, particularly his honesty, leadership ability, and temperament.

In terms of character, Trump was critiqued heavily for his contradictory policy statements, involvement with Trump University, off-the-record comments about immigration, and support from racist groups. For example,

Rubio, in response to a question from moderator Bret Baier about his use of personal attacks, started the debate by arguing that, "...if there is anyone who has ever deserved to be attacked [personally], it has been Donald Trump, for the way he has treated people in the campaign" (Peters & Woolley, 2016). And despite his claim that he would rather focus on policy issues instead of personal attacks, Rubio frequently referred to Trump as a "con man" who was "trying to con people into giving them their vote" (Peters & Woolley, 2016). Later in the debate, Rubio further called into question Trump's competence to be the Commander-in-Chief when he referred back to Trump's seeming inability to answer a question about nuclear deterrence in the December 15 Las Vegas debate. Rubio noted that "...someone who thinks the nuclear triad is a rock band from the 1980s" is not fit to be president (Peters & Woolley, 2016). Another central line of attack on Trump's character dealt with his conservative credentials. For instance, Rubio argued several times that Trump's policy stances were not conservative enough. One key line of attack for both Cruz and Rubio was to demand that Trump ask the *New York Times* to release his off-the-record comments about his immigration stance, suggesting that Trump had something to hide, implying that his position might be more moderate than previously suggested. Similarly, Cruz focused largely on Trump's past financial support for Hillary Clinton and other high profile Democrats over the last four decades.

In addition to remarks about his character, Trump was also criticized for lacking the temperament to be president. For example, after a number of heated back-and-forth exchanges with Trump, Rubio highlighted that the debate was getting "personal" as Trump repeatedly called Rubio "little Marco" (Peters & Woolley, 2016). In response to the numerous insults, Rubio pointed out to the audience, "...he's asking us to make him the president of the United States of America.... This is not a game" (Peters & Woolley, 2016). In what would become one of the most memorable comments of the evening, Trump made the debate even more personal when commenting on Rubio's attacks on his hand size and the suggestion that his manhood was insufficient: "...he referred to my hands, if they are small, something else must be small. I guarantee you there is no problem. I guarantee" (Peters & Woolley, 2016). While attempting to stay out of the personal fracas between Rubio and Trump, Cruz mockingly offered Trump a number of techniques to remain claim. For example, Cruz asked Trump to "learn not to interrupt. It's not complicated" and to "[c]ount to 10, Donald" and breathe (Peters & Woolley, 2016). Summarizing the evening's theme about Trump's temperament, Cruz noted that the debate was, "...not about what attacks we can throw at each other.... I don't think the people of America are interested in a bunch of bickering school children" (Peters & Woolley, 2016). Overall, there was a concerted effort made by Cruz and Rubio to call into question Trump's intrinsic credibility during the debate. Given the culmination of Never Trump and other developments leading up to the debate, Cruz and Rubio had hoped that a powerful assault on Trump's credibility during the debate would serve as a knock-out blow against him.

Trump's Inconsistencies

In almost every modern presidential election, policy statement reversals–known colloquially as a "flip-flop"–are often an important barometer of a candidate's integrity. Many times, inconsistencies and reversals can be damning. As *Washington Post* columnist Hunter Schwarz (2015) notes, "Flip-flopping in politics can be deadly for candidates. Just ask Mitt Romney about health care or John Kerry or Hillary Rodham Clinton about Iraq." In the Detroit debate, Fox News dedicated a significant amount of time interrogating Trump on his economic policy numbers

296

and inconsistent statements about his stance on the Afghanistan war and Syrian refugees and his claim that President George W. Bush lied to justify the Iraq war. Early in the debate, moderator Chris Wallace pressed Trump about his tax cut estimates, noting that Trump's plan "would add $10 trillion to the nation's debt over 10 years" and that his stated savings in other areas "don't add up" (Peters & Woolley, 2016). Trump responded that Wallace failed to account for savings made by making cuts to executive agencies or negotiating with pharmaceutical companies for lower Medicare drug prices. But Wallace continued to point out that even taking these savings into account, Trump's calculations did not make sense.

Later in the debate, moderator Megan Kelly led a segment that specifically examined three policy or statement reversals by Trump. Kelly acknowledged that "one of the things people love about [Trump] is they believe [he] tell[s] it like it is," thus highlighting that trustworthiness is an important part of his appeal to voters. Yet, she follows up by noting, "…time and time again in this campaign, you have actually told the voters one thing only to reverse yourself within weeks or even sometimes days" (Peters & Woolley, 2016). When pressed about his stance about the Afghanistan war, Trump claimed that he was misunderstood and he clarified that he was critiquing the Bush administration's justification for the Iraq, not Afghanistan, war. On the issue of Syrian refugees, Trump claimed that he initially supported bringing refugees into the U.S. because he believed that there would be very few of them. However, he asserted that he changed his position once he learned of the scale of the program. Kelly pointed out that this seemed dubious as he changed his stance the very next day. Yet, Trump continued to maintain that he received new information immediately after offering his tentative support for the program.

In addition to this segment, Trump was pressed on two other claims. During an exchange with Rubio about Trump University, Trump claimed that Rubio was wrong about the university's Better Business Bureau rating insisting that it was upgraded from a "D-" rating to an "A." As Rubio and Trump went back and forth over the issue, Kelly interjected, noting that the BBB rating was currently a "D-". Much later in the debate, Baier noted that, in the past, Trump endorsed an assault weapons ban. Baier followed up by asking, "So do you think there should be any restrictions on the Second Amendment?" (Peters & Woolley, 2016). In this instance, Trump quickly stated that his position had changed and he no longer supported an assault weapons ban. In sum, all of these questions raised a number of questions about Trump's trustworthiness as a presidential candidate.

In response to the substantial challenge to his character, honesty, and temperament, Trump used ad hominem attacks and tit-for-tat exchanges, evasion, and emphasis on his previous success. Nothing about his aggressive style in this debate was different from his general strategy throughout the previous primary debates. However, what was significant about these tactics in this debate was he chose to use them in a context that was shining an intense spotlight on his credibility. Particularly in light of Romney's speech early that day, rather than back away from his aggressive approach, Trump seemed to double-down on the strategy.

Ad hominem Attacks and Tit-For-Tat Exchanges

Trump's primary debate tactic was to use personal attacks, particularly against Romney and Rubio. For example, the first question of the evening was about Romney's speech. Trump responded by calling Romney "a failed candidate" who was "an embarrassment to everyone" (Peters & Woolley, 2016). Later, replying to Rubio's argument about where Trump Collection clothes were manufactured, Trump began his "little guy" attacks against Rubio. For instance, Trump claimed that, in regards to clothing issue, "[t]his little guy lied so much…" (Peters & Woolley, 2016). In several other moments during the debate, Trump continued to call Rubio, "little Marco." Besides name-calling, Trump also criticized Rubio for his congressional voting record. While this could have been a more substantive challenge to Rubio's professionalism, it quickly became a personal attack. For example, in an exchange about Trump University, Trump responded to Rubio's accusation that he is a con artist by calling into question Rubio's trustworthiness. According to Trump, "The real con artist is Senator Marco Rubio…who has the worst voting record in the United States Senate…. He couldn't get elected dogcatcher" because he was so unpopular in Florida. To conclude the attack, Trump accused "little Marco" of "defraud[ing] the people of Florida" (Peters & Woolley, 2016).

While much of his attention was focused on Rubio, Trump also attacked Cruz, focusing on his trustworthiness as well. In a discussion of H1-B guest worker visas, Cruz related the issue to Trump's hiring of foreign workers at his Florida hotel. After a lengthy round of back-and-forth accusations and denials, Trump called Cruz a "liar" and "the lying guy up here." Eventually this morphed into Trump's favorite label for Cruz–"Lyin' Ted"–during a round of questions about the Second Amendment (Peters & Woolley, 2016).

In addition to using ad hominem attacks, Trump frequently interrupted and talked over other candidates, particularly Rubio, to initiate tit-for-tat exchanges that devolved into personal attacks. Five times during the debate, Rubio and Trump repeatedly disrupted each other to bicker back and forth about smaller details discussed in questions about conservative principles, employer records, and Trump's admiration of Russian President Vladimir Putin. Later in the debate, Cruz was twice embroiled in similar exchanges with Trump about Trump's financial support of key Democrats and Trump University's fraud case. In all, Trump was the center of seven lengthy blow-for-blow exchanges that attempted to call into question Trump's integrity and temperament.

While this kind of aggressive behavior likely would undermine other candidate's credibility, there is a prior expectation that this is how Trump debates. Throughout the campaign, Trump has billed himself as a strong person that speaks off-the-cuff and "tells it like it is"; this is how he framed his extrinsic credibility. While the other GOP candidates had hoped the Detroit debate would be their best opportunity to undermine Trump's perceived credibility, the attacks against his intrinsic credibility during the debate either magnified Trump's extrinsic credibility–e.g., he is a tough brawler–or it was outweighed by Trump's established credibility. According to Benoit and Benoit (2008), prior reputation has a more consistent effect on the persuasiveness of a speaker than intrinsic credibility. While the name-calling and aggressive exchanges might not have substantially increased Trump's credibility, as we now know, it did little to undermine his extrinsic ethos.

Compounding this effect is Trump's celebrity status. For traditional politicians, this type of performance would devastate a candidate's ethos. Take for example the reaction to Vice President Al Gore's excessive sighing during the first presidential debate against George W. Bush in 2000. Gore was heavily criticized as being impatient and rude because viewers expected him to behave more professionally (Wolf, 2012). However, Trump's celebrity status in a social media-age has changed the rules entirely. As Van Jones (2015) contends,

> "In the old [campaign] system...going widely off message with bombastic statements would terminate a campaign. But

not on a reality TV show . . .. Under the old
system, scathing attacks on
individuals…would scare away voters. But
on Twitter, insulting people and throwing
rhetorical bombs doesn't cost you followers.
It usually gains [them]."

During the debate, Senator Rubio noted this effect, by arguing, "The media has given these personal attacks that…Trump has made an incredible amount of coverage" (Peters & Woolley, 2016). However, what Rubio fails to observe here is that these attacks are ideal for a social media environment. In many ways, the insults operate just like sound bites for traditional news media. As Jim Rutenberg (2016) suggests, "…shocking comments…and personal insults…keep Americans glued to their screens," both big and small.

Evasion of Questions

Another tactic used by Trump was to dodge questions that he did not want to answer. Rather than just outright ignore the question, Trump often made a response that tangentially related to the question and then he followed up with a personal attack on another candidate as a distraction. For instance, when asked about Romney's criticism of his character, Trump never refuted the claims; instead, he counter-attacked Romney's character. Additionally, when pressed about where his Trump Collection clothing was manufactured, Trump launched into a lengthy discussion of how other countries cheat the United States by devaluing their currency, which undermines U.S. apparel manufacturing. While the answer is indirectly related to the question, he never answers the attack on his honesty; rather, he evades and distracts. Thus, while the Fox News moderators and other presidential candidates had numerous opportunities to challenge many aspects of Trump's credibility, they failed to capture Trump as he evaded a number of difficult questions.

Focus on Contest Results

Another tactic used by Trump throughout the Detroit debate was to frequently remind the audience that he was leading the other candidates in primary victories and national polls. For example, in response to an argument by Cruz, Trump pointed out, "...I have won 10 [contests]. He has won three or four." Later in the debate, Trump summarized his focus on the contest in arguing, "[In a recent CNN poll], I'm at 49 [percent]. [Cruz] is at 15.... Then he goes, we have five [victories]. And–well, excuse me, I won 10.... Everybody knows that on Super Tuesday,

Trump was the winner" (Peters & Woolley, 2016). In an insightful retort, Cruz noted, "…Donald lives by the polls every day. He tweets about the polls" (Peters & Woolley, 2016). Senator Cruz was correct in his observation: Trump constantly attempts to keep media focused on his status as the frontrunner. This type of framing of media coverage is known as horse-race campaign coverage. It is often favored by news media because it is dramatic, newsworthy, and, as noted media scholar Shanto Iyengar (2004) and his colleagues conclude, "[it] is what attracts the most viewers" (p. 2). Trump appears to be very aware of this effect and rather than depend on the news media to focus on this, he augments media horse-race coverage by constantly reminding viewers that he won the most primaries and led in national polls. This was effective for Trump because it highlighted his extrinsic perception as a winner, regardless of the frequent attacks to his credibility during the debate. Additionally, this tactic fed the next morning's news cycle, where readers and viewers were reminded that Trump was winning with his aggressive and outlandish style. When the horse-race and theatrics are the focus, there is little room to consider Trump's flip-flops or evasions (Rutenberg, 2016).

Post-Debate Perceptions of Trump's Performance

Reactions to the Detroit debate were mixed in declaring who won the debate. For example, unscientific snap polls favored Trump by large margins. For instance, the *Detroit News* (2016) poll had Trump winning with 78.96 percent of respondents and Kasich was a distant second with 14.18 percent of the votes. On the conservative news source, Newsmax (2016), Trump was named the winner by 75 percent of the vote and Cruz was second with 15 percent. Conservative pollster Frank Luntz led a post-debate focus group of 25 people. Fifteen people picked Kasich as the winner, six selected Cruz, one picked Trump, and none selected Rubio (Weber, 2016). Likewise, editorialists and journalists were divided in their reactions. The most common response was that the entire debate was "dirty" and "ugly" (Lee, 2016; Voorhees, 2016). Yet, Chris Cillizza of the *Washington Post* declared Cruz and Kasich the winners of the evening, largely because they appeared most presidential and rose above the fray. In comparison, Trump lost because he was "juvenile" and Rubio self-destructed in "kamikaze missions against Trump" (Cillizza, 2016). Similarly, Douglas Schoen (2016) of Fox News declared Cruz and Kasich the winners because they were far more professional and presidential than Rubio and Trump.

However, despite the number of criticisms of Trump's performance in comparison to Cruz and Kasich, the debate worked in Trump's favor on several levels. First, while he was battered by claims of policy inconsistency and poor character, Trump lead 62 percent of all Twitter and 73 percent of all Facebook discussion about the debate (Allen, 2016). While we typically think of candidate control of the traditional news cycle as important, Trump has demonstrated that a candidate can be highly successful at reaching supporters by controlling social media conversations (Rutenberg, 2016). As Van Jones (2015) observes, "...every political era is shaped by the media environment of its time. The most successful politicians have an innate understanding of that environment and the skill to act on it. In our era, that could be Trump." Thus, while traditional media commentators and political insiders denounced Trump's debate performance, there were a number of signs suggesting that Trump effectively controlled the focus of discussions about the debate, which had favored him the entire primary season.

Second, an ugly blow-for-blow debate advantaged Trump. Returning to the understanding of credibility as extrinsic and intrinsic, voters have come to expect Trump to act in a bellicose and unscripted manner; it defines his extrinsic credibility. Up to this point, Trump's antagonistic behavior worked in his favor and it was unclear why it would undermine his overall credibility in this debate (Voorhees, 2016). More importantly, rather than harm Trump, the extended and fierce tit-for-tat argumentative exchanges hurt Trump's opponents more than they harmed him. As Graham (2016) observes, "The funny thing about Trump's rough performance was that no one else did especially well, either." For Trump, the constant attacks in the wake of Romney's denunciation of him only bolstered his extrinsic status as a political outsider (Lee, 2016). For a candidate like Rubio, there was only a risk that using Trump's aggressive tactics against him would backfire. As Bruni (2016) argues, Trump "...has done so well at dragging his rivals so far down into the sewer with him that portions of what we watched on Thursday night were a fetid farce.... [T]his tone favors Trump...and if rivals join him there, they merely become his subjects." In other words, viewers expected candidates like Rubio to behave as traditional presidential candidates in the debates because the candidates had invested so much importance in maintaining that candidates should behave appropriately.

Yet, in debating Trump in a blow-by-blow battle, these candidates undermined their own character (Jeffers, 2016).

Third, given the intensity of both the previous Houston debate and this one, the last question asked in the debate handed Trump a major victory. In the last segment of the debate, Baier asked each candidate this question: "Tonight, in 30 seconds, can you definitively say you will support the Republican nominee, even if that nominee is Donald J. Trump?" (Peters & Woolley, 2016). Cruz, Kasich, and Rubio all answered "yes," even if reluctantly. After calling into question Trump's character, expertise, and trustworthiness for almost two hours, the candidates' answers to this question deflated any force the attacks on Trump's credibility might have had. Oddly enough, at the peak of the Never Trump campaign, Trump's opponents destroyed any legitimacy the effort might have had.

Implications for the General Election Debates

Since becoming the Republican nominee, Trump has made it apparent that he is not going to change his argumentative style very much. Recently, during a scripted speech shortly after the tragic shooting at the Pulse nightclub in Orlando, Trump's style and tone matched his aggressive argument style in the Detroit debate (Jan, 2016). Given that Trump never paid a price for his debate strategy in the primary debates, it seems rather unlikely that he will reverse course now, particularly in a format where keeping on script will be very difficult.

If Trump continues to use debate tactics like the ones we saw in the Detroit debate, it would seem unwise for Clinton to directly engage these aggressive tactics. As the Detroit debate demonstrates, diving into the fray with Trump only harms the credibility of the person we expect to act in a more controlled and professional manner. If she should model her response to Trump from anyone, she should follow the example set by Kasich, who refused to answer questions that attempted to bait him into blow-for-blow exchanges with Trump as he transcended those moments to discuss his achievements. The difficulty for Kasich was that he received very little airtime during debates because he was competing with four other candidates; Clinton will not have this problem. Moreover, Cruz had his best debates when he chose to largely stay away from Trump's antics, further demonstrating the success of this tactic.

The best play for Clinton in the general election debates will be to preserve and enhance her appearance as presidential and trustworthy. Given her background, she already enters the debates with a considerable amount of extrinsic credibility in areas such as competence, empathy, and leadership, particularly in foreign policy matters (Dann, 2016). However, the weak spot for Clinton's credibility is her character, particularly in terms of trustworthiness. While Clinton would like to run a "high-minded, policy-focused campaign," she has "a more visceral problem. Voters just don't trust her" (Chozick, 2016). This problem has only grown worse as more reports have come out about her questionable use of email as Secretary of State (Chozick, 2016). In confronting this problem, it would be disastrous if she engaged Trump during debates in ways that allowed him to make the small sound-bite friendly jabs that he favored against Rubio in the Detroit debate. Instead, Clinton should use other speeches and paid media to improve her extrinsic trustworthiness to an extent that Trump's ad hominem attacks–e.g., "Lyin' Hillary"–ring hollow in comparison. In response to these jabs during the debates, it would be wise if Clinton refused to engage them and simply used them as an opportunity to discuss her credentials, leadership capabilities, and her specific policies. Instead, the response to attacks and counterattacks are best left to campaign allies and surrogates such as former President Bill Clinton, President Barack Obama, and Senator Elizabeth Warren, who lose little in such exchanges with Trump. Unlike Trump's campaign, Clinton has allies who can bombard Trump on a daily basis and erode his extrinsic credibility; Clinton should ignore the attacks and engage issues and themes on her own ground.

References

Allen, C. (2016, March 4). Top takeaways from the Detroit Republican debate. *USA Today.* Retrieved from http://www.usatoday.com/story/news/politics/onpolitic s/2016/03/04/takeaways-detroit-republican-debate-trump-cruz-rubio-kasich/81298794

Benoit, W., & Benoit, P. (2008). Persuasive messages: The process of influence. Malden, MA: Wiley-Blackwell.

Bruni, F. (2016, March 3). Five big questions after a vulgar Republican debate. *The New York Times.* Retrieved from http://www.nytimes.com/2016/03/03/opinion/five-big-questions-after-a-vulgar-republican-debate.html

Chozick, A. (2016, May 25). Emails add to Hillary Clinton's central problem: voters just don't trust her. *The New York Times.* Retrieved from http://www.nytimes.com/2016/05/26/us/politics/hillary -clinton-emails-campaign-trust.html

Cillizza, C. (2016, March 3). Winners and losers from the 11th Republican presidential debate. *The Washington Post.* Retrieved from https://www.washingtonpost.com/news/the-fix/wp/2016/03/03/winners-and-losers-from-the-11th-republican-presidential-debate

Dann, C. (2016, June 2). NBC/WSJ polling shows Clinton with foreign policy advantage. *NBC News.* Retrieved from http://www.nbcnews.com/politics/2016-election/nbc-wsj-polling-shows-clinton-foreign-policy-advantage-n584536

Detroit News. (2016, March 3). Poll: debate Detroit's debate. Retrieved from http://content-static.detroitnews.com/pages/polls/detroit-gop-debate-poll.htm

Graham, D. (2016, March 4). Motor City meltdown. *The Atlantic*. Retrieved from http://www.theatlantic.com/politics/archive/2016/03/republican-debate-detroit/472245

Iyengar, S., Luskin, R. C., & Fishkin, A. J. (2004, April 23-24). Deliberative public opinion in presidential primaries: evidence from the Online Deliberative Poll. Paper presented at the Voice and Citizenship: Re-thinking Theory and Practice in Political Communication conference, Seattle, WA. Paper retrieved from https://pcl.stanford.edu/common/docs/research/iyengar/2004/primaries.pdf

Jan, T. (2016, June 15). Trump's staying the same–and that worries the GOP. *The Boston Globe*. Retrieved from https://www.bostonglobe.com/news/politics/2016/06/14/donald-trump-general-election-new-boss-same-old-boss/yXxgpCfAQ40klZSNnIwGON/story.html

Jeffers, G. (2016, March 2). Cruz, Rubio expected to come gunning for Trump at Detroit debate. *Dallas Morning News*. Retrieved from http://www.dallasnews.com/news/politics/headlines/20160302-cruz-rubio-expected-to-come-gunning-for-trump-at-detroit-debate.ece

Jones, V. (2015, October 26). Trump: the social media president? *CNN News*. Retrieved from http://www.cnn.com/2015/10/26/opinions/jones-trump-social-media

Kinder, D. (1986). Presidential character revisited. In R. Lau & D. Sears (Eds.), *Political cognition: the 19th annual Carnegie Symposium on cognition*. Hillsdale, NJ: Erlbaum.

Lee, M. J. (2016, March 4). Republican debate turns dirty. *CNN*. Retrieved from http://www.cnn.com/2016/03/03/politics/republican-debate-highlights

Newsmax. (2016, March 4). Trump dominating Newsmax TV GOP debate poll. Retrieved from http://www.newsmax.com/Headline/Donald-Trump-Ted-Cruz-GOP-debate-Newsmax-TV-poll/2016/03/04/id/717379

O'Keefe, E. (2016, March 3). Mitt Romney slams 'phony' Trump: He's playing 'the American public for suckers'. *Washington Post*. Retrieved from https://www.washingtonpost.com/news/post-politics/wp/2016/03/03/mitt-romney-trump-is-a-phony-a-fraud-who-is-playing-the-american-public-for-suckers

Rutenberg, J. (2016, June 5). The Trump show, a hit for now, face a test in the fall. *The New York Times*. Retrieved from http://www.nytimes.com/2016/06/06/business/media/can-trump-productions-content-be-a-kingmaker.html?_r=0

Peters, G., & Woolley, J.T. (2016, March 3). Presidential candidates debates: "Republican candidates debate in Detroit, Michigan." The American Presidency Project.

Retrieved from
http://www.presidency.ucsb.edu/ws/?pid=111711

Schoen, D. E. (2016, March 4). A rattled Trump debates in Detroit. Kasich, Cruz are night's big winners. *Fox News*. Retrieved from http://www.foxnews.com/opinion/2016/03/04/presidential-donald-trump-skips-gop-debate-kasich-cruz-walk-away-as-winners.html

Schwarz, H. (2015, July 17). The art of the political flip-flop. *The Washington Post*. Retrieved from https://www.washingtonpost.com/news/the-fix/wp/2015/07/17/the-art-of-the-political-flip-flop

Voorhees, J. (2016, March 3). The Fox News debate was ugly, rowdy, and immature. Of course Trump won. *Slate*. Retrieved from http://www.slate.com/blogs/the_slatest/2016/03/03/the_fox_new_debate_in_detroit_was_ugly_and_immature_of_course_trump_won.html

Weber, P. (2016, March 3). Frank Luntz's Fox News GOP focus group crowns John Kasich winner of March 3 debate. *The Week*. Retrieved from http://theweek.com/speedreads/ 610373/frank-luntzs-fox-news-gop-focus-group-crowns-john-kasich-winner-march-3-debate

Wolf, Z. B. (2012, October 1). The 12 most cringe-worthy debate moments in history. *ABC News*. Retrieved from http://abcnews.go.com/Politics/OTUS/12-cringe-worthy-debate-moments/story?id=17367100#6

CHAPTER TWELVE

<<<<<<<<<<<<<<<<<<<<<<<◇>>>>>>>>>>>>>>>>>>>>>

GOP Primary Debate #12
Miami, Florida, March 10, 2016
Patrick Waldinger

<<<<<<<<<<<<<<<<<<<<<<<◇>>>>>>>>>>>>>>>>>>>>>

The election results from the slate of 16 primaries and caucuses held on March 1, 2016 buoyed Donald Trump's chances for the Republican presidential nomination. Ben Carson dropped out shortly after and only Ted Cruz, John Kasich, Marco Rubio and Donald Trump were left in the race. While the odds were looking good for Trump in early March, he had not yet reached the 1237 delegates needed to win the nomination. There were still several important Republican primaries and caucuses, and three determined candidates, between Trump and the Republican nomination for President.

In the previous chapter, Young (2016) discussed the 11th Republican primary debate on March 3 in Detroit. The Detroit debate had many points of interest, but it will always be known for its lack of civility. With media headlines such as, "The Detroit GOP debate was presidential politics' worst day ever" (Marcus, 2016),

"Detroit Republican Debate: An Ugly Train Wreck" (Alberta, 2016) and "The Fox News Debate Was Ugly, Rowdy, and Immature. Of Course Trump Won." (Vorhees, 2016), the concern was that the Republican primary debaters were derailing focus away from the issues toward personal insults.

In the week after the Detroit debate, Trump won a majority of the delegates in the Republican primaries and caucuses. Despite big wins in the first two weeks of March, as of March 9, Trump had earned 458 delegates—only about 37% of the delegates he needed to win the nomination—whereas, Cruz was second with 359 delegates (Collins, 2016). Trump, however, did have a lot of momentum heading into the March 15 primaries, which included the delegate-rich states of Florida and Ohio.

The Florida and Ohio primaries offered several unique challenges to Trump as a frontrunner. First, Florida and Ohio's combined delegate count was 165, accounting for roughly 6.6% of the overall total delegates and a little more than 13% of delegates any candidate would need to win the nomination. Second, despite there being only four candidates left in the race, two of them were from these states. Rubio was the junior Senator from Florida and

Kasich was the Governor of Ohio. Finally, the Florida and Ohio primaries were the first, and largest, winner-take-all states of the contest. If Trump could win one or both of these states, he would likely have the momentum to win the nomination. If Trump lost both, his path to the nomination would be a lot more difficult (Balz, 2016a).

It was with this backdrop that on Thursday, March 10, CNN, Salem Radio and the Washington Times sponsored the 12th Republican primary debate hosted at the University of Miami. Jake Tapper of CNN was the head moderator. Tapper's co-moderators were CNN Chief Political Correspondent Dana Bash, Stephen Dinan from the Washington Times and Hugh Hewitt of Salem Radio.

Unlike the affair in Detroit, the Miami debate took a turn away from insults and focused on debating the issues. The contrast between the two debates offers ample opportunity to analyze the issues discussed and the media's reaction to the Miami debate. Given the potential political costs of a poor debate performance, the Miami debate provides an excellent opportunity to analyze Donald Trump as a debater – both in terms of style and substance.

In addition, the Miami debate was Trump's final official debate before he squares off with Hillary Clinton on September 26 in the first Presidential debate, because Trump withdrew from the Fox News' March 21 debate in Salt Lake City, Utah. The Miami debate, then, becomes the last opportunity to analyze Trump's strategy and what it might foreshadow for the Presidential debates.

Issues in the Miami Debate

The Miami debate, more so than any of the other Republican primary debates, focused on the issues. Interestingly, though, the biggest "issue" of the night was the debate's civility. A little more than a half an hour into the debate, during an exchange between Cruz and Trump on Social Security that turned to immigration, Trump (2016) stated, "[S]o far I cannot believe how civil it's been up here." In many ways, civility was the meta-issue in the debate–an issue that influences all the others.

As a meta-issue in the debate, civility impacted the debate in two ways. First, the tone of the responses steered the candidates away from personal attacks for fear of sounding unappealing to the voters. Hinck, Hinck & Dailey (2008) explain the importance of politeness in political debates. They describe politeness as a "construct that audience members bring to debates and use to evaluate candidates" (Hinck et al., 2008, p. 7). Given audience expectations, the way the candidates treat each other has an influence on how an audience will perceive the candidates and the overall debate. The candidates were aware of the backlash after the Detroit debate and acted accordingly.

Second, given the lack of insults, there was plenty of time dedicated to discussing the issues in the debate. The Miami debate in many ways was the antithesis of the Detroit debate. With a winnowing field of only four candidates and more time to discuss policies, the audience really had a chance to assess the candidates' knowledge, or lack thereof, of the issues. Many of the questions in the debate were focused on policy specifics rather than having candidates defend against personal attacks.

A debate that focused on the issues showed that Trump was lacking in specific policy knowledge and details. When a debater does not have a strong depth of knowledge on the issues, he or she should try to bring the debate back to issues that are his or her core strengths. Throughout the Miami debate, Trump used this strategy when pressed for policy specifics.

Trump has two core strengths he consistently relies upon. First, Trump talks about reasons why only he would make a great President–specifically, that only he can fix the problems of the current system because he knows them the best and that he has the ability to make great deals for America. Second, Trump talks about issues that matter a lot to Americans, specifically regarding economic security, such as, jobs, trade, wage depression, taxes and immigration.

During the first question in the Miami debate, which combined the issues of trade, immigration and jobs, Trump used the opportunity to express that only he can effectively change the system. Tapper asked Trump about the potential hypocrisy of running as a candidate for the domestic worker while running businesses that bring in foreign workers and manufactures from other countries. Trump (2016) responded that people should trust him because "nobody knows the system better than me." Trump (2016) admitted he used these laws but acknowledges they need to change, saying, "I'm the one that knows how to change it. Nobody else... knows how to change it like I do, believe me."

Trump's core strength about making better deals for America was certainly a theme Trump focused on in the Miami debate. In fact, Trump mentioned the great deals he would make for America 23 times in the Miami debate. In any other previous debate, the maximum number of times he mentioned his deal making skills was seven (Zhong, 2016). Specifically, on the issues of Social Security and Cuba, you can see Trump's pivot away from specific policies and toward his deal making acumen.

On Social Security, Dana Bash asked Trump for specifics on what he would do to prevent Social Security from running out of money in 20 years. Trump (2016) vowed to leave Social Security alone but promised he will, "[M]ake this country rich again; to bring back our jobs; to get rid of deficits; to get rid of waste, fraud and abuse." Bash challenged Trump, explaining that getting rid of fraud and abuse would only save $3 billion of the $150 billion needed to make Social Security solvent and asked where he would make up the rest. Trump, then, talked about how the United States military protects many countries and gets nothing in return. To make up the deficit, Trump (2016) said, "We're going to negotiate real deals now, and we're going to bring the wealth back to our country."

On a policy that is especially important in Miami given its large Cuban-American population, the candidates were asked about the United States' policy toward Cuba, specifically Obama's recent rapprochement. Bash asked

Trump whether he would continue diplomatic relations with Cuba if he were President. Again, Trump (2016) pointed out that the current deal Obama made with Cuba was bad, and added the Iran deal as well, saying, "I would want to make a good deal, I would want to make a strong, solid, good deal because right now, everything is in Cuba's favor ... the same ... as the Iran deal." Unfortunately, while there was lot of talk of bad deals, there was not much in the way of substance to explain what exactly a good deal is for America and how Trump would be able to negotiate it.

The most memorable issues in the debate surrounding Trump were his attacks on Islam and criticism of the recent violence at his rallies. Trump was asked about his statement in an interview with Anderson Cooper the night before the Miami debate that "Islam hates us" (Schlefier, 2016). Tapper (2016) asked Trump specifically, "Did you mean all 1.6 billion Muslims," to which Trump (2016) replied, "I mean a lot of them." For Trump, his attacks on Islam are tied to immigration. He has called for a moratorium on Muslims immigrating to the United States because of this supposed hatred (Campbell, 2016).

Trump focused the question of whether or not he encourages violence back to some of his core strengths:

trade, taxes and jobs. Tapper asked about an incident that occurred earlier on the day of the debate–when one of Trump's supporters sucker-punched a protester at a Trump rally in North Carolina. Tapper (2016) asked Trump, "Do you believe that you've done anything to create a tone where this kind of violence would be encouraged?" Unlike the answer to the Islam question, Trump tried to walk back some of his previous rhetoric and stated, "I hope not. I truly hope not." Trump, then, tried to explain the root cause of some of the anger his supporters display. Trump was very good about placing the locus of the anger on issues he promises to fix. Trump (2016) said, "They don't like seeing bad trade deals, they don't like seeing higher taxes, they don't like seeing a loss of their jobs."

Media's Reaction

After the Miami debate, the media covered a few different stories. Much of the media's analysis was about how civil the debate was, especially compared to the Detroit debate one week earlier (Altman & Miller, 2016; Hemmingway, 2016; Johnson, 2016). Several sources pointed out that the more civil tone opened up a debate on the issues, rather than insults (Appelbaum, 2016; Newmyer, 2016). While most praised a return to civility, there were some analysts who pointed out that the more civil Miami debate was boring and, therefore, bad for ratings (Barry, 2016; Whalen, 2016).

Perhaps it is obvious that the Miami debate was much more civil than the previous one, but the fact that Trump mentioned it in the debate only made it more so. Many sources pointed out Trump's own words about how civil the debate was (Benac & Bykowicz, 2016; Newmyer, 2016). In fact, before the debate even began, Trump promised a "softer" debate (Holland, 2016). While it would have been difficult to have a debate more unruly than Detroit, save a fistfight breaking out, it turns out Trump's prophecy was correct. Trump was already trying to set the media narrative before the first question was even asked.

An interesting media take was the distinction between civility in tone and substance of the debate (Lee, 2016; Ornstein, 2016). While the tone of the debate was very civil, i.e., the candidates did not resort to insults, the substance of the debate was anything but. Specifically, the discussions of whether all Muslims hate America and the violence at Trump rallies show the dichotomy in the tone and substance. While Trump was polite saying it, arguing that most members of a religion are violent and hate

America and encouraging violence against protesters at rallies, is anything but.

In political debates, the media tries to identify winners and losers. The media's reaction to the Miami debate was mixed. Since there was a focus on the substance, the media had a difficult time determining a clear winner. With a more subdued Trump and a lack of direct attacks on him, several outlets reported that Trump won simply by not losing (Decker, 2016; Lee, 2016; Stanage, 2016). There were even some media outlets that said Trump both won and lost the debate (Cillizza, 2016; Morrissey, 2016). Trump was said to win the debate because he did not harm his frontrunner status. However, Trump lost the debate because he did not show he had a command of the issues.

One other issue reported on after the Miami debate was that Trump was hinting about not debating the final Republican primary debate on March 21 in Salt Lake City. Immediately after the Miami debate, CNN interviewed Trump who said, "[W]e've had enough of the debates, wouldn't you say?" (Associated Press, 2016) Trump, in fact, used the civil tone of the Miami debate to help make his argument for canceling the Salt Lake City debate. On March 12, the day after the Miami debate, Trump referenced the tone of the Miami debate and said, "It would be nice to finish off with this one" (Alter, 2016).

In the morning of March 16, just one day after Trump won every primary the previous night except Ohio, he announced on Twitter that he would not attend the Salt Lake City debate (Canham, 2016). Upon hearing the news that Trump was not going to attend the debate, Kasich dropped out and Fox News promptly canceled the debate without ever hearing from Cruz (Canham, 2016). Thus, the Miami debate became the last official debate Trump participated in before the Presidential debates.

Trump's Debate Strategy

Trump's debate strategy was clear from the beginning: he was trying to win the debate by not losing. Given that Trump had already won 30% of the vote and was leading in Florida, he had the luxury of playing it safe in the debate. (Tapper, 2016) Much like the hyped Floyd Mayweather and Manny Pacquiao boxing match in May of 2015, many tuned into the Miami debate expecting a lot action, especially coming off the heels of the Detroit debate. Instead, like the Mayweather-Pacquiao fight, what we saw was Trump, like Mayweather, get ahead on points and play defense the entire time (Eligon, 2015). Trump knew he did not have to knock out his opponents; he just needed to make sure he did not get hit too hard. Make no mistake, though, like the boxing match, Trump was ready to attack if he needed to.

As we saw above, the media deemed Trump the winner because he did not lose. As the frontrunner, his strategy for the debate changed radically–he no longer needed to go on the offensive (no pun intended) to win the debate (Balz, 2016b; Bender & Kapur, 2016; Crilly, 2016). This strategy is common for frontrunners in political debates. If a candidate is the frontrunner, then he or she tends to view debates as a burden or, even, a trap. A frontrunner is afraid that any gaffe could cost him or her, but as a candidate trailing, he or she views debates as an opportunity to score some political points and gain momentum (Perry, 2016).

In many ways the strategy Trump took in the Miami debate was the antithesis of the way he had run his campaign and his previous debate performances. Trump's style is brash and in-your-face. He is often unapologetic in his views and usually comes out swinging, metaphorically. The outsized influence of Florida and Ohio likely caused

Trump to tread more cautiously. There was still much to lose if Trump had a poor debate performance.

In addition, Trump took a more genteel approach to the debate to help his argument that he will help unite the party, not divide it. A close look at Trump's opening and closing statements in the debate show that he was making the case that the Republican Party should rally around him as the nominee. In his opening statement, Trump (2016) explains how he has mobilized millions of enthusiastic voters to the Republican Party:

> "One of the biggest political events anywhere in the world is happening right now with the Republican Party. Millions and millions of people are going out to the polls and they're voting.... I think, frankly, the Republican establishment, or whatever you want to call it, should embrace what's happening."

In Trump's (2016) closing statement, he encourages the Republicans to embrace the new political movement and unify around him:

> "The Republican Party has a great chance to embrace millions of people that it's never

known before. They're coming by the millions. We should seize that opportunity…. So I just say embrace these millions of people that now for the first time ever love the Republican Party. And unify. Be smart and unify."

Trump realized that a more civil tone was necessary to help unite the party around him. Trump could see the nomination within his grasp. He not only took a subdued approach to the debate to prevent his opponents from gaining momentum but also to help shift toward uniting the party around his nomination. Trump could not keep using insults like "Little Marco" and "Lyin' Ted" and expect Rubio and Cruz supporters to embrace his nomination with open arms. Instead, Trump tried to take a more conciliatory tone to look more magnanimous to the Republican voters. While it is possible to debate the overall effectiveness of Trump embracing a unifying message, there can be no doubt that an aggressive Trump in the debate but a unifying Trump in the opening and closing statements would make unification more difficult, if not impossible.

Foreshadowing the Presidential Debates

Looking forward to the Presidential debates between Clinton and Trump, what, if any, lessons can we learn from the Miami debate? There are four big takeaways from the Miami debate: 1) Trump's "winning by not losing" strategy is unlikely to be employed in the Presidential debates, 2) Trump lacks serious knowledge of the policy issues, 3) to make up for the lack of knowledge he relies on his core strengths, and 4) Trump does have the ability to reign himself in and have a civil debate.

The first lesson is that Trump's "winning by not losing" strategy is unlikely to be employed in the Presidential debates. Unlike the Republican primary debates where there were several candidates to share the airtime, the Presidential debates focus on you and your opponent. The debates will likely be one-on-one, unless a third party candidate happens to get 15% of the vote, which seems unlikely (Scher, 2016). Trump simply does not have the luxury of debating passively when the spotlight is on him. For every answer Clinton gives, Trump is expected to respond. There will be one winner and one loser in the debate. This means that Trump either needs to debate aggressively or the voters and media will deem Trump the loser.

Second, the Miami debate showed that Trump has limited policy knowledge of the issues. Even when the moderators challenged Trump to explain further, Trump went back to his core issues, lacking policy nuance. The lack of specific policy knowledge would hurt Trump in a one-on-one debate, especially against Clinton. She is known as a policy wonk–someone who knows a lot about the details. The audience could see a glaring difference and think that Clinton is more prepared for the job and vote accordingly.

Third, when Trump is pressed for specifics on his policy proposals he often brings the debate back to his core strengths. Clinton needs to be aware that Trump will attempt to pivot many of issues in the debates. On domestic issues, Trump will try to bring the issues back to economic security. On foreign issues, Trump will try to explain that the United States is weak because of bad deals negotiated in the past. Trump will paint himself as a great dealmaker. So far, Trump has shown that he does not need policy specifics if he tells the audience what they want to hear (Appelbaum, 2016).

Regardless, Trump should study policy issues and be prepared to debate the substance. Given that there is just over six months between the last Republican primary debate and first Presidential debate, it is possible that Trump could become familiar enough with the policy specifics to have a substantive debate. Trump is unlikely to win a one-on-one in a debate with Clinton on the issues; however, showing some proficiency might allay fears that he is not fit for the presidency.

The final lesson is that Trump has the ability to rein it in and have a civil debate. The media can now hold Trump to a higher standard for the debates. If Trump leads the debates to an ugly place, some will likely comment that it is just "Trump being Trump." However, the media's reporting after such a Presidential debate could include mention of how Trump intentionally chose to eschew civility, since the Miami debate shows he can be civil if he wants to be. The negative media coverage could outweigh any advantage Trump gets from being ill-mannered.

Trump needs to be careful about the insults he pursues in the debates. Trump has not been shy calling Clinton "Crooked Hillary." If the audience is looking for the Presidential debates to show who is more presidential, then insults could really backfire. Direct insults would likely offend an audience that is wider than the Republican base

Trump was focusing on in the primary debates. Trump does not need to attack Clinton directly in the debates. Trump has many surrogates and other opportunities, such as, television advertisements to get that message across before November.

Clinton should prepare for hostile debates, should they come to that. In many ways, Trump defies the conventional wisdom of what a Presidential candidate can get away with saying. The more Clinton can explain that Trump's temperament, while possibly appealing or entertaining, cannot function in the Oval Office on the day-to-day issues of the job, the better off she will be with voters.

As the Miami debate shows, it is not enough to just point out Trump's seeming lack of knowledge and details on many issues. Trump has done well by addressing questions many voters have with America's future. The challenge is answering the meta-issues relating to economic insecurity and foreign policy strategy, especially when they are offered as truisms rather than specific policy proposals. On these issues, Clinton would be wise to not only point out Trump's lack of specifics but to get ahead of the debate and offer her own policies and experience to the voters.

While it seems unlikely, Clinton should also be prepared for Trump acting passively in the debates to make it appear that she is the aggressor. If the narrative becomes that Clinton is the bully, then the media may report on the style of the debates, rather than the substance. Since Clinton is very policy-focused, more media attention of style distracts voters from her core strengths. In the end, Clinton needs to prepare for both a naughty and nice version of Trump, or somewhere in between, in the debates.

Donald Trump ended up winning Florida and losing Ohio on March 15. Rubio, after failing to win his own state, quickly dropped out of the race. Of Trump's two remaining Republican opponents, neither Cruz nor Kasich could get enough momentum to overtake Trump for the nomination. Trump won the Republican nomination for President and is scheduled to square off against Hillary Clinton in three Presidential debates, starting on September 26.

The 12th and final Republican primary debate in Miami was a fascinating one. In the Miami debate, we all got to see Trump debate like he never has before, literally. Trump set a civil tone that no opponent really dared to challenge. We saw a Trump looking to unite a party, rather than maintain cleavages. We got to see a debate on the issues rather than character. Trump failed to impress in his answers to the policy questions but his demeanor and focus on his core issues allowed him to survive the debate without much damage.

Before the Miami debate, we saw Trump debate in an aggressive and bombastic way. In Miami, we saw a Trump who debated in a more subdued, civil and conciliatory style. So which Trump will show up in the Presidential debates against Clinton? While we are likely to see Trump on the attack with a less civil tone, given the dynamic nature of Trump's debating style, the Presidential debates are must-see television. You can be assured that no matter his strategy, many people will be watching when Hillary takes her turn debating The Donald.

References

Alberta, T. (2016, March 4). Detroit Republican Debate: An Ugly Train Wreck. *National Review*. Retrieved from http://www.nationalreview.com/article/432348/detroit-debate-republican-train-wreck-gets-ugly

Alter, C. (2016, March 11). Donald Trump: 'We've Had Enough Debates'. *Time*. Retrieved from http://time.com/4256083/donald-trump-skip-republican-debate-salt-lake-city

Altman, A., & Miller, Z.J. (2016, March 11). Why Republicans Pulled Their Punches at the Debate. *Time*.

Retrieved from http://time.com/4255204/republican-debate-miami-twelfth-miami-analysis

Appelbaum, Y. (2016, March 10). Trump's Popular Appeal. *The Atlantic.* Retrieved from http://www.theatlantic.com/politics/archive/2016/03/republican-debate-miami/473307

Associated Press. (2016, March 10). Donald Trump says he'd had enough with these weekly GOP presidential face-offs. *U.S. News & World Report.* Retrieved from http://www.usnews.com/news/politics/articles/2016-03-10/the-latest-oh-state-coach-meyer-backs-kasich-in-gop-race

Balz, D. (2016b, March 10). A subdued Trump plays it safe; rivals say his policies don't add up. *Washington Post.* Retrieved from https://www.washingtonpost.com/politics/a-subdued-trump-plays-it-safe-rivals-say-his-policies-dont-add-up/2016/03/10/5964a366-e6d8-11e5-b0fd-073d5930a7b7_story.html?hpid=hp_hp-top-table-main_take-1117pm%3Ahomepage%2Fstory

Balz, D. (2016a, March 8). As Trump rolls again, opposition has one week to stop him.

Washington Post. Retrieved from https://www.washingtonpost.com/politics/as-trump-rolls-again-opposition-has-one-week-to-stop-him/2016/03/08/2d60c582-e53a-11e5-b0fd-073d5930a7b7_story.html

Barry, D. (2016, March 11). Finally, a GOP debate on the issues! Zzzzzzzz… *Miami Herald.* Retrieved from http://www.miamiherald.com/living/liv-columns-blogs/dave-barry/article65445777.html

Benac, N., & Bykowicz, J. (2016, March 10). Trump, GOP rivals rumble — politely — in crucial debate. *Las Vegas Review Journal.* Retrieved from http://www.reviewjournal.com/politics/elections/trump-gop-rivals-rumble-politely-crucial-debate

Bender, M.C., & Kapur, S. (2016, March 11). Donald Trump, Fierce in Past Debates, Shows His Cautious Side. *Bloomberg Politics.* Retrieved from http://www.bloomberg.com/politics/articles/2016-03-11/donald-trump-fierce-in-past-debates-shows-his-cautious-side

Campbell, C. (2016, March 10). TRUMP: 'Islam hates us'. *Business Insider.* Retrieved from http://www.businessinsider.com/donald-trump-islam-hates-us-2016-3

Canham, M. (2016, March 17). Debate scrapped after Donald Trump says he won't show in Salt Lake City, and Kasich follows suit. *Salt Lake City Tribune.* Retrieved from http://www.sltrib.com/home/3669839-155/donald-trump-says-he-wont-show

Cillizza, C. (2016, March 10). Winners and losers from the 12th Republican presidential debate. *Washington Post.* Retrieved from https://www.washingtonpost.com/news/the-fix/wp/2016/03/10/winners-and-losers-from-the-12th-republican-presidential-debate

Collins, E. (2016, March 9). Delegate count: Who has what? *Politico.* Retrieved from http://www.politico.com/story/2016/03/how-many-delegates-do-2016-candidates-have-220484

Crilly, R. (2016, March 11). Republican debate: Donald Trump strikes moderate tone with eye on general election. *The Telegraph.* Retrieved from http://www.telegraph.co.uk/news/worldnews/us-election/12190597/Republican-debate-CNN-Miami-Donald-Trump.html

Dailey, W.O, Hinck, E.A., & Hinck, S.S. (2008).*Politeness in Presidential Debates: Shaping political face in campaign debates from 1960 to 2004.* New York, NY: Rowman & Littlefield.

Decker, C. (2016, March 11). An intently civil Republican debate fails to dethrone Donald Trump. Will anything? *Los Angeles Times*. Retrieved from http://www.latimes.com/politics/la-na-republican-debate-analysis-20160311-story.html

Elgion, J. (2016, May 3). A Letdown for the Masses, but a Treat for Aficionados. *New York Times.* Retrieved from http://www.nytimes.com/2015/05/04/sports/mayweathers-defensive-tactics-frustrate-pacquiao.html?_r=0

Hemmingway, M. (2016, March 11). 5 Quick Takeaways From Last Night's GOP Debate In Miami. *The Federalist.* Retrieved from http://thefederalist.com/2016/03/11/5-quick-takeaways-from-last-nights-gop-debate-in-miami

Holland, S. (2016, March 10). Republicans may generate less heat at Miami debate. *Reuters.* Retrieved from http://www.reuters.com/article/us-usa-election-republicans-idUSMTZSAPEC3ATLMWMB

Johnson, E. (2016, March 11). A Low-Energy Debate in Miami. *National Review*. Retrieved from http://www.nationalreview.com/article/432662/miami-republican-debate-donald-trump-and-rivals-avoid-attacks

Lee, T.B. (2016, March 11). 3 winners and 3 losers from Thursday night's Republican debate. *Vox.* Retrieved from http://www.vox.com/2016/3/11/11200318/republican-debate-miami-trump

Marcus, R. (2016, March 4). The Detroit GOP debate was presidential politics' worst day ever. *Washington Post.* Retrieved from https://www.washingtonpost.com/opinions/the-detroit-gop-debate-was-presidential-politics-worst-day-ever/2016/03/04/9c78e858-e235-11e5-8d98-4b3d9215ade1_story.html?utm_term=.7630924424a0

Morrissey, E. (2016, March 10). GOP debate winners and losers — the envelope please... *Hot Air.* Retrieved from http://hotair.com/archives/2016/03/10/gop-debate-winners-and-losers-the-envelope-please

Newmyer, T. (2016, March 10). Who Won the Republican Debate? *Fortune.* Retrieved from http://fortune.com/2016/03/10/who-won-the-republican-debate-8

Ornstein, N. (2016, March 11). How the GOP Debate in Miami Changed the Race. *Newsweek.* Retrieved from http://www.newsweek.com/trump-rubio-republicans-gop-debate-miami-cruz-kasich-tapper-bash-hewitt-dinan-435967

Perry, D. (2016, March 3). Why the next Republican debate matters: Donald Trump rivals' last stand (time, channel, analysis). *The Oregonian.* Retrieved from http://www.oregonlive.com/today/index.ssf/2016/03/why_the_next_republican_debate.html

Scher, B. (2016, August 16). Did Gary Johnson just get boxed out of the debates? *Politico.* Retrieved from http://www.politico.com/magazine/story/2016/08/gary-johnson-debates-214168

Schlefier, T. (2016, March 10). Donald Trump: 'I think Islam hates us'. *CNN*. Retrieved from http://www.cnn.com/2016/03/09/politics/donald-trump-islam-hates-us

Stanage, N. (2016, March 11). GOP debate winners and losers. *The Hill*. Retrieved from http://thehill.com/homenews/campaign/272650-gop-debate-winners-and-losers

Tapper, J. (2016, March 15). Transcript of Republican debate in Miami, full text [Debate transcript]. *CNN*. Retrieved from http://www.cnn.com/2016/03/10/politics/republican-debate-transcript-full-text

Trump, D. (2016, March 15). Transcript of Republican debate in Miami, full text [Debate transcript]. *CNN*. Retrieved from http://www.cnn.com/2016/03/10/politics/republican-debate-transcript-full-text

Vorhees, J. (2016, March 3). The Fox News Debate Was Ugly, Rowdy, and Immature. Of Course Trump Won. *Slate*. Retrieved from http://www.slate.com/blogs/the_slatest/2016/03/03/the_fox_new_debate_in_detroit_was_ugly_and_immature_of_course_trump_won.html

Whalen, B. (2016, March 10). Republican Debate Lessons: A Tame Trump Makes For Lame TV. *Forbes*. Retrieved from http://www.forbes.com/sites/billwhalen/2016/03/10/the-republican-debate-in-miami-a-tame-trump-makes-for-lame-tv/#174e98a94e44

Young, K (2016). GOP Primary Debate #11. In A. Kall, editor, Debating The Donald.

Zhong, W. (2016, March 11). How the GOP Debate in Miami Changed the Race. *Newsweek*. Retrieved from http://www.newsweek.com/trump-rubio-republicans-gop-debate-miami-cruz-kasich-tapper-bash-hewitt-dinan-435967

CONCLUSION

<<<<<<<<<<<<<<<<<<<<<O>>>>>>>>>>>>>>>>>>>

Aaron Kall

<<<<<<<<<<<<<<<<<<<<<O>>>>>>>>>>>>>>>>>>>

The March 10 debate in Miami marked the end of the Republican primary debate season for Trump. The civil and substance-based affair was a nice conclusion to eight months of sharp exchanges and zingers. In some ways it was his finest debate and represented a stark contrast from the Detroit debacle. Trump acknowledged as much in a press conference the following day by complimenting the Miami event and expressing disdain for any additional primary debates. When reminded of the Salt Lake City debate scheduled for March 21, he feigned ignorance, and it was canceled a few days later because of a scheduling conflict with the American Israel Public Affairs Committee Policy Conference in Washington, D.C. Ted Cruz challenged Trump to debates in Pennsylvania, Wisconsin, and Indiana to no avail. He briefly flirted debating Bernie Sanders for charity on the eve of the California primary, but quickly reversed course on this pledge.

Trump's had a love-hate relationship with debates, and this will likely continue through the fall. He appeared on

CNBC's *Squawk Box* on May 5 to proclaim that he won every single primary debate. Trump offered faint praise to Secretary Clinton, who he described as "not a bad debater." He said there was a lot going on in the world, and perhaps there should be more than the typical three debates during the general election. Trump's tune changed a bit in late July while criticizing the Commission on Presidential Debates for scheduling two debates opposite National Football League games. He floated the possibility of a conspiracy to limit the debate audience size with no supporting evidence. In early August, Trump said that certain moderators would be unacceptable, and participation could be conditioned upon several factors.

The Republican and Democratic primary debates of the 2016 election cycle attracted a total of nearly 250 million viewers, and a tremendous amount of excitement exists for the trio of debates scheduled between Trump and Clinton: Hofstra University (September 26), Washington University in St. Louis (October 9), and University of Nevada, Las Vegas (October 19). Despite the competing event between the Atlanta Falcons and New Orleans Saints on September 26, the inaugural presidential debate could garner close to 100 million viewers, which would approach Super Bowl-like television ratings. An estimated 67 million people watched the first debate between President Obama and Mitt Romney in 2012, and the star power of the two current candidates should have no trouble surpassing this impressive number. The Commission on Presidential Debates finally unveiled the slate of moderators on September 2, which is much later than usual. Trump's prior comments about fairness no doubt contributed to additional scrutiny. Lester Holt of NBC News, Anderson Cooper of CNN, Martha Raddatz of ABC News, and Chris Wallace of Fox News are all excellent selections, but they will certainly have their work cut out for them.

The winners and losers of this year's presidential debates will largely be determined by the expectations of the candidates set by the media and voters. Clinton is an experienced debater who has participated in dozens of contests and possesses a strong policy background as well. She participated in nine Democratic primary debates this cycle, 26 total debates during the 2008 election, and had three tangles with Rick Lazio while running for the Senate in 2000. Trump has only participated in a total of 11 debates ever and is considered to be a novice politician. He did an excellent job of lowering expectations before the Cleveland debate, while touting the distinguished political careers of many opponents. Trump was mostly successful during the primary debates, and his reality television star background helped assist with the reading of audiences and opponents. The expectations game will continue to be played by both campaigns until the debates are under way. George W. Bush and Sarah Palin both benefited from relatively low expectations and were perceived to have solid performances. Longtime friend Susie Tompkins Buell recently said Clinton's debate against Trump will resemble Serena Williams playing tennis with Chris Christie (Pace & Thomas, 2016). This is exactly the type of lofty expectation the Clinton campaign wants to avoid in order to maximize her chances of prevailing in the long run.

The unpredictability associated with the first debate at Hofstra University is the major reason so much anticipation surrounds the event. Trump last debated six months ago, and it's anyone's guess whether Miami Nice or the version from the first ten contests will appear on stage in New York. Trump has publicly said he would prefer not to attack Clinton but reserves the right to counterpunch if circumstances warrant. He engaged in several nasty exchanges with Rand Paul, Ted Cruz, Marco Rubio, and Jeb Bush during the primary debates, so Clinton must be well prepared for the emergence of this version of Trump. If Stephen Bannon and Roger Ailes continue to be involved in Trump's debate preparations, Clinton's mental and physical stamina, as well as past infidelities of President Bill Clinton could be on the table. Trump's worst moment in the primary debates came via a well-delivered zinger from Carly Fiorina during the Simi Valley debate. Rick Lazio's aggressive posture toward Clinton during their first Senate debate in New York completely backfired. Trump would be wise to tread carefully regarding this subject matter, especially considering some of his own personal vulnerabilities.

The structure and style of the three presidential debates will be especially fascinating. All the debates are 90 minutes in duration with no commercials or breaks. The moderators solely control the content of the questions and have autonomy for appropriate and substantial follow-ups. Clinton participated in five head-to-head debates with Sanders, six such debates with Obama in 2008, and three with Lazio in 2000. Conversely, Trump has never participated in a debate with fewer than four candidates. The largest amount of airtime he received in a primary debate was 30 minutes while in Houston. In several other debates, he spoke for approximately 10 minutes and was largely absent from the event for large stretches at a time because of the crowded stage. It doesn't appear that a third-party candidate will qualify for any of the general election debates, so Clinton certainly has the experience and advantage in this scenario.

Trump will also be lacking several arrows from his quiver that were of great assistance during the primary debates. He's now unable to brag about leads he once enjoyed in national and state polls. The self-funding of his campaign and aversion to super PACs was a popular line that can no longer be uttered. Trump picked fights with moderators and said audible boos in the crowd were from lobbyists and special interests. General election debate audiences are usually reserved and polite. When asked about the planned release of his tax returns by Hugh Hewitt during the Houston debate, Trump criticized the ratings of his radio show instead of answering the question. Tactics like this won't be successful with an esteemed moderator and respectful audience. Similar to the Trump campaign's general election pivot, his debate tactics must also adapt and moderate in order to be successful on the big stage.

Both Trump and Clinton have numerous vulnerabilities not thoroughly vetted during the primaries that will likely receive a new wave of scrutiny during the fall debates. Trump was largely given a pass on his temperament to be president by opponents like Bush, Cruz, and Fiorina, who said it should be left up to the voters. This issue has been a major focus of Clinton stump speeches and advertisements. Numerous former national security officials have publicly opposed Trump's candidacy because of behavioral and other concerns. Trump has tried to walk back his public bromance with Russian president Vladimir Putin, but this attempted distancing has been made tougher by the hacking of the Democratic National Committee and sordid relationship with former campaign chairman Paul Manafort. The hiring of people like Manafort, Bannon, Earl L. Phillip, and Corey Lewandowski casts serious doubts on Trump's hiring judgment. He claims to only hire the best and brightest, while criticizing current government employees for getting fleeced by other countries and their negotiators.

Although Trump committed numerous major errors during the primary debates, he never paid a tremendous political cost. He didn't have a firm grasp of the U.S. nuclear triad during the Las Vegas debate, thought China was part of the Trans-Pacific Partnership in the Milwaukee debate, and claimed his confusing of the Kurds and Quds Force was caused a mispronunciation during the Simi Valley debate. A Rick Perry-like gaffe while debating isn't an impossibility. Finally, Trump is vulnerable to flip-flopping. George W. Bush got a lot of mileage out of this charge against Massachusetts Senator John Kerry during the 2004 debates. Trump has switched positions on issues such as the assault weapons ban, raising the minimum wage, Syrian refugees, H-1B visas, the Iraq war, criminalizing abortion, the auto bailout, and so on. Such inconsistency on major policies hurts the brand of a candidate who continually repeats the phrase "believe me" during debates.

Clinton similarly has numerous shortcomings that weren't thoroughly explored in the Democratic primary debates. During the inaugural contest in Las Vegas, Sanders gave her a pass on the private server controversy by saying the American public was "sick and tired of hearing about the damn e-mails." Trump will not be as kind and likely rehash testimony from FBI Director James Comey regarding her being extremely careless in the handling of highly classified information. Favorable opinions of Clinton have recently hit a record low and the e-mail scandal and Clinton Foundation fallout are major contributors to this (Blake, 2016). It was recently announced that the Foundation will no longer accept corporate or foreign money if Clinton is elected president, but Trump will likely demand this process cease immediately. Other areas of vulnerability include free trade, the Iran nuclear deal, and even Clinton's record while a New York Senator. Although she has come out against the Trans-Pacific Partnership in its current form, there are some concerns bolstered by surrogates that she will switch positions on this issue once in the White House (Karni, 2016). Clinton will likely be tied to the alleged $400 million cash for hostage swap with Iran, even though she was no longer Secretary of State at the time, and Trump repeatedly erred about there being video footage of this transaction. Even her job creation record while a New York Senator could be scrutinized. There remains scant evidence that Clinton's economic development programs had a major impact on upstate employment in New York while a senator (Markon, 2016). Trump will attempt to contrast this with his successful business career and track record of creating tens of thousands of jobs. The New York setting of the first debate makes the raising of this particular issue more likely.

Just like Romney's impressive debate performance in Denver four years ago, Trump has the opportunity to fundamentally alter the trajectory of the race during the New York debate and given the location and connection to both candidates, he relishes this potential scenario. The respective political conventions offered a good preview of contrasting messages that will be conveyed on the debate stage. Trump argues that America is a mess and in real trouble, while Clinton strikes a more upbeat tone and says the country is already great. Following a general election pivot and major speech on immigration, the fall debates offer the opportunity for in-depth policy discussions that were severely lacking during the primaries because of a crowded field and abundance of moderators. It remains unclear which debate version of Trump will appear in New York, however, he will be ready and willing to counterpunch at a moment's notice, which continues to be his greatest strength on stage and a potential blind spot for Clinton. Trump may also have one final trick up his sleeve. During the Las Vegas debate, he announced that he wouldn't run for president as an independent, and at the conclusion of the Detroit debate, Trump said he would support the Republican nominee no matter who it was. Making news by deciding to release his tax returns, additional medical records, or the naming of Cabinet positions or judges during a debate wouldn't be totally unexpected. Debating The Donald never involves a dull moment, and that's precisely why millions will continue to view his debate performances from the edge of their seats wondering what will come next.

References

Blake, A. (2016, August 31). A record number of Americans now dislike Hillary Clinton. *Washington Post*. Retrieved from https://www.washingtonpost.com/news/the-fix/wp/2016/08/31/a-record-number-of-americans-now-dislike-hillary-clinton/

Karni, A. (2016, July 26). Clinton friend McAuliffe says Clinton will flip on TPP, then walks it back. *Politico.* Retrieved from http://www.politico.com/story/2016/07/terry-mcauliffe-hillary-clinton-tpp-trade-226253

Markon, J. (2016, August 7). As senator, Clinton promised 200,000 jobs in Upstate New York. Her efforts fell flat. *Washington Post*. Retrieved from https://www.washingtonpost.com/world/national-security/as-senator-clinton-promised-200000-jobs-in-upstate-new-york-her-efforts-fell-flat/2016/08/07/339d3384-58d2-11e6-831d-0324760ca856_story.html

Pace, J., & Thomas, K. (2016, August 24). Before debates, Clinton aims to keep Trump expectations high. *Associated Press*. Retrieved from http://bigstory.ap.org/article/5242ea5375f44871a2baa6 88ec19e70d/eyeing-debates-clinton-aims-keep-trump-expectations-high

ACKNOWLEDGEMENTS

This book is dedicated to my friend and mentor, Dr. J.W. Patterson of the University of Kentucky. He gave me the opportunity of a lifetime, and I owe much of my professional success to Dr. P, to whom I will forever be grateful. I would like to thank my wife Rachel for all her support and help with the book. As a former collegiate national champion debater, she never misses an opportunity to mention her 2-0 record against me. Rachel's own experience as an author was invaluable to the completion of this book. Thankfully, she introduced me to copy editor Helen Page, who did a terrific job in record time. Ronald and Arlene Kall are the greatest parents and role models. I will never forget their tremendous sacrifices. Finally, I would like to thank the eleven other contributors to the book. They are my friends and devoted a significant amount of time and energy to this project during their summers, which is greatly appreciated.

Patrick Waldinger wishes to thank Leandra Lopez for all her help and support in writing Chapter Twelve, the GOP Debate in Miami.

Cover art by Perry Elisabeth Design.

Photo of Donald J. Trump courtesy of Jared Wadley, University of Michigan News.

<<<<<<<<<<<<<<<<<<<O>>>>>>>>>>>>>>>>>>

COPYRIGHT

<<<<<<<<<<<<<<<<<<<O>>>>>>>>>>>>>>>>>>

<<<<<<<<<<<<<<<<<<<<<◇>>>>>>>>>>>>>>>>>>>>
CONTACT
<<<<<<<<<<<<<<<<<<<<<◇>>>>>>>>>>>>>>>>>>>>

Please direct any queries or comments to Aaron Kall:
akall@umich.edu

Follow us on Twitter @michigandebate

Please like our Facebook page:
facebook.com/UMichDebate

For more information see: www.michigandebate.com

<<<<<<<<<<<<<<<<<<<O>>>>>>>>>>>>>>>>>>

PLEASE LEAVE A REVIEW

<<<<<<<<<<<<<<<<<<<O>>>>>>>>>>>>>>>>>>

Thank you for your interest in our book. Please feel free to leave a review on Amazon to help share this important work with other interested readers. Many thanks for your support.

www.ingramcontent.com/pod-product-compliance
Lightning Source LLC
Chambersburg PA
CBHW030417290526
45786CB00001B/22